More Praise for *The BS Dictionary*

"When I worked with Bob Wiltfong at *The Daily Show* it was clear he was full of BS. I'm glad to see he's found an outlet for it."

—Stewart Bailey, Former Co-Executive Producer,
The Daily Show with Jon Stewart

"This is the book I wish I had written."

—Tripp Crosby (of Tripp & Tyler), Entertainers and Creators
of "A Conference Call in Real Life"

"As a corporate executive, I thought I understood all the business jargon known to (wo)man. But no BS, this dictionary has shown me I've only scratched the surface. I'm now on a mission to *push the envelope* and *circle back* to this hilarious, sometimes cringe-inducing book again and again whenever I need a *magic bullet* for corporate translation."

—Christine Walters, Television Development Executive

"Page-turner is not a word I would normally associate with a dictionary, but this book is just that. It is filled with one delicious entry after another, giving insight into some of the most commonly used business words and phrases in today's corporate world. At Four Day Weekend, we have taught thousands of business leaders the power of 'yes, and' at their jobs. I say 'yes, and' to another volume of *The BS Dictionary!*"

—David Ahearn, Co-Founder, Four Day Weekend Comedy

"I referred to Bob Wiltfong's *Daily Show* field pieces to learn how to do the job. I'm glad he wrote a book I can use to finally figure out what the hell everyone in the office is saying."

—Ronny Chieng, Standup Comedian and Reporter,
The Daily Show with Trevor Noah

T0273816

"*The BS Dictionary* is a cross between an old school dictionary and an Urban Dictionary, with a huge dose of biting personality. This book is hilarious and addictive."

—Bob Kulhan, Founder and CEO, Business Improv

"This is fantastic book not only clearly defines many of the business words and phrases in the corporate world, but it also gives the origin of each phrase in a very fun and informative way. I can't think of a better way to learn (and laugh about) the foreign language that is today's business speak."

—Kathleen O'Connor, Professor, London Business School, Visiting Associate Professor, Cornell Johnson Graduate School of Management

"In addition to being an actually helpful resource, *The BS Dictionary* is also a joke book, a history lesson and a trivia fan's delight. If you love to learn and laugh, you'll agree it gets on the green."

—Jane Borden, Journalist
Author, *I Totally Meant to Do That*

"One thing I know about Bob Wiltfong—he's a funny guy. And that's no BS! If anyone can make 'business humor' more than an oxymoron, it's him. This book should be required reading for anyone who thinks an occasional laugh is a good way to cope with the corporate world. I'll force all my employees to keep a copy on their desk. Or is that pushing the envelope?"

—Pat Dolan, Owner, *Newsday*

The BS Dictionary

Uncovering the Origins and True Meanings of Business Speak

BOB WILTFONG
TIM ITO

PRESS

Alexandria, VA

ATD Press is an internationally renowned source of insightful and practical information on talent development, training, and professional development.

ATD Press
1640 King Street
Alexandria, VA 22314 USA

Ordering information: Books published by ATD Press can be purchased by visiting ATD's website at www.td.org/books or by calling 800.628.2783 or 703.683.8100.

Library of Congress Control Number: 2020933993

ISBN-10: 1-950496-16-3
ISBN-13: 978-1-950496-16-7
e-ISBN: 978-1-950496-17-4

ATD Press Editorial Staff
Director: Sarah Halgas
Manager: Melissa Jones
Community Manager, Management: Ryan Changcoco
Developmental Editor: Kathryn Stafford
Production Editor: Hannah Sternberg
Text Design: Shirley E.M. Raybuck
Cover Design: Rose Richey

Printed by BR Printers, San Jose, CA

Bob

To my wife, Jill: You are my unicorn, my rock star,
my GOAT. In a nutshell, I love you!
To my kids: If you ever feel like you're in the weeds and life has left you holding the
bag, know that we are all attending a series of lunch & learns on this Earth and
that Mom-and-Pop love you to the ends of the universe.

Tim

To my mom and dad, the two best people I know.
To my wife, Julie, and sons, Alex and Eric: You give me joy every day.
To the town and people of Lakewood, Ohio: You are where you come from.
And I'm proud to say I come from there.
Lastly, to my friends: Thank you for always being there.

CONTENTS

SIDEBARS

PREFACE

Dear Reader,

We're going to take off our kid gloves and be aboveboard with you. At the end of the day, most of us have to work 24/7 to survive. We could give you the blow-by-blow on why that is, but that's like putting lipstick on a pig, yes? Why boil the ocean to find the reasons? It is what it is.

As such, we believe it's important to disambiguate the common phrases of our jobs and to open the kimono on idioms and clichés that stretch our bandwidth of understanding and make us wonder if our careers are scalable. Plainly put, how we communicate in our jobs is where the rubber meets the road for our future and can determine whether we can establish the mind-share necessary to move the needle. Trust us, as professionals who are long in the tooth in the world of corporate training and marketing, this is not our first rodeo!

We've gone beyond the low-hanging fruit of just giving you parts of speech and red-flagging definitions. For all intents and purposes, that's table stakes here. Look, we went against the grain by giving you what we think each word or phrase really means when used in the business world. Some thought leaders might suggest these "BS definitions" aren't worth their salt and are just a white elephant meant to increase SEO for the book. We realize the BS definitions certainly represent a thinking-outside-the-box approach to a standard dictionary, and we had a SWOT team of editors throwing shade at us for doing them. However, we stuck to our guns and put our John Hancocks on these Easter egg definitions, if you will, because we think the sweat equity results in great deliverables and a USP for a client-facing book such as this. The net-net is a win-win for you and for us.

That is why we wrote this game-changing book: to give you cut-and-dry definitions of some of the most cookie-cutter words and phrases used in today's business environments. Hence, what follows is a deep dive into what these words really mean. The upshot of this 360-degree approach is making you the master of the universe with the new normal of communication in the business world! Kudos to you for leaning in to this content!

—Bob and Tim

P.S. Seriously, we hope you enjoy this book. We had a great time discovering the origins of these words and phrases, and writing the definitions for what businesspeople are really thinking when they say them! We hope it provides useful insight into how we speak to one another on the job, and the way communication has evolved over time through various influences. The reality is there wouldn't be business without business speak, but we hope this book will inspire us all to be more original and use just a little less of it when communicating our thoughts on the job.

ACKNOWLEDGMENTS

Writing a book like this obviously takes a tremendous amount of research, and many sources have played an integral part of bringing these pages to life. In particular, the Internet has a vast amount of information—some of it verifiable and correct, some of it misleading, and some of it specious at best, but always a good lead for what people believe about word origins. What is true is that we relied on Internet sources to start our research, and where possible, found other valid resources to back up any claims we found online. With that said, any factual errors you see in these pages are ours alone at this point.

The following sources proved invaluable in our research:

- The *Oxford English Dictionary* (*OED*). Called the "definitive record of the English language," it is indeed a great resource for many of the first documented uses of words and phrases.
- *The Field Guide to Sports Metaphors* by Josh Chetwynd. This book is essential for all of you interested in the influence that sports has had on our language. Josh is a friend and a great guy. So please read his work.
- Google's Ngram Viewer (https://books.google.com/ngrams). The ability to look up books and see manuscripts from the 1500s is frankly amazing, and provided a whole new window into the origin and age of some terms, many of which hadn't been documented before.
- Websites
  - The Phrase Finder (www.phrases.org.uk); this is a terrific site we used to find some original citations and as a starting point for learning more about the terms
  - Online Etymology Dictionary (www.etymonline.com)
  - The Word Detective (www.word-detective.com)

- Wikipedia; it's not only a wealth of information, but also a great reality check on competing sources
- Dictionary.com
- Thesaurus.com
- *Merriam-Webster Dictionary* (M-W.com)

• There are too many other books, message boards, and websites to mention that at least helped provide a starting point for what others have found.

We also couldn't have done this without the expert guidance of key individuals at the Association for Talent Development, including our remarkable editors, Kathryn Stafford and Melissa Jones; our marketing guru, Kay Hechler; our book's honcho, Justin Brusino; and our all-around management-communications Sherpa, Ryan Changcoco.

Bob would also like to thank his agent, Duvall Osteen at Aragi, for believing in him and this project from day one. Duvall, you are the best! In addition, a huge thank you to Zack Stovall, whose animations supplemented an earlier version of this material. Zack, your drawings may not exist in the finished product, but know that your spirit is in these pages. Finally, Tim Ito, without your work and vision this book would simply not exist. Bob thanks you for your guidance and help. It is an honor to have you as a co-author.

In closing, we'd like to thank our wives and children, who have indulged us (particularly as we've waxed poetic about the origin of this or that term). We wouldn't be the cutting-edge, rubber-meets-the-road kind of guys we are without you.

There are almost 300 entries in this book. Want to help us pass that milestone? Drop us a line at info@thebsdictionary.com, and we'll try to include your suggestion in the second edition.

—Bob Wiltfong and Tim Ito, April 2020

INTRODUCTION

The idea for this book started one day at my home, when the woman who I thought was my wife turned into someone I did not recognize. Jill is a very smart and accomplished businesswoman. On this fateful day, she was about to jump on a conference call with colleagues. I had just finished talking to her about something (I forget what), and we'd had crystal-clear communication, both sides understanding every word, every idea. This is a woman I've known for more than 25 years. We "get" each other. We're simpatico.

Then the business call started.

Jill began using words that I had never heard come out of her mouth before. Things like *straw man*, *table stakes*, and *SEO*. To make matters worse, she was using the words with confidence, and amazingly, her co-workers were throwing other foreign-sounding phrases—*Internet of Things*, *blockchain*, *pivot*—right back at her with total understanding. It was almost like discovering that your spouse is a spy after being married to the person for years and never suspecting. I envisioned confronting her after she hung up: "Who are you, woman?! I want answers now. No more lies!"

Where in the heck did Jill learn all these words, and why did they make sense to her and her co-workers, but no sense to me? They were part of a foreign language that I did not know how to speak (and was afraid to admit I didn't).

That's when I started researching the terms that you'll find in the following pages. I didn't intend to write a book. I just wanted to learn more. It was only after I was introduced to the phrase *the tallest midget* at one of my consulting gigs that I started to think, "There should be a dictionary devoted to this stuff."

Business has always had its own language, with legions of speakers across generations and continents, but its dictionaries have been few. While that might not seem like a pressing problem, there are larger issues here that need to be explored.

First, business speak (BS for short . . . pun intended) changes quick-ly. "Our technology spreads things fast," says Angela Noble-Grange, senior lecturer of management communication at the Cornell SC Johnson College of Business, "and it kills things fast, so something that's cool today might have a life of a week, and then it's gone." That means you're not alone if you've found yourself in a business meeting wondering what that word or phrase everyone else is using means (but are afraid to say you don't know it).

When my co-author, Tim Ito, was working as a researcher at *U.S. News & World Report*, a seasoned reporter turned in his work and then announced he would be "out of pocket" for the next few days. Tim had never heard that phrase before and was confused by what it meant. From the context, he knew it was something important, but did it mean the reporter was broke? Maybe he didn't have any clean clothes? A colleague finally cleared up his confusion (see *out-of-pocket* in these pages for a full definition).

Further evidence of the problem presented itself to a friend of mine who's been working for 30 years in journalism and real estate. She told me she didn't know what B2B stood for when she first heard it. Concerned about showing her ignorance, she muddled through the first few times it came up in conversation, and then privately googled the phrase to figure it out.

This book addresses that problem by giving you the latest, up-to-date definitions of some of the most well-known BS terms in the English language. You don't have to be a recent business school grad, or a foreign traveler trying to parse the crazy things we English speakers say while doing business, to get something out of it. We're sure even the most experienced, English-speaking businessperson will find a few surprise meanings and origins in these pages.

Speaking of origin, there's a famous saying that "history is written by the victors."[1] In the case of word origins and what the public believes, the same is perhaps true if you add "of search engine optimization" at the end. Certainly, one natural place to begin understanding the origin of terms is the Internet, given the voluminous amount of data and information it contains. But what comes up on the first page of Google results—because let's face it, no one reads page 2—can be a red herring (see page 194) in many ways. There are message boards with different people of varying expertise weighing in. There are websites for which someone has perhaps written a very authoritative-seeming blog post. There are brand-name websites (such as the History Channel and Merriam-Webster) that also give their take. There's the work of the late William Safire, the renowned *New York Times* writer on language; Ben Zimmer, who writes the *Wall Street Journal* column on language; Anne Curzan, of the University of Michigan; and other highly cited etymologists.

At times (well, perhaps more often than not), websites copy one another's sources—even reputable sites will take a shortcut and point to the first source that came up in search results. Sometimes that source is correct; other times, it's one that merely espouses great conspiracy theories.

Add to this the difficulty that comes from someone just saying a term versus it being documented in history. We have several examples where that appears to be the case—*push the envelope*, for example, seems to originate from American pilots who worked on the Mercury space program in the late 1950s and early1960s, but it seemingly wasn't documented on paper until Tom Wolfe's book *The Right Stuff*, published in 1979.

In other cases, the origin is buried deep in the bowels of the Internet because some sources don't rise to the level of Google's algorithm. Take *lunch & learn* for example. If you do a search for "What's the origin of 'lunch & learn'?" or "Who coined the term 'lunch & learn'?" as we did, you won't find an answer—at least within the first 10 pages. We then looked at the *Oxford English Dictionary* (the *OED*, known as "the definitive record of the English language"), and they didn't even have a starting reference for it.

What to do? We next looked at Google Books, which now has an archive of published works going back to the 1500s, and found an obscure 1973 reference to a "lunch & learn" concept that was recorded in the U.S. Department of Agriculture's *Extension Service Review* journal. We found a partial passage in that Google Books document, which led us to the full document online, in which it was revealed that two housewives—Sandra Stockall and Jeanette Grantham of Nebraska—were said to have originated the term.[2] (It makes sense really. Only geeks like us actually want to know the origin of the term *lunch & learn*, and it's definitely not something that occupies people's minds on a daily basis.)

In this book, Tim and I have tried to lighten up the subject matter some with the comedic aspects of business speak. It is, in a way, its own kind of folly. But when it comes to origins, we were dead serious. We relied heavily on trusted sources (which we detail in the acknowledgments), including the *OED*, which really is an amazing resource.[3] And where possible, to supplement what we found, we tried to locate the original documentation or confirm with other reputable sources.

One thing we've realized in this whole process is that if you want to be known for coining something, make sure to document it. For example, if you want to invent a new term—let's say it's a new style of music called "thrash disco"—you have to put it somewhere in writing so the Internet will see it. Then, you need to spread the word about your new term and how you invented it. By doing so, you will become the "victor" of that phrase's history, and all the spoils will flow to you—and reward you with Internet glory.[4]

But why does this dictionary even have to exist? Why do so many people in the business world feel the need to use words and terms that they may not really know the origins of and don't use anywhere else in their daily lives? Noble-Grange has two theories.

"One reason is influence," she says. "How do you get people to do what you want them to do? Persuade them or influence them. It's called likability. You want people to like you, so you use the language that they use. You might start copying some of the stuff that they do. That helps build your likability. The other reason is credibility. You sound smart if you're using the words that the people who are above you are using. Some people will buy it. They'll listen to you and say, 'Wow, you sound smart,' not even questioning what it is that you're saying. [You] say it with such a tone, with such authority, [that you] sometimes [get] from a lot of people instant credibility, because it just sounds good."

And that, my friends, is why *The BS Dictionary* is now in your life. We hope it increases your likability and credibility on the job, and that you enjoy it as much as we've enjoyed putting it together for you.

—Bob Wiltfong

24/365 *adv., adj.* twenty-four/three sixty-five **1.** 24 hours a day, 365 days a year. **2.** The ability to go for a full year with no rest and not dying.

> **BS Definition:** I am not human. I am a cyborg. I feel no pity, remorse, or fear. I don't need to apply sunblock. Xbox is my spouse. I am Elon Musk.

> **Origin:** The *OED* attributes the first usage of this phrase to basketball player Jerry Reyn-olds, who was quoted in *Sports Illustrated* in 1983 as saying his jump shot was "good 24 hours a day, seven days a week, 365 days a year." Reyn-olds, at the time, played in college for Louisiana State University, and he evidently thought very highly of himself. Otherwise, why would he say his jump shot never took a break like, literally, ever?[1]

24/7 *adv., adj.* twenty-four/seven **1.** 24 hours a day, seven days a week. **2.** The ability to go all day and night without sleep.

> **BS Definition:** I'm serious; I'm Elon Musk. Tell me how to find Sarah Connor or die.

> **Origin:** Score another one for Jerry Reynolds! The origin for 24/7 can also be traced to the basketball player (see *24/365*). We wanted to know if he was really that good. I mean, we're basketball fans, and we've never heard of the guy, so we researched his stats. Turns out, Reynolds would go on to an eight-year career in the NBA playing for the Milwaukee Bucks, Seattle Supersonics, and Orlando Magic. Not bad. With that

said, his career 41.8 percent field-goal percentage is below the NBA's 43.5 percent average for players of that same era. So, perhaps Reynolds wasn't everything he claimed to be. Mathematically speaking, a more accurate fraction to describe his jump shot would be 4/10 (or . . . carry the two . . . 2/5). However, saying your jump shot is good for about 10 out of 24 hours a day or about three out of seven days a week doesn't sound nearly as cool as "24/7" or "24/365," so good on you, Jerry Reynolds. Good on you.[2]

360° *adj.*, *n.* three hundred sixty degree 1. From a variety of workplace sources, usually done in a confidential way. 2. The name given to a kind of leadership assessment that comprises feedback from a variety of colleagues.

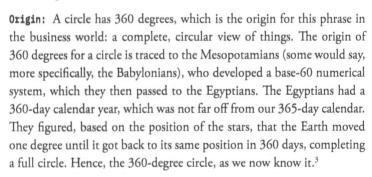

BS Definition: Going around real sneaky-like and only getting the opinions that help get that [*beep*] in marketing fired.

Origin: A circle has 360 degrees, which is the origin for this phrase in the business world: a complete, circular view of things. The origin of 360 degrees for a circle is traced to the Mesopotamians (some would say, more specifically, the Babylonians), who developed a base-60 numerical system, which they then passed to the Egyptians. The Egyptians had a 360-day calendar year, which was not far off from our 365-day calendar. They figured, based on the position of the stars, that the Earth moved one degree until it got back to its same position in 360 days, completing a full circle. Hence, the 360-degree circle, as we now know it.[3]

According to the *OED*, the first known figurative reference to a "360-degree" view of things comes from the July 11, 1965, edition of the *New York Times Book Review* (its review of *The Liberation of Lord Byron Jones* by Jesse Hill Ford): "Seen in the purest perspectives of fiction, this book . . . is curiously disappointing. As a 360-degree examination of the 'situation' in the South of the 1960s, however, it has stunning sociological relevance."

In popular parlance, this term is often misused (particularly in the United States), with people saying things like, "He's made a complete 360-degree turn in his life." If you do the math, that means the person is back where he started.[4]

A

aboveboard *adj.*, *adv.* **1.** Legitimate, honest, open. **2.** In open view, without tricks, concealment, or disguise.

> **BS Definition: 1.** Usually just the opposite. **2.** Trust us. You don't want to see what's below board.
>
>
>
> **Origin:** Researchers at the *OED* say references to this term first appeared in print in 1594 with an origin in gambling, particularly cards. To play "aboveboard" meant keeping your cards above the level of the playing table (as opposed to being in one's lap) to avoid any suspicion of cheating. The board, in this case, is a table. Conversely, playing "under board" meant you might be dishonest. That 1594 citation comes from *Terrors of the Night*, first edition, by Elizabethan pamphleteer Thomas Nashe: "Now that he [Satan] is thoroughly steeled in his scutcherie, hee playes aboue-boord boldly, & sweeps more stakes than euer he did before." In 1623, clergyman Richard Carpenter used a closer version of the BS phrase in *The Conscionable Christian*: "All his dealings are square and above the boord."[1]

across-the-board *adj.* **1.** Taking into account all classes or categories. **2.** Applying to every part or individual.

> **BS Definition:** Looking at more than the top four returns on the first page of your google search (and maybe venturing to the second page if you're feeling really inspired).

Origin: As opposed to aboveboard, where *board* refers to a table, in this case *board* refers to the tote board, common at racetracks across the country, which shows odds or payouts useful for racetrack patrons. The reference to across-the-board comes from when a bet can be made across the board to win, place, or show—the three main payouts on the tote board for horses that finish first, second, or third. The first known documented reference to across-the-board as its own term came in 1901 in *The Atlanta Constitution*: "Cousin Jess won the steeplechase after a hard drive in the stretch, lowering the best previous time of 4 09 by seven seconds. Dr Einus in the fourth race, a 100 to 1 shot, heavily played across the board, ran second."[2]

action *v.* **1.** To put into practice. **2.** To deal with.

BS Definition: 1. To use a noun in a verb-y kind of way. **2.** Ironically, when used as a verb, it's the first hint that the person speaking won't actually be taking any real action.

Origin: Using action as a verb has been around for centuries. Its use as a noun came first in the legal world, derived in the 14th century from the old French word accion, meaning "lawsuit" or "case."[3] The *OED* reports that its first written reference as a verb wasn't until 1734, in Henry Fielding's play *Don Quixote in England*: "I don't question but to action him out on't." Then the *OED* says action was used for the first time in its glorious BS form in the *Times* of London in 1960: "Full details taken, the message is actioned straight away." We could give you more early citations of action as a verb, but we think it's best that we action that item later.

action man/man of action *n.* **1.** A person who prioritizes performance and deeds over words or contemplation. **2.** A person whose life is defined by physical activity rather than intellectual matters.

A

BS Definition: How you see yourself when the boss tells you to do something, and you, in turn, tell your employees to do it.

Origin: A cow named Dinah is responsible for the earliest known reference of *action man* in writing. In 1943, the *Fresno Bee Republican* ran a piece about this record-breaking cow: "Maybe Dinah [a cow that produced 17 times her own weight in milk] and her owner . . . have caught some of the 'miracle production' philosophy of Henry J. Kaiser, the famous ship building action man of that state." Action Man toys from the United Kingdom may also have played a role in making this a popular BS phrase. From 1966 to 1984, a company called Palitoy marketed Action Man dolls and figures based on the popular GI Joe action figures sold in the United States by Hasbro.[4] For people who remember that, *action man* may very well mean "superhero figure who died a horrible death over and over again in the worst play-fighting seen this side of Ken and Barbie's breakup."

actionable *adj.* **1.** Anything on which action can be taken. **2.** Liable to a lawsuit.

BS Definition: Literally nothing on the list of items that comes from the innovation team.

Origin: The first known use of the word actionable—in the sense of providing grounds for a legal action—came in the early 1600s from an English antiquarian named William Lambarde and his work, *Archion: or, A Commentary Upon the High Courts of Justice in England*: "Baited, & bitten with libells & slanders that be not actionable."[5] Eventually, the term evolved to mean anything that is capable of being acted on, coming into usage in the 20th century. One early citation comes from Christine Frederick's 1913 book *The New Housekeeping: Efficiency Studies in Home*

Management: "Refuse to let the mind wallow and dawdle around a problem without arriving at definite, actionable conclusions."[6]

admin *n.* Administrative assistant.

BS Definition: **1.** Personal slave. **2.** Officially, an individual who isn't supposed to exercise independent judgment or discretion. Practically, the individual who makes all the decisions in the office. **3.** The person you refer to as "what's-his-face" or "what's-her-face" in moments of forgetfulness.

Origin: Although *admin* can refer to a system administrator, the primary reference for our *BS Dictionary* purposes is the reference to the role once occupied by a secretary. *Admin* itself is an abbreviation originating in the 15th century from the Middle French *administrateur*, meaning "one who has been given authority to manage." However, today the word is often connected with the role of an administrative assistant (who, ironically, has no authority to manage or has all the authority in the world, depending on the role). The first known reference to an "admin" as an administrative assistant comes from Armistead Maupin's series of novels, *Tales of the City*—specifically the first volume, from 1978: "I was . . . an admin assistant for the past year and a half."[7] Eventually, admin became the *nom de rigueur* as the term *secretary* went out of style in the late 20th century. The big turning point came in 1998, when Professional Secretaries International (formerly the National Secretaries Association) changed its official name to the International Association of Administrative Professionals, recognizing the larger societal shift.[8]

against the grain *idiom* **1.** Different from the standard. **2.** Counter to what is usual or normal.

A

BS Definition: 1. That Halloween office party where you intentionally dressed up as a Hershey's kiss (even though you knew some would think you were the poop emoji instead). **2.** Decorating your office cubicle with Jonas Brothers posters.

Origin: Although this phrase invokes images of cutting against a wood grain (which woodcutters say you do at your peril), there are no references to wood in early uses of the phrase.[9] Indeed, the first documented use of against the grain comes from Shakespeare in the 1607 play *Coriolanus*, a tragedy based on the life of Roman leader Gaius Marcius Coriolanus.[10] It is one of the last two tragedies written by The Bard, the other one being *Antony and Cleopatra*. The citation reads as follows:

> Say, you chose him
> More after our commandment than as guided
> By your own true affections, and that your minds,
> Preoccupied with what you rather must do
> Than what you should, made you against the grain
> To voice him consul: lay the fault on us.[11]

all-hands meeting *n.* A mandatory meeting for all employees.

BS Definition: 1. When management tells you that, despite the poor financial outlook, you're ready to rise up like Simba in Act III of *The Lion King*. **2.** When company leaders interrupt your day to give you the reasons you should be back at your desk working.

Origin: This expression is believed to have evolved from the late 16th century naval term *all hands*, which referred to an entire ship's company. A related term includes *all hands on deck*, which was a call for all sailors to come to the deck of a ship, particularly to help in times of crisis.[12] In 1655, the term started to appear for the first time in a work context: "Then would all hands be set a-work, and every one would become instrumentall to serve himselfe and his Neighbours in Love."[13] An all-hands meeting doesn't necessarily connote a crisis, though it certainly can be an occasion for one (see the Google or Facebook all-hands meetings of 2018).[14] Before the days of the Internet, all-hands meetings were relatively closed affairs, and the information presented was available primarily to employees who attended. Today, however, many companies are learning that information presented in an all-hands meeting can quickly end up on a reporter's Twitter feed.

an ax to grind *idiom* **1.** To have a selfish reason for saying or doing something. **2.** To have an ulterior motive of revenge.

BS Definition: 1. The feeling you get when you see your former boss—the one who laid you off by saying the company was "rightsizing"—at the grocery store and immediately start thinking of ways to beat them to the checkout aisle. **2.** For those classic literary types, think Edmund Dantes' long-awaited revenge against Mondego in the Alexander Dumas' *The Count of Monte Cristo*. For those comic-book types, think Marv avenging the death of Goldie in Frank Miller's *Sin City*.

Origin: This phrase is commonly attributed to Benjamin Franklin, though some claim its first use was by a fellow Pennsylvania writer, Charles Miner; both men wrote cautionary tales regarding the sharpening of axes. Franklin's autobiography, which was written in his later years and published posthumously in 1791, has a story of a man who asks a blacksmith to sharpen his ax, but ends up working the grindstone himself. Meanwhile, Miner is believed to be the author of an anonymous 1810 piece in the Pennsylvania newspaper *The Centinel*, under the title "Who'll Turn Grindstone?" in which he first uses the phrase *axe to grind*:

A

When I see a man holding a fat office, sounding 'the horn on the borders' to call the people to support the man on whom he depends for his office. Well, thinks I, no wonder the man is zealous in the cause, he evidently has an axe to grind."[15]

anointed *n.* A blessed or preordained person or thing.

BS Definition: 1. An employee who can't seem to do anything wrong in the eyes of management. **2.** The last person in the office invited to Friday's happy hour.

Origin: This BS term is derived from the mid-14th-century French word *enoint*, meaning to spread oil on or to smear with oil, ointment, milk, butter, or other fat. Such acts have been used in various religions to introduce a divine presence of some kind or as part of a ceremonial consecration. For example, one anointing of Jesus is said to have occurred when Mary of Bethany poured oil over his feet. According to the *OED*, the term started to be used as a noun as early as the 1500s. Today, anointing can have a more secular connotation, though it does still typically involve a "chosen one" assuming a position of power. And while there is not a physical spreading of oil or butter on that individual, we're sure some co-workers would like to smear that person in one form or fashion.[16]

ask *n.* A request or an inquiry.

BS Definition: 1. We're efforting a solve for this first BS definition. The takeaway is, we'll give the share as soon as the build is complete. **2.** Used when you feel like the word *request* or *question* isn't cool enough.

Origin: There is some debate about using *ask* as a noun—that is, whether or not it's a real usage. In truth, *ask* has been used as a noun for about 1,000 years.[17] In particular, the *OED* has three early citations of

A

it, between roughly 1000 and 1230, although the way we encounter it today is primarily a 1980s phenomenon. (Again, more evidence of how the '80s screwed up everything.) By 2004, *ask* as a noun had become so obnoxious that Raymond Chen, a senior Microsoft programmer, wrote about the ubiquitous appearance of the word in a corporate context:

Ask (as a noun)

This has taken over Microsoft-speak in the past year or so and it drives me batty. "What are our key asks here?", you might hear in a meeting. Language tip: The thing you are asking for is called a "request." Plus, of course, the thing that is an "ask" is usually more of a "demand" or "requirement." But those are such unfriendly words, aren't they? Why not use a warm, fuzzy word like "ask" to take the edge off?

Answer: Because it's not a word.[18]

at the end of the day *idiom* **1.** After analyz-ing all possibilities. **2.** Equivalent to saying, "When all is said and done," "At this moment in time," or "Bottom line."

BS Definition: Another way to say, "I like to say unnecessary words before giving my opinion."

Origin: The earliest documented use of the phrase comes from a sermon first published posthumously in 1826 by Reverend Ebenezer Erskine (1680–1754), a Scottish minister. Erskine and his fiery orations led to the establishment of the Secession Church (formed by dissenters of the Church of Scotland). He used the phrase much like one would today:

Christ's flock is but a little flock, comparatively considered. . . . They are but little in respect of their numbers. Indeed abstractly considered, at the end of the day, they will make an "innumerable company, which no man can number"; but, viewed in comparison of the wicked, they are but few.[19]

The term gained more popularity in the 1980s (again, more evidence that the '80s helped destroy the world as we know it), but by 2008, *at the end of the day* was so despised that it was voted the most annoying cliché in a British poll.[20]

authoritatively *adv.* Having the sanction or weight of authority.

BS Definition: The ability to be bossy and bullsh*t people at the same time while keeping a straight face.

Origin: According to the *OED*, the first documented use of "authoritatively" occurred around 1443 in Reginald Pecock's *The Reule of Crysten Religioun* (edited by William Cabell Greet): "Alle hem which he knowiþ certeynly be synners and brekers of þi law, god, þat he denounce auctoritatively." Derived from the medieval Latin word *auctoritativus*, the term implied anything from describing dictatorial behavior to someone acting with approval or sanction.

Today, the term is sometimes used to ridicule others who seem to act in an authoritative manner, yet perhaps lack such actual influence.[21] Our favorite references include the hard-throwing, rough-around-the-edges minor league pitcher Nuke Laloosh in the film *Bull Durham*, who wanted "to announce my presence with authority," and Dwight Schrute from the TV show *The Office*, who said of showing his authority over his co-workers, "I love catching people in the act. That's why I always whip open doors."[22]

BS IS LIKE A BOX OF CHOCOLATES—PART I

Bull Durham with its BS-friendly dialogue of "announc[ing] my presence with authority" is just one example of movie lines that are creeping into the world of business speak. Famous lines from films have become a fun way for some people to communicate in business. Other examples include:

- "Coffee's for closers" from *Glengarry Glenross*
- "May the force be with you" from *Star Wars*
- "I'll be back" from *Terminator*
- "You talkin' to me?" from *Taxi Driver*
- "We're on a mission from God" from *The Blues Brothers*.

It's a reminder of how much Hollywood shapes how we communicate on a day-to-day basis. Here are our top eight most influential movie lines that apply to the working world and why they translate so well as business speak.

No. 8
"Show me the money!" (Jerry Maguire)

Why It's Influential: A great line from a great scene, this is perfectly applicable to any business situation. However, its brilliance is sometimes overshadowed by an even better line from that same movie: "You had me at hello."

Why It Works in Business Speak: "Money talks; bullsh*t walks" (without any cursing)—this movie line suggests to any business partners that the best way for them to show they value you or your contributions is to pay you money for it.

No. 7
"If you build it, [they] will come." (*Field of Dreams*)

> *Why It's Influential:* This movie will make you laugh. It will make you cry. Set in a small town in Iowa, it tells the story of farmer Ray Kinsella (played by Kevin Costner), who hears voices that tell him to build a baseball park in the middle of one of his corn fields. When he does, ghosts appear to him (including his own dead father) that demonstrate the power of second chances in life.

> *Why It Works in Business Speak:* This line is often used to justify investments in things with no strong customer base at the moment. Starbucks, for instance, followed this mantra when building a demand for coffee shops. Apple leaned on the idea when marketing the iPad. The reality is, Kevin Costner's character almost lost his farm building his baseball park in a corn field—a possible outcome that many businesses seem to ignore when embracing the idea that simply building a great business will draw a customer base to you.

No. 6
"I'm gonna make him an offer he can't refuse."
(*The Godfather*)

> *Why It's Influential:* So many great lines came from this movie. Our personal favorite is "leave the gun; take the cannoli." However, "I'm gonna make him an offer he can't refuse" is perfectly applicable to business, and has become a popular line when someone is trying to close a deal.

> *Why It Works in Business Speak:* Nothing says you're serious about making a business deal better than quoting the Mafia. This is an organization that is willing to put a dead horse's head into a movie producer's bed just to send a message, for goodness sake!

No. 5.
"What we've got here . . . is failure to communicate"
(Cool Hand Luke)

> *Why It's Influential:* The Captain (Strother Martin) hits Luke (the always cool Paul Newman), knocking him to the ground, and then delivers this famous line:
>
> > What we've got here is . . . failure to communicate. Some men you just can't reach. So, you get what we had here last week, which is the way he wants it . . . well, he gets it! I don't like it any more than you men.
>
> What makes this particularly memorable is Martin's delivery, a kind of stuttering, staccato-like emphasis on various words, which was memorably replicated at the beginning of the Guns N' Roses song Civil War from 1991.
>
> *Why It Works in Business Speak:* Ever been in that meeting where two colleagues are simply talking past each other and nothing gets accomplished? This is a great one-liner to use *after* that meeting, when walking out with the other staff present. That said, a word of caution: Don't even try to replicate Martin's vocal-gymnastic cadence. It won't work out well.

See part II of this sidebar for our top four movie lines used in BS on page 40.

B

B-school *n.* Business school.

> **BS Definition:** **1.** The place where you spend a lot of money trying to learn how to make a lot of money. **2.** The primary institution responsible for inspiring the 1978 Bob Seger song "Feel Like a Number."

> **Origin:** We don't know who first coined the phrase B-school, but our guess is it was some hipster student in Paris around 1819. That's because the world's first business school, ESCP Europe, was founded in Paris that year. If it wasn't then and there, then it had to be around 1881, when the Wharton School of the University of Pennsylvania became the United States' first business school.[1] If our hunch is correct about its origin, our guess is the term *B-school* was invented in this fashion: "Hey, Henri. Do you want to join me and our fellow students at the library for some studying?" "Nah, Antoine. You guys go ahead. I've got some girls coming over to listen to the latest cuts from Beethoven's piano sonata. We're going to do some B-school studying of our own tonight."

b to b *or* **B2B** *adj.* **1.** In which one business makes a commercial transaction with another. **2.** Business conducted between companies, rather than with individual consumers.

> **BS Definition:** What Terry in accounting often mistakes for a cozy little guesthouse in the New England countryside.

> **Origin:** According to the *OED*, the first written reference to B2B happened in 1994 with this line from *Marketing News*:

B

The AMA has launched the B2B Marketing Exchange, an Internet bulletin board designed to provide information on coming events, research sites, courses, and articles of interest to business-to-business marketing academics and practitioners.[2]

However, any 12-year-old South Korean girl can tell you that this term didn't *really* come into existence until 2012. That's when the all-boys group consisting of Seo Eun-kwang, Lee Min-hyuk, Lee Chang-sub, Im Hyun-sik, Peniel Shin, Jung Il-hoon, and Yook Sung-jae debuted as BtoB. They released their debut EP, *Born to Beat*, that year, which included "Insane" and "Imagine," but you already knew that, right? OMG! C'mon, we're talking BtoB here!! They're, like, soooo Gucci!!![3]

back burner *n.* **1.** A place of less importance. **2.** A condition of low priority or temporary deferment.

BS Definition: Usually equivalent to saying, "This idea will never be seen or heard from again."

Origin: The Cold War gave us so much: the beginnings of Bluetooth (thank you, Hedy Lamarr), worldwide access to GPS (shame on you, USSR), and, of course, bears being used to test ejector seats on supersonic jets (What the . . . ?!?).[4] *Back burner* can also be added to this list. According to the *OED*, the first known written reference to *back burner*—as a way to describe postponing something—was in April 1963 in the *Times* of London: "With Mr. Khrushchev showing no interest in the Anglo-American proposals, the test ban, with Berlin and the Soviet evacuation of Cuba, will have to be put on the back burner, as the Americans have it."

Some have speculated that *back burner* came into existence before that, with old-fashioned wood or coal-burning stoves that predate the mid-1960s.[5] However, we know our stoves (or at least Google says it

B

does), so let us settle this feud between stove enthusiasts once and for all, before any more blood is shed over the matter. Wood- and coal-burning stoves did *not* have back burners. Sure, different areas of the stove would have warmer or cooler temperatures depending on the position of the firebox underneath, but there were no back burners, per se. Only when gas ranges were introduced (as early as the 1830s) would the idiom of a back burner have made sense and thus been extended to activities other than cooking.[6]

back of the envelope *n.* **1.** A rough calculation done in a quick, casual manner. **2.** More than a guess but less than an accurate answer.

BS Definition: The kind of hurried calculation that leads you to race after the CEO, who's headed into a closing elevator, only to have the door shut painfully on your foot.

Origin: Oh snap! You thought the struggle between stove enthusiasts over the BS term *back burner* was fierce? Wait until you get a load of the battle for who's responsible for *back of the envelope*!

In this fight for origin superiority, we have the creator of the world's first nuclear reactor, physicist Enrico Fermi (1901–1954), versus the inventor of the maser, Nobel laureate Charles Townes (1915–2015).[7] Supporters of the Fermi side of things (we'll call them "Fermites") say he was well known for using simple calculations to help communicate complex scientific ideas, and developed a series of calculations called "Fermi questions" or "back-of-the-envelope calculations." Townes and his fans (we'll call them "Townies") counter that one day in 1968, while waiting for breakfast in Washington, D.C., he took a walk and had a deep insight about some research he was working on. "I pulled out an envelope from my pocket and wrote down the equation and it looked like it really would probably work. Wow."[8]

So, who's actually the originator of this BS term? We can't say for sure, but we do know the Townies and Fermites are going to settle this once and for all on the playground after school today. Be there!

bait and switch *n.* **1.** The action of advertising a low price or special feature but then adding extra fees (or taking away the special feature) when the purchase becomes final. **2.** The intention of substituting inferior or more expensive goods compared with what was advertised.

BS Definition: Any timeshare offer.

Origin: Bait-and-switch techniques have probably been around since the first days of commercial transactions. One of the earliest references on record comes from 17th-century China, where Zhang Yingyu's book about fraud, *The Book of Swindles* (published in or around 1617), contains 84 short stories about rip-offs and deceptions—including bait-and-switch schemes.[9] The purported purpose of the book was to teach the reader about various detailed scams that had flourished during the latter part of the Ming dynasty, and how to avoid them. Zhang, though, is somewhat mysterious in his leanings, at times condemning the swindlers' deceptions, and at other times praising their ingenuity. According to the *OED*, the first known reference to *bait and switch* in English comes much later, in an August 1953 volume of *Reader's Digest*:

> This was my introduction to the "bait 'em and switch 'em" racket.
> . . . I learned that "bait advertising" is the biggest gyp and the most widespread abuse in advertising today."

ballpark *n.* **1.** Approximate. **2.** Rough estimate.

BS Definition: Pulling a number out of one's you-know-what.

B

Origin: The origin of this phrase likely begins with American baseball.[10] However, the earliest mentions of it suggest it was actually popularized in the U.S. Air Force during World War II as slang for an approximate area. The *OED* cites the first write-up of ballpark as occurring in 1943. In an article in the *Charleston* (West Virginia) *Gazette* from October of that year, this line appears: "This, as air force officers put it, will bring the whole Ruhr valley 'within the American fighters ballpark.'" In 1943, the Ruhr Valley in Germany was subject to a five-month strategic bombing campaign by Allied forces, who saw it as a large industrial complex for the Nazis. By July, about one-third of all antiaircraft guns in Germany were positioned there, prompting British crews to nickname it "The Valley of No Return."[11]

balls in the air *idiom* **1.** Having a number of tasks going on at the same time. **2.** An allusion to the situation of a juggler who is attempting to juggle an excessive number of objects at once.

BS Definition: A phrase often used by those who can't even keep one ball in the air.

Origin: This American expression was preceded by the similar British phrase *keep the ball up*. Both ideas speak to the same idea: keeping an activity going despite what's going on around it. In 1781, a radical social philosopher in the United Kingdom named Jeremy Bentham mentioned it in a letter: "I put a word in now and then to keep the ball up."[12] In America, we embraced the juggling term *balls in the air* to capture the idea. When exactly did the activity of juggling originate, you ask? Well, the oldest known depiction of juggling took place about 2,000 years before the birth of Christ. It is reflected in the wall paintings of a tomb in Egypt. Oddly enough, it was another 1,500 years before evidence of juggling reappeared, in the art of the Greeks.[13] That's a long time to keep your balls in the air.

bandwidth *n.* **1.** A range of frequencies in telecommunications. **2.** The speed of data transfer in digital technology. **3.** The ability to complete work given available resources. **4.** Your capacity to handle a task.

B

BS Definition: Your personal threshold for being treated slightly better than a 12th-century medieval serf.

Origin: In electronics, bandwidth is the width, measured in hertz, of an electromagnetic (EM) spectrum band (a contiguous interval of frequencies) that is allocated to a particular use. Wider frequency bands allow more "channels" of data to flow through. The first discovery of an EM band other than visible light came in 1800, when William Herschel discovered infrared radiation. The earliest citation for *bandwidth*, per the *OED*, comes from 1930's *Proceedings of the Institute of Radio Engineers*: "The greater band width being required as the standard of quality becomes higher." In the 1990s, bandwidth began to be used to describe data transfers over the Internet, representing the total capacity of any system, regardless of whether it was using an EM band or not. In recent times, the meaning of the word has broadened further from "data capacity" to "personal capacity"—as in, "Brian, I really would like to hear more about how smart you are, but I don't have the bandwidth to smile and nod at you anymore."[14]

bang for the buck *n.* Getting the most return for your money.

BS Definition: **1.** When you spend millions of dollars recruiting and onboarding new employees and they stay longer than a year. **2.** The chalupa that $5 can get you on your lunch break at Taco Bell.

Origin: This saying was popularized in the 1950s. Most sources credit U.S. Defense Secretary Charles Wilson as the source. However, according to the *OED*, the first written citation of *bang for the buck* happened

B

in December 1953, in an article written by Stewart Alsop in the *New York Herald Tribune*: "They believe that the 'more bang for a buck' theory is an excuse for the cutbacks, rather than a real reason, and that the 'buck' came first by an easy margin, with the 'bang' a poor second."

There are a couple of popular theories as to what source might have spawned this phrase.[15] One is that it originated in the explosives and mining industry, where it referred to the amount of dynamite power per unit of explosive purchased. Others are convinced that the saying comes from the world of prostitution—with the *OED* citing the first written use of the word bang to mean "having sexual intercourse with" as having occurred in 1937.[16] However, we found no credible sources to support an origin story that connects either of these meanings with our BS phrase here.

banner year *n.* **1.** The best year in a company's history. **2.** A year in which something is especially successful.

BS Definition: When your percentage merit increase actually exceeds the cost of living (see *once in a blue moon*).

Origin: This one may go all the way back to 1014 in Ireland, when the Dalcassians (known in Irish as Dál gCais or "peoples of Cas") carried banners into the battle of Clontarf. (That sounds like a made-up town, doesn't it? Or the name of a planet being explored on *Battlestar Gallactica*.) Fast forward to the 1800s, and the custom of trade guilds (bakers, butchers, stonecutters, and so forth) carrying banners to political meetings became common in parts of the country. The more banners supporting a candidate, the more likely that candidate would win the election and have a "banner year."[17]

baseline *n.* **1.** One's current performance on a project or activity. **2.** A basic standard or level. **3.** A starting point used for comparisons later.

BS Definition: Doing something half-ass early on so you look better doing it later.

Origin: The first literal use of the word baseline comes from math—more specifically, geometry. One example from the 16th century is *A Book Called Tectonicon* by Leonard Digges, in which the author notes: "The base line of the Triangle." However, it took almost 300 more years before anyone would use the word figuratively. The *OED* cites the first figurative use of *baseline* in a book written by Thomas Chalmers sometime between 1836 and 1842. Chalmers was a Scottish minister and social reformer who has been called "Scotland's greatest 19th-century churchman." In addition, for all you New Zealand fans out there, Port Chalmers, in New Zealand, is named after him, so there you go. His use of *baseline* was as follows: "The article of our guilt or corruption by nature may be regarded as a base line on which to construct or to estimate many of the other and these the chief articles of our faith."[18]

bean counter *n.* A derogatory term for an accountant.

BS Definition: When *number cruncher* and *pencil pusher* just won't do.

Origin: *Bean counter* has had several meanings throughout the years, including the counters where beans were sold in the United States during the late 19th and early 20th centuries. One  early reference came in the June 1, 1907, issue of the *Lewiston Evening Journal*: "The Handsome Slender Clerk, seeing himself worsted by the numbers . . . walked over to the bean counter where he again busied himself putting up packages for the evening trade."[19]

However, the main way it's used today (as another word for an accountant) likely stems from an expression translated from German. The German word *erbsenzähler* (*erbsen* = beans and *zähler* = counter) was used in print by Hans Jakob Christoffel von Grimmelshausen (sounds like a name from a Wes Anderson movie, but we digress) in his 1668 book, *Simplicius Simplicissimus*, in the same context. That novel, which revolves around some autobiographical experiences in the Thirty Years War, is considered among the greatest German literary works of the 17th century, by the way—right up there with *How Not to Die From the Black Death in 5 Easy Steps!*

beat a dead horse *idiom* **1.** To expend effort on something when there's no chance of succeeding. **2.** To waste energy on a lost cause or unalterable situation.

BS Definition: The fifth, no wait, sixth time you asked your boss for a raise.

Origin: This phrase (or a variation thereof) first appeared in print in an 1859 report of a U.K. parliamentary debate in the London paper *Watchman and Wesleyan Advertiser*: "It was notorious that Mr. Bright was dissatisfied with his winter reform campaign and rumor said that he had given up his effort with the exclamation that it was like flogging a dead horse." The origin of that expression—to flog or beat a dead horse—comes from a time when the practice of beating horses to make them move faster was often viewed as acceptable.[20]

beauty contest *n.* **1.** In a literal sense, a competition between people to be crowned most attractive. **2.** In a business sense, potential suitors pitching for the same business at the same time.

BS Definition: Usually involves people in the business world who are not beautiful enough to be involved in the literal activity.

Origin: The first modern beauty contest was staged by P.T. Barnum in 1854, but it was closed down by public protest. Barnum had previously held dog, baby, and bird beauty contests. Modern beauty pageants, as we know them today, are traceable to the Miss America Beauty Pageant, which was first held in Atlantic City in 1921 under the title "Inter-city Beauty Contest."[21]

Around that same time, the term *beauty contest* started to show up in descriptions of political races in which the outcome was thought to be influenced more by the personalities and media image of the candidates than their policies or capabilities: "The same strictures hold against the 'beauty' contests which have marked the choice of state librarians in some of the southern states." The OED says the first written reference to the business definition of this term was in

a 1976 *Forbes* article: "The distributorship selection turned into a beauty contest that was the talk of Texas bar-rooms for three months."[22]

beef up *v.* **1.** To make stronger. **2.** To add strength.

BS Definition: Something your résumé could almost always use.

Origin: According to the *OED*, the first literary reference to beef, with this meaning, was in 1851 innone other than Herman Melville's classic novel *Moby-Dick*: "Oh, do pile on the beef . . . Oh! my lads, do spring." The exact phrase of beef up, meaning to "add strength," first appeared in 1941 in Alfred Oliver Pollard's book *Bombers Over the Reich*: "When the Fortresses reach Britain from the United States certain alterations are made; the larger guns are . . . 'beefed up' so as to give them a rate of fire of 900 rounds a minute."[23]

best of breed *n., adj.* **1.** The best of its type or category. **2.** A product considered best of its class.

BS Definition: It's OK. I mean, it's not awful or anything, especially when you compare it with the rest of the crap out there. Wait. Why

B

are you getting upset? You asked my opinion, so I . . . Oh, man. Don't cry.

Origin: The first "best of breed" dog show was held in Newcastle upon Tyne, England, in June 1859. The largest and most prestigious dog show in America is the Westminster Kennel Club Dog Show, which was established in 1877 and is held annually at Madison Square Garden in New York City. According to the *OED*, it wasn't until 1984 that the phrase was written for the first time in its business meaning, in an advertisement in *PC* magazine: "Now you can buy the finest PC compatible boards, accessories and software from a single, trusted source. The Heath Company. We guarantee these to be the best of breed for your PC."

best practice *n*. A method or technique that delivers superior results compared with other methods and techniques.

BS Definition: A great name for a new hospital TV drama. We can hear the promo now: "NYU medical student Andrea Best reluctantly accepts a match in small-town Alaska only to fall in love with the place and people, making her realize her life is more than just medicine. It's *Best Practice*!"

Origin: The term *best practice* began appearing with great frequency in books in the 18th century. One early example comes from 1746's *Agriculture Improv'd: or, The Practice of Modern Husbandry Display'd* by William Ellis, a farmer:

> For this Lady takes great Delight, and indeed makes it part of her Business, to pry into, and inform her judgment of, the latest and best Practice of Husbandry; and therefore very much encourages and receives Advice on this Account.[24]

This citation predates the *OED*'s first reference, which is a 1927 issue of *Popular Science*: "Can the home builder rely on city plumbing codes to specify best practice?"

beta testing *v.* **1.** A phase of new development in which a sampling of the intended audience tries out a product. **2.** A trial period in which a new product is usually given free to employees of the developing organization to verify that it performs as intended.

> **BS Definition: 1.** Trying new stuff out on an unsuspecting public and hoping nobody sues you when somebody gets hurt. **2.** Another way of saying "throwing spaghetti at the wall."

> **Origin:** According to a *BS Dictionary* search of usage on the Google Ngram Viewer, the term beta test was used as early as the 1920s in various documents, primarily in scientific studies. One reference we found contained many examples of alpha (first-stage testing) and beta (second stage), including multiple data tables where both are labeled. Here's one example: "After segregation according to literacy, the alpha examination is given in groups up to 500; the beta test in groups as large as 100."[25] However, the phrase became popular in BS during the golden age of IBM (the 1960s), when engineers used it to denote the second stage of development. Alpha testing represented the feasibility and manufacturability evaluation done before any commitment to design and development, and the beta test represented a demonstration that the engineering model functioned as specified.[26]

big data *n.* **1.** A collection of data that is too big and complicated for processing by traditional database management tools. **2.** A collection of data from traditional and digital sources inside and outside your company that represent a source for ongoing discovery and analysis.

> **BS Definition:** A term used when you want to sound like what you're working on is super important or hard (instead of something your 10-year-old could figure out, if given the chance).

Origin: Some credit Roger Magoulas from O'Reilly Media as the one who popularized the term *big data* in 2005. (Interestingly, it was only a year after the media company had created the term *web 2.0*.) However, others suggest that the term was first used long before Magoulas. John Mashey, who was the chief scientist at Silicon Graphics in the 1990s, gave hundreds of talks to small groups in the middle and late '90s to explain the concept, including one entitled "Big Data and the Next Wave of Infrastress" in 1998.[27] Meanwhile, the *OED* cites a 1980 research paper from the University of Michigan as the birth year for big data: "None of the big questions has actually yielded to the bludgeoning of the big-data people."[28] Regardless of its exact origin, big data has become one of the most popular BS buzzwords of the 21st century.

binary *adj.* 1. Of or relating to something programmed or encoded using only the digits of 0 and 1. 2. Having only two elements or aspects.

BS Definition: If you use this word conversationally, chances are you are A) socially awkward, and B) smarter than most of the people you work with.

Origin: "It's not binary!" Seth Rogen's character, Steve Wozniak, says to Steve Jobs (played by Michael Fassbender) in the 2015 movie named after the Apple founder. "You can be decent and gifted at the same time."[29]

While those lines were written by screenwriter Aaron Sorkin for a movie, the use of binary to describe only two potential (incompatible) outcomes is showing up more and more in business speak in the new millennium. The immediate reason is its origin in technology, particularly computing. But the term itself—and the modern concept of binary numbers—goes back centuries to Gottfried Leibniz in 1689, appearing in his article "Explication de l'Arithmétique Binaire." Almost 200 years later, two men, George Boole and Claude Shannon, are credited with applying binary numbers to computing. Boole, who in 1854 published a landmark paper on an algebraic system of logic that would become known as

Boolean algebra, proposed that logic problems could be solved by math equations, assigning a value of 1 to true statements and 0 to false statements. Meanwhile, Shannon, an electrical engineer who happened to take a philosophy course at the University of Michigan covering Boole's work, later applied this principle in his 1937 master's thesis, "A Symbolic Analysis of Relay and Switching Circuits," in which he combined Boole's logic system with telephone-call-routing technology to figure out a way to transmit any type of information electronically.[30] Basically, that was the key insight on which computers would eventually rely, and the 1s and 0s that form the basis for all binary code—which is used to write data, such as the instructions that computer processors use. Said Shannon on the happenstance of his discovery in applying two different fields, philosophy and technology: "It just happened that no one else was familiar with both those fields at the same time."[31] As Seth Rogen's character said, that's not binary!

bio break *n.* A pause to go to the bathroom during a meeting.

BS Definition: 1. A polite way of saying, "Hey, why don't we take 10 minutes here to run to the bathroom before I embarrass myself?" **2.** An opportunity to sit in a bathroom stall, check your social-media feeds, and drift into daydreams of what your life could have been.

Origin: In terms of a way to say one is relieving oneself, biological break first started to appear in print in the late 20th century. One early reference occurs in the 1991 book *Shocco Tales: Southern Fried Sagas* by Jim Ritchie, who notes on page 50: "The tight space in the booths did have one disadvantage. When you had to take a biological break and adjourn to the rest room, you had to squeeze out past the other scrunchers and lose your seat." Bio break as a shortened form was popularized soon thereafter, in the mid-1990s. *Wired* magazine reported in 1994 that it was "techie slang for using the bathroom." Older euphemisms for the same thing include "visit the powder room," "use the facilities," and, of course, "Get out of the way! I need to go!"[32]

Bitcoin *n.* **1.** A digital payment system introduced in 2009. **2.** A type of digital or virtual currency that uses state-of-the-art peer-to-peer technology to facilitate instant payments.

BS Definition: Something that, 20 years from now, could be considered as revolutionary as email (see *game changer*) or as outdated as a Laser-Disc (see *miss the boat/bus*).

Origin: Of all the origin stories in this book, Bitcoin (and its related BS term, *blockchain*) may have the coolest one. In 2008, a scientist using the pseudonym Satoshi Nakamoto published a nine-page whitepaper on a mailing list for people interested in cryptography (the practice and study of techniques for secure communication).[33] *Bitcoin: A Peer-to-Peer Electronic Cash System* outlined in detail how to make a completely novel cryptocurrency called "Bitcoin."

Unlike government-issued currencies, Bitcoin is operated by a decentralized authority (no banks or governments issue or back it), and it offers the promise of lower transaction fees than traditional online payment mechanisms. There are no physical Bitcoins, only balances kept on a public ledger in the cloud that—along with all Bitcoin transactions—is verified by a massive amount of computing power (see *blockchain*). As you might guess, that whitepaper featured the first public record of the word: "I've been working on a new electronic cash system that's fully peer-to-peer, with no trusted third party . . . Bitcoin: a peer-to-peer electronic cash system."

Ever since, Bitcoin has received a fair amount of media attention from supporters and critics alike.[34] In December 2012, *Foreign Policy* magazine said, "Bitcoin . . . is either the future of global commerce or a high-tech form of money laundering—depending on whom you ask." And in 2014, the business section of the *Sunday Independent* (Ireland) newspaper reported, "Bitcoin is not really a currency, it's a commodity. It has no value other than what people are willing to pay for it."

Regardless, one thing is certain about Bitcoin: Whoever Nakamoto is, they have potentially made *a lot* of money off it. Experts estimate that those who were in on Bitcoin at the beginning (in 2009) could easily be billionaires by now.[35]

bleeding-edge *adj.* **1.** Extremely cutting-edge. **2.** Brand-new or visionary, but also carrying a high level of risk. **3.** At the forefront of innovation or development.

BS Definition: 1. So cutting-edge that we had to kill someone to make it. **2.** Cuts like a knife (yeah, and it feels so right).[36]

Origin: First used in the 1980s, the saying has a lot in common with *leading-edge* and *cutting-edge*. The first documented example of *bleeding-edge* dates to early 1983, when an anonymous banking executive used it in reference to Storage Technology Corporation, a company later bought by Oracle: "We ended up on the bleeding edge of technology, instead of the leading edge," he said.[37] Although most commonly used in reference to new technologies, the term can also describe new styles in the fine arts. *Bleeding-edge* may have originated as a pun on leading-edge. In aeronautics, *leading edge* is a technical term for the airfoil or propeller blade at the front of the plane, leading the movement of the plane. Metaphorically, the *leading edge* refers to the most recent development in a field. *Bleeding edge* comically alludes to a leading edge as a dangerous weapon.[38]

B

blockchain *n.* **1.** Digital pieces of information ("blocks") stored in a public database (the "chain"). **2.** Uniquely coded data that, depending on the tracking required, can document a huge amount of transaction history in one spot.

BS Definition: Something that most of us still don't really understand, so we just smile and nod whenever it's talked about in front of us.

Origin: Remember that story we told you about the origin of Bitcoin? Well, that same story applies to blockchain, because it too came from the same whitepaper mysteriously posted by the pseudonymous Satoshi Nakamoto in 2008 on a mailing list for people interested in cryptography (the practice and study of techniques for secure communication).[39] *Bitcoin: A Peer-to-Peer Electronic Cash System* outlined in detail how to make a completely novel cryptocurrency based on a sophisticated mathematical formula and architecture. That architecture eventually included the first blockchain—which helps ensure that people are exchanging actual value in cyberspace when they use cryptocurrency.

The first-ever work on a cryptographically secured chain of blocks (what we would later consider a "blockchain") took place from 1991 to 1992, when mathematicians Stuart Haber and W. Scott Stornetta published some of the first ideas on it.[40] However, it was Nakamoto who cracked the code and actually made the first one. Nakamoto's identity is unknown to this day, but speculation is that they are a computer-science expert of non-Japanese descent, living in the United States and various European countries. Personally, we think it's George Clooney. He just looks like an international man of mystery to us (see *action man*).

blue sky *v.* **1.** To come up with new ideas or new approaches. **2.** To think creatively. **3.** To explore an idea with no immediate commercial goal.

BS Definition: To waste time thinking about ideas that will never get approved for production.

Origin: This term is said to have originated in the early 1900s, when a Supreme Court justice declared his desire to protect investors from speculative ventures that had "as much value as a patch of blue sky." In the years leading up to the 1929 stock market crash, there were instances of companies making lofty, unsubstantiated promises of greater profits to come. In the 1930s, states enacted "blue sky laws" intended to protect investors from those practices in the future.[41] Over time, the term *blue sky* took on a more positive connotation. In 1959, the *OED* says, a Duke Law School publication gave us the first written use of *blue sky* in that positive light: "Many large firms set aside a significant portion of their research and development budget for 'undirected' or 'blue sky' research with the full confidence that over the long run, the new knowledge gained will pay off."

boil the ocean *v.* **1.** To undertake an impossible task or project. **2.** To make a task or project unnecessarily difficult.

BS Definition: To try to understand U.S. tax codes.

Origin: Usually attributed to American humorist Will Rogers, who is said to have suggested boiling the ocean as a way to deal with German U-boats during World War I: "You just boil the oceans. The U-boats will turn pink and pop to the surface. Then, you just pick them off."[42] Shrugging off the question of how to actually boil the ocean, Rogers just said that he never worries about details. Sounds like Rogers would have been a good collaborator for us on this book!

boondoggle *n.* **1.** An unethical use of public money. **2.** Work or activity that is wasteful or pointless but gives the appearance of having value.

BS Definition: 1. Checking your social media feeds at work and calling it "market research." **2.** An adorable name for a basset hound.

Origin: Among the things Boy Scouts did at summer camps in the late 1920s and early 1930s was braid and knot colorful strands of plastic and leather to fashion lanyards, neckerchief slides, and bracelets. Eagle Scout Robert Link of Rochester, New York, coined the term for this new handicraft: "boondoggling."[43]

Few Americans had heard of it until it suddenly became front-page news on April 4, 1935.[44] That's when the *New York Times* reported that the federal Works Progress Administration (WPA) had spent more than $3 million on training for unemployed white-collar workers that included instruction in ballet dancing, shadow puppetry, and making boondoggles. Even though this expenditure helped hundreds of unemployed teachers and taught children in poor neighborhoods creative uses for material that otherwise would have been trash, critics of President Franklin D. Roosevelt's New Deal pounced on the frivolous-sounding "boondoggling" activities as indicative of what they considered the WPA's wasteful spending. "It is a pretty good word," Roosevelt admitted in a January 1936 speech, before adding, "If we can boondoggle our way out of the Depression, that word is going to be enshrined in the hearts of Americans for many years to come."

The word indeed became part of the American political lexicon, but not in the way Roosevelt had hoped. Ironically, an activity that was part of an effort to encourage children to reuse waste materials has become synonymous with waste itself.

bootstrap *v.* **1.** To start a business without external help or capital. **2.** To do a difficult task using very little outside resources to complete it.

BS Definition: What you have to do every single time the bozos (*incompetent fools*) in accounting open their yappers (*mouths*) and say your ideas cost too much moolah (*money*).

Origin: Let's put aside the fact that it is impossible to lift yourself off the ground by pulling on straps attached to your boots and just look at the origin of this phrase.

B

"Pulling yourself up by your own bootstraps" was a phrase known by the early 20th century. One of the earliest citations comes from the April 1918 issue of *Upton Sinclair's: A Monthly Magazine*, in which the famed social activist mockingly refers to bootstrap-lifters:

> Bootstrap-lifting? says the reader. It is a vision I have seen: upon a vast plain, men and women are gathered in dense throngs, crouched in uncomfortable and distressing positions, their fingers hooked into the straps of their boots. They are engaged in lifting themselves; tugging and straining until they grow red in the face, exhausted.

James Joyce also mentions it in *Ulysses*, published in 1922: "There were others who had forced their way to the top from the lowest rung by the aid of their bootstraps."

Some early computers used a process called *bootstrapping*, which alludes to this phrase. The process involved loading a small amount of code that was then used to progressively load more complex code until the machine was ready for use. This led to the use of the term *booting*, to mean starting up a computer.

However, some researchers say the true origin of this phrase is as an insult. It used to describe people who were basically delusional—you know, like people who spend hundreds of hours writing a book about business speak, thinking it will actually make them money down the line. This meaning makes sense (because, as we mentioned earlier, it's physically impossible to pull yourself up by your own bootstraps), but, at some point in history, this phrase went from defining delusional behavior to denoting fortitude and resourcefulness.[45]

bottom line *n.* **1.** The final total of an account, a balance sheet, or another financial document. **2.** The end result (see *at the end of the day*).

BS Definition: What people see when you bend over too far to pick up that sticky note that fell on the floor.

Origin: The most likely inspiration for this BS term is the world of accounting. The *OED* says that starting in 1831, *bottom line* began showing up in writing as a way to describe the last line of an account or a bill (which customarily displayed the final profit or loss). The first write-up with this meaning was in the *Providence* (Rhode Island) *Patriot* newspaper on April 15, 1831: "The managers of the opposition have a long account to settle with the farmers; and, if we mistake not, the bottom line will show a balance in favor of the farmers."[46]

brainstorm *v.* **1.** To come up with ideas in an unprepared way. **2.** To produce an idea or solve a problem spontaneously.

BS Definition: Your brain + a storm = the opposite conditions of what you would need to think clearly and quickly on short notice.

Origin: Originally, the word *brainstorm* referred to individuals who were, at least temporarily, deranged or enraged and unable to control themselves.[47] One early reference comes from 1861's *Dark Cloud With Silver Lining* by Samuel Bracebridge Hemyng: "Then a fierce brainstorm swept over her. There was a gloom on her brow, clothing the dimly visible gnomes of the future in dark, shapeless shadows."

In terms of a creative attempt to solve a problem, the term is often credited to an advertising executive by the name of Alex Osborn at BBDO, who was frustrated with the output of his employees and felt there could be a better way to tap their creativity.[48] He was said to have coined the word *brainstorming* to describe his solution in the late 1930s, *but* we found that's not true.[49]

B

The term *brainstorm*, in its BS context, had existed for more than a dozen years before Osborn allegedly invented it. In February 1925, *College Humor* magazine out of Chicago ran an article that included the following line with the word's BS meaning behind it: "He had a brainstorm." With that said, possibly Osborn's real brainstorm with this term was simply to co-opt it and brand it as his own—which while not completely original, is kind of genius in itself.

bullish *adj.* **1.** Hopeful; optimistic. **2.** Potentially profitable.

BS Definition: Often used on CNBC by commentators who probably should be more bearish.

Origin: The first known instance of the market term *bull* was in 1714. At the time, it was a relatively common (and gruesome) practice to bear- and bull-bait. That means people would chain a bear (or bull) up in an arena, and then set some other animals (usually dogs) to attack it as a form of entertainment for spectators seated in the arena. Sick, right?

It is speculated that the popularity of bear- and bull-baiting at that time—along with the association of bulls charging—is why bull (aggressive and optimistic) became the antithesis of bear (conservative and pessimistic) in the stock sense. By the way . . .

The leading theory as to why *bear* became synonymous with pessimism is derived from a 16th-century proverb: "selling the bear's skin before one has caught the bear," or alternatively, "Don't sell the bear's skin before you've killed him," equivalent to, "Don't count your chickens before they've hatched." By the early 18th century, when people in the stock world started selling something they didn't yet own (in hopes of turning a profit by eventually being able to buy the thing at a cheaper rate than what they'd sold it for, before delivery was due), this gave rise to the saying that they'd "sold the bear-skin," and the people themselves were called "bearskin jobbers."[50]

burning platform *n.* **1.** An impending crisis. **2.** An urgency to make a choice or change behavior.

BS Definition: When the CEO of your tech company in Silicon Valley suggests you expand into winemaking (check out AltaVista true stories).

Origin: This origin story is the stuff of nightmares. In July 1988, Andy Mochan was working on the Piper Alpha oil-drilling platform in the North Sea off the coast of Scotland. An explosion rocked the rig one night, causing a huge fire on the platform. Mochan managed to escape the flames and find his way to the edge of the platform. Facing certain death from the approaching fire, Mochan jumped more than 100 feet into the freezing North Atlantic waters. Fortunately, he survived the jump and was rescued by boat. When asked later why he took that potentially fatal leap, Mochan said, "It was either jump or fry."[51] Since then, businesspeople have started using *burning platform* as shorthand for the conditions that exist when hard choices of survival have to be made.

buy-in *n., v.* **1.** Agreement or acceptance. **2.** Support.

BS Definition: Peer pressure from your boss to make you agree to something stupid.

Origin: A shortened form of *buy into*, this colloquialism can be used as a noun or verb. Early uses of the term *buy into* emerged around the concepts of buying into stocks, starting in the late 17th century and into the 18th century. One of the earliest references comes from Sir Josiah Child, an economic writer and a merchant, who wrote in the publication *Treatise E.-India Trade* in 1681: "I . . . had rather buy in this Stock . . . at

300l. for 100l. then come into any New Stock at even Money." According to the *OED*, the first colloquial instance of *buy in*, as in subscribing to an idea, came in 1972 in *Philosophical Quarterly* magazine:

> Everybody else subjects himself to a rule requiring that he keep his promises . . . on the understanding that I will do the same (an understanding I give whenever I buy into the institution by using the word 'I promise' in the relevant circumstances).

BS IS LIKE A BOX OF CHOCOLATES—PART II

Here are our top four movie lines that are used in the world of BS.

No. 4.
"Greed . . . is good" (Wall Street)

Why It's Influential: In the movie, Wall Street financier Gordon Gekko (played by Michael Douglas) utters the phrase "Greed, for lack of a better word, is good" when addressing a stockholders meeting of Teldar Paper. At the time, the line shocked audiences, most of whom had never heard an argument in support of that particular vice. Interestingly, that writer and director Oliver Stone envisioned this film to be a cautionary tale about the evils and excesses of Wall Street, but Douglas's portrayal was so compelling that it opened the floodgates of business-school graduates wanting to join investment banks and other Wall Street institutions.

Why It Works in Business Speak: If you're talking business, you're talking money. If you're talking money, you're talking about the possibility of greed. That's why this saying gets a lot of play in the business world—especially when being used facetiously. If you really want to mess with people, we encourage you to memorize the whole speech Gekko gives in the film, and use it as a response the next time your legal team suggests strictly adhering to any environmental, financial, health, or safety regulations that stand in the way of making money.

No. 3.
"We're not in Kansas anymore" (The Wizard of Oz)

Why It's Influential: After a tornado whips through her home state of Kansas, Dorothy, played by Judy Garland, arrives in the magical land of

Oz with her dog, Toto, and utters the somewhat obvious phrase, "Toto, I have a feeling we're not in Kansas anymore." The line wasn't in the original book by L. Frank Baum, so some see it as perhaps a subtle dig at what Hollywood considered the general naivete of the flyover states. And c'mon, it's *The Wizard of Oz*, one of the greatest movies in history.

Why It Works in Business Speak: If you live, work, or have roots in Kansas (like *BS Dictionary* co-author Bob Wiltfong), you may not have the same fondness for this phrase that others do. That's because the phrase is usually used by non-Kansans as a way to belittle the lack of refinement of people from that part of the world, and everyone who says it to a Kansan thinks it's, somehow, the first time that person has ever heard the line used outside the film. It's sort of like going up to a native New Yorker and going "Bada-bing!" or a native Californian and saying, "Duuuude." With that said, it's definitely a BS-friendly line from *The Wizard of Oz*, along with others like, "There's no place like home," "If I only had a brain," "Follow the yellow-brick road," "Ding-dong, the witch is dead," and "Pay no attention to the man behind the curtain."

No. 2
"You're going to need a bigger boat" (*Jaws*)

Why It's Influential: Martin Brody, the chief of police for Martha's Vineyard (played by Roy Scheider), gets his first glimpse of the massive great white shark in the film and backs away toward Quint (played by Robert Shaw), uttering the famous line: "You're going to need a bigger boat," with his lit cigarette dangling from his mouth. What's interesting about the film is that the line was never in the original screenplay, but was ad-libbed in various takes by Scheider because it was a running joke that the boat being used wasn't actually conducive to filming the scenes.

Why It Works in Business Speak: We love using this literally anytime we can. Try this: The next time you suggest a marketing budget and the CEO cuts it in half, employ this line and see how it goes. Likely you will get the reaction that Brody eventually got from Quint in the movie—to trash the boat even more. Oh, it's also a great line for poker too (when you have a hand that trumps someone else's).

No. 1.
"These go to 11" (*This Is Spinal Tap*)

Why It's Influential: Guitarist Nigel Tufnel, played by Christopher Guest, is explaining the configuration of his amps to documentarian Marty DiBergi (played by Rob Reiner). The amp has dials that go to a maximum setting of 11 rather than the standard 10; DiBergi asks, "Why don't you just make 10 louder and make 10 be the top number and make that a little louder?" Tufnel, not seeing the logic, simply says, "But these go to 11." The original mockumentary, *This Is Spinal Tap* contains some of the best one- and two-liners in the history of movie comedy:

> » "It's such a fine line between stupid . . . and clever."
> » "They're two distinct types of visionaries; it's like fire and ice, basically. I feel my role in the band is to be somewhere in the middle of that, kind of like lukewarm water."
> » "We'd love to stand around and chat but we gotta sit down in the lobby and wait for the limo."

Why It Works in Business Speak: Honestly, feel free to use any of these lines to mock the always-way-too-confident individuals in your organization—especially that product VP who seems to relish the idea of including every single feature set known to humankind in the new release.

C

cannibalize *v.* **1.** To launch a new product that takes market share away from a company's established products. **2.** To remove parts, equipment, assets, employees, and so forth from an item, a product, or a business in order to use them in another.

BS Definition: To cut off your nose to spite your face . . . and then eat that nose.

Origin: Derived from the Spanish word *canibal*, the term was first applied by the Spaniards to West Indies natives, who the Europeans believed were anthropophagites (eaters of human flesh). Apparently, the term was Christopher Columbus's interpretation of how the natives referred to themselves (*kalino, karina*).[1] How he got canibal out of that, we'll perhaps never know. Edmund Burke, the famed Irish-born philosopher and member of British Parliament, also used the phrase in 1798, writing in his memoirs:

> It was to stimulate their cannibal appetites (which one would think had been gorged sufficiently) by variety and seasoning; and to quicken them to an alertness in new murders and massacres, if it should suit the purpose of the Guises of the day.[2]

Outside of people eating one another, the business meaning of cannibalize was first mentioned in 1920. According to the *OED*, the *Logansport* (Indiana) *Pharos Tribune* wrote in April of that year: "The Herald and the Examiner were combined, the Herald having previously cannibalized the *Record*, the *Times*, and the *Inter-Ocean*." However, it wasn't until the 1940s that the term started to become more common in business circles.

C

The theory is that's because soldiers in World War II adopted parts from things that weren't being used to repair other machines—in a process they referred to as "cannibalizing"—and used the term more commonly in everyday conversations as a result.[3]

career suicide *n.* **1.** An action that causes you to lose both your current job and any chance you'll find another one in your field. **2.** To do something that will totally discredit you and nullify any chance of personal advancement.

BS Definition: Drinking with and/or initiating a conversation on politics with any member of the board of directors.

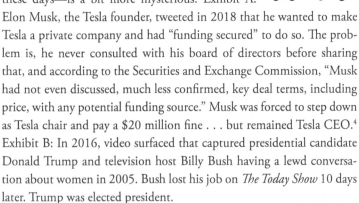

Origin: If you're looking for the hard-core punk band Career Suicide, they originated in Toronto, Canada, in 2001. However, the origin of *career suicide* in a business sense—and what results in it these days—is a bit more mysterious. Exhibit A: Elon Musk, the Tesla founder, tweeted in 2018 that he wanted to make Tesla a private company and had "funding secured" to do so. The problem is, he never consulted with his board of directors before sharing that, and according to the Securities and Exchange Commission, "Musk had not even discussed, much less confirmed, key deal terms, including price, with any potential funding source." Musk was forced to step down as Tesla chair and pay a $20 million fine . . . but remained Tesla CEO.[4] Exhibit B: In 2016, video surfaced that captured presidential candidate Donald Trump and television host Billy Bush having a lewd conversation about women in 2005. Bush lost his job on *The Today Show* 10 days later. Trump was elected president.

And when did this phrase first appear in print? According to the *OED*, the earliest reference comes from the *Huron* (South Dakota) *Huronite and Daily Plainsman*, which contained the following in its Friday, September 17, 1948, edition: "That they are afraid to say 'yes' shows that

Communists know that they are disliked and unpopular and would be committing career suicide to accept membership."[5]

catalyst for change *n.* **1.** The thing that sparks a new action or movement. **2.** A person or an event that precipitates a shift in action or thinking.

BS Definition: The opposite of Riley in accounting, who's been here way . . . too . . . long.

Origin: Most sources cite the year 1902 as when the first documented use of the word *catalyst* occurred in English. Derived from Greek, it's a combination of *kata* ("down") and *lyein* ("loosen"), and it's defined as a substance that enables a chemical reaction to proceed at a faster rate or under different conditions than would otherwise be the case.[6]

While it's not exactly clear who said the words *catalyst for change* first, the term appears to have started to take hold in the early 1960s. One of the first references we could find was in a 1961 journal called *Managing Major Change in Organizations*: "'How can similar ability to anticipate problems and plan their solution be developed by those actually engaged in managing major changes, perhaps for the first time?' It was in this setting that a new role for change catalyst emerged."[7] The term has also been associated with several key figures who have pushed for advancements within society or business. One example: Shirley Chisholm, the first African American *and* woman to seriously run for president of the United States, in 1972. She was also the first African American woman elected to Congress, in 1968. The title of her biography? *Shirley Chisholm: Catalyst for Change.*

client-centric *adj.* **1.** A specific approach to doing business that focuses on the customer. **2.** Putting the customer at the center of a business's philosophy, operations, or ideas.

BS Definition: What our company is. I mean, ahem, we always make decisions based on what's best for our customers. Sure. Right. *Avoids eye contact and changes subject*

Origin: The word *client* is believed to have first appeared in the lexicon in the 14th century as a reference to a dependent, or one who was reliant on or under the protection of another. The meaning of client as a lawyer's customer is believed to have been first used in the 1400s, and by the 1600s the word was extended to any customer who put a particular interest in the care and management of another.[8]

The exact origin of *client-centric* is less clear, but it could stem from any number of industries, including psychology and social work. One of the earliest citations, according to the *OED*, comes from *Social Forces* in 1931: "Her [sc. the social worker's] thought ceases to be client-centered." In the 1940s, one of the biggest influencers in this field was American psychologist Carl Rogers, who founded a more humanistic approach to psychology called client-centered therapy. Another possible origin source for this BS term is one of the more well-known thinkers on the customer-client relationship, Peter Drucker, who in 1954 wrote about a customer-centric approach in *The Practice of Management*: "It is the customer who determines what a business is, what it produces, and whether it will prosper."[9]

cookie-cutter *adj.* 1. Generic; unimaginative. 2. Denoting something mass-produced or lacking any distinguishing characteristics.

BS Definition: Giving your boss a coffee mug that says "World's Best Boss."

Origin: The term, of course, alludes to the utensils, which are used to cut out cookie shapes for baking. Most reliable etymological sources date the first citations of these actual baking tools to the mid-19th century, and later figurative references to the 20th century.[10] But we at *The BS Dictionary* didn't go with the cookie-cutter approach to our research. We found an even earlier reference to both the tool and the figurative use of it! Yes, we actually got excited by making that discovery.

C

In 1834, a *Conversation on Decrees and Free Agency, Between James and John* (basically a doctrine explaining and defending the Presbyterian Church) was published. It included the following passages:

> When the dough had been prepared and rolled flat, there was the interesting work of cutting out the cookies. Down went the cookie cutter and out came a cookie. . . . We employ the cookie-cutter method in religious education. . . . There is no serious attempt in most communities to provide for the children, young people, and older people, too, whom our cookie-cutter method misses.[11]

core competency *n.* **1.** The fundamental strength of a firm or person. **2.** A defining capability or advantage that distinguishes an enterprise from its competitors.

BS Definition: What you might say you've achieved when you can hold a plank position for more than 30 seconds.

Origin: The first known attribution of the term *core competency* is relatively recent. It comes from a 1990 *Harvard Business Review* article titled "The Core Competence of the Corporation," by C.K. Prahalad and Gary Hamel, who suggested that business executives in the coming decade "be judged on their ability to identify, cultivate and exploit the core competencies that make growth possible." They observed that successful enterprises viewed themselves as "a portfolio of competencies versus a portfolio of businesses," and these competencies "empower individual businesses to adapt quickly to changing opportunities." In later years, the term evolved to suggest company strengths in various businesses as well as individual strengths in certain areas.[12]

cost-effective *adj.* Producing good results without costing a lot of money.

BS Definition: A term you use when you want to "talk dirty" with an accountant. We know this for a fact. After all, how many of you have been to the Accounting Hall of Fame at The Ohio State University? We have.

Origin: The *OED* and *Merriam-Webster* cite the first use of this term as occurring around the mid-to-late 1960s. One example, from the *Washington Post* on October 31, 1963: "These significant wartime military advantages cannot and should not be assigned to a bargain basement price tag for peace time cost effectiveness study purposes." But other lesser-known sources suggest that the term was used in print as early as 1836, and appeared in documented works as early as 1887. We were unable to verify the documents from the 1800s, but if true, we would certainly empathize with *Merriam-Webster* and the *OED*, which may have found it more cost effective to not research texts going back to the 1800s.[13]

creatives *n.* 1. Designers. 2. The materials designers make (see *deliverable*).

BS Definition: The people who know how to do PowerPoint.

Origin: According to *Merriam-Webster*, creative as a noun has been around since at least the 1830s, albeit as a synonym for creation. In 1839, the *Bombay Times* of India wrote:

> It is to be lamented certainly that the three Armies of India do not form one great whole, but, while the distinctions do exist, the good policy of promoting harmony amongst them should dictate to the Government the avoidance of all such creatives of jealousy as this staff dispute has unavoidably proved.

Creatives stems from the adjective *creative*, which comes from the Latin *creō* ("to create," "to make"). *Create* appeared in English as early as the 14th century in Chaucer's *The Parson's Tale*, indicating divine creation.[14] In modern parlance, the use of *creatives* to describe the actual product produced by designers, particularly in advertising, comes from the 1930s. Hope Hale wrote the following in the *New York Tribune* to describe the "mad men" of the day:

> A dose of the anonymous Groucho is recommended to the college creatives who think of the advertising "game" as a promised land where one may deign to accept a great deal of money for having fun among the pencils and paint pots and typewriters.[15]

critical mass *n.* **1.** A majority or tipping point when something becomes dominant. **2.** The minimum size or amount of something required to start or maintain a venture.

BS Definition: When your corporate YouTube video gets more than 15 views—not including the friends and family you told to watch it.

We went viral!

Origin: The term *critical mass* is now so widely used it can refer to any number of things. In social dynamics, it's a stage of adoption in a social system; in engineering, it's a level in the product life cycle of software; in cycling, it's the name of a series of worldwide racing events; in politics, it's a U.K. political pressure group or an antinuclear umbrella group founded by Ralph Nader; in design, it's an agency headquartered in Calgary, Canada; and in robotics, it's a team at the Dwight-Englewood School in Englewood, New Jersey.[16]

However, the modern use of *critical mass* in business is commonly thought to have evolved from physics, referring to the smallest amount of fissile (capable of undergoing nuclear fission) material needed for a sustained

C

nuclear chain reaction.[17] During the race to build the atomic bomb in the 1940s, many physicists, for example, used the term *critical* with other words: size, volume, condition—in addition to mass—to describe this condition. *Critical mass* has been cited in two works in particular: the *Smyth Report* in August 1945 and the *Los Alamos Primer* in 1943.[18]

Another contributing factor to the popularity of this BS term is the work of game theorist Thomas Schelling and sociologist Mark Granovetter in the field of social dynamics. Schelling first established, although did not exactly name, the idea in his essay about racial segregation in neighborhoods, published in the *Journal of Mathematical Sociology* in 1971. He later refined the concept in his book, *Micromotives and Macrobehavior*, published in 1978, in which he used the term *critical density* with regard to pollution. Granovetter is credited with defining the term in its current and more-popular BS form in his essay "Threshold Models of Collective Behavior."[19]

cross-functional *adj.* **1.** Having different specialties or skills. **2.** Different areas of expertise working toward a common goal.

BS Definition: 1. In theory, a system in which people from different areas of an organization work together as a team. If only it worked that way every time. . . . **2.** Being able to use your middle finger to say hello *and* goodbye at the same time.

Origin: Northwestern Mutual life insurance is credited with pioneering the use of cross-functional teams in the 1950s, when the CEO gathered people from the financial, investment, actuarial, and other departments to study the effect that computers would have on the business world. As a result of that first team, Northwestern was among the first companies in the country to create an information-systems department. Today, cross-functional teams are put together for other reasons, including encouraging diversity, innovation, business alignment, and leadership responsibilities.[20]

cross-pollination *n.* **1.** Generating ideas by bringing together people from different backgrounds and experiences. **2.** Sharing knowledge from different disciplines for mutual benefit.

C

BS Definition: Stealing ideas from other people you don't think will sue you (see *dovetail*).

Origin: Pollination, the term to describe the transfer of pollen from male to female reproductive organs in seed plants, was first used in the 18th century by German naturalist Christian Konrad Sprengel. When he published his first work on the topic in 1793 it was hardly ground-breaking because many contemporaries dismissed his ideas. However, he did have his supporters—among them, Charles Darwin—who posited that cross-pollination (what he called "cross-fertilization"), rather than self-fertilization, was responsible for keeping wild species homogenous yet vigorous. In 1876, he wrote in *The Effects of Cross and Self Fertilisation in the Vegetable Kingdom*: "Cross-fertilization is sometimes ensured by the sexes being separated." The first known use of the term cross-pollination came later—in 1882, per the *OED*—in *Text-Book of Botany: Morphological and Physiological*, by botanist Sydney Howard Vines: "The contrivances for cross-pollination in Orchids."[21]

cross-sell *v.* To give an additional product or service to an existing customer in exchange for money.

BS Definition: To make more money off your customers by selling them things they don't really need.

Origin: You might think that Amazon invented cross-selling with its "Customers who bought this item also bought . . ." feature, but the truth is that cross-selling is as old as retail and sales itself. However, the practice has only been recently labeled as such. The *OED* cites the first published use of *cross-selling* in 1972, in an article in *Bankers* magazine: "The best products for new bank services come from cross selling [to] those customers who already have one type of relationship with the bank."

C

However, we found an even earlier first reference of the term—in 1960, during a U.S. Senate hearing of the Committee on Interstate and Foreign Commerce on the topic of "automobile dealers' territorial security." The transcript from June 20-22 of that year reads: "Sixty-three percent of dealers said that cross-sales and intra-territorial sales were equally profitable to them," and then the next line contains this heading: "2. Effect of cross-selling on sales and profits."[22]

While it's unclear if the auto industry coined the term, there are certainly some businesses that are better known for cross-selling techniques than others. McDonald's standardized the use of "Would you like fries with that?"; Best Buy employees asking if you'd like to buy the extended warranty on your new TV also comes to mind.[23]

cutting-edge *adj.* **1.** Innovative, pioneering. **2.** On the forefront of advancement.

BS Definition: The adjective bosses use to describe a new business or product instead of saying, "Potentially a career killer," "I have no idea if this thing will actually work," or "This could ruin all of us."

Origin: As ironic as it may seem (as well as contrary to popular wisdom), *cutting-edge* is a pretty old term. References to *cutting edge* as part of a tool or instrument that makes an incision go back as far as the early 19th century in literature. Some sources suggest that the metaphorical usage (the way we currently understand the term) also dates back to that same timeframe, although we couldn't independently confirm this.[24]

What we do know is that references to the non-tool-based meaning of *cutting-edge* began to spike after the 1960s. One citation we found comes from the 1960 book, *The Edge of Objectivity: An Essay in the History of Scientific Ideas* by Charles Coulton Gillispie: "Physics has been the cutting edge of science since Galileo, and its mathematization in dynamics was, therefore, the crucial act in the scientific revolution."[25]

D

data dump *n.* **1.** A large amount of information transferred from one system or location to another. **2.** The act of handing over a bunch of unedited research.

> **BS Definition:** Giving your bosses volumes of completely useless information and hoping they see it as a sign that you've been working hard.

> **Origin:** Originally believed to have been derived from *database dump*, this term has been used to describe the downloading of information from a database, typically an overwhelming amount. Computerized databases started to appear in U.S. companies in the 1960s.

There were two popular data models back then: a network called CODASYL and another called IMS. However, the database system that proved to be the biggest commercial success was the SABRE system—used by IBM to help American Airlines manage its reservations data.[1] The *OED* lists the first published reference of *data dump* in 1965. However, we found an earlier reference in a 1962 NASA document, *Computer Program Retrieval and Data Analysis*, in which a section heading reads: "AUTOMATIC CHECK-OUT EQUIPMENT COMPRESSED DATA DUMP PACKAGE."[2]

deep-dive *v.* **1.** To study in-depth. **2.** To immerse yourself in a situation for problem solving or idea creation.

BS Definition: To say you're going to study something really, really hard, but then kinda half-ass it when no one's looking.

Origin: According to *Merriam-Webster*, there have been several developments in the evolution of *deep-dive* as a common term. *Dive* itself has been used as word for more than 1,000 years, but in the sense of plunging into an activity, it is relatively more recent—the 16th century. As for *deep* modifying the word *dive*, one of the first documented cases was Samuel Jackson Pratt, writing in *Miscellanies* in 1785: "Lord, what a whirl! at one deep dive, In this blest region to arrive." However, deep-dive in the "thorough examination" sense came much later, dating to the late 20th century. One example is Martin Norman, who wrote in *Automotive Industries* in 1998:

> Microsoft officials say the project, known internally as Apollo, aims to create a standard Windows CE operating system platform for in-car computing, integrate a speech-based interface, establish a standard for navigation applications, and take a deep dive into in-car data communications.[3]

deliverable *n.*, *adj.* **1.** Something, such as merchandise, that is or can be delivered to fulfill a contract (see *creatives*). **2.** A realistic expectation of something that can be done.

BS Definition: The opposite of the Fyre Festival (see *dumpster fire*).

Origin: The adjective *deliverable*—meaning "that is or can be delivered"—was first used in the 1700s. However, it wasn't until 1948 that the *OED* says the word was first used in print as a noun. From the *Journal of Marketing*: "Of the original mailing 955 solicitations were delivered. . . . Of the deliverables, 185 families, or 19.4 percent agreed to join the panel."[4]

deploy *v.* **1.** To execute. **2.** To position something for use.

BS Definition: 1. To yell at planes in the sky like Tattoo from *Fantasy Island* after having one too many mai-tais.[5] **2.** Did you know only five verbs start with the letters "depl": Deploy, deplane, deplete, deplore, deplume? You're welcome. Now, maybe you can deploy that knowledge somewhere. **3.** A word that makes you feel like a military general when you say it.

Origin: The man credited with bringing the printing press to England, William Caxton (1422-91), used the words *deploye* and *dysploye* in books he printed at that time.[6] Those words have their roots in French. However, the actual adoption of *deploy* as we know it today didn't take place until the end of the 18th century. The *OED* records the first published mention as happening in 1786, in an article titled "Progress of War" in *European Magazine*: "His columns . . . are with ease and order soon deploy'd."

digital native *n.* A person who grew up during the age of digital technology and is therefore familiar with computers and the Internet from an early age.

BS Definition: 1. A person who half-listens to you because they're too busy taking pictures for their 1 million followers on Instagram. **2.** Similarly, anyone who makes up those 1 million followers on Instagram.

Origin: Many credit author Marc Prensky for having popularized this term in 2001 with his article "Digital Natives, Digital Immigrants," in which he relates the decline in American education to educators' failure to understand the needs of modern students.[7] However, the term *natives*  was used to describe this digital-age generation as early as 1996 in a widely distributed early paper—"A Declaration of the Independence of Cyberspace" by John Perry Barlow—on the governance of the rapidly growing Internet: "You are terrified of your own children, since they are natives in a world where you will always be immigrants."[8]

disruptive *adj.* **1.** Relating to a new product, service, or idea that radically changes or displaces an industry or business. **2.** Uprooting an existing market, industry, or technology and producing something new and more efficient. **3.** Destructive and creative at the same time.

or

D

disruptive innovation *n.* **1.** A new product, service, or idea whose application significantly affects the way a market or industry functions. **2.** Shaking up a market or industry by introducing something completely new and different. **3.** A process whereby a smaller company with fewer resources is able to successfully challenge and gain competitive advantage over established incumbent businesses.

> **BS Definition:** Applying a term to your own work or business without fully appreciating that it truly isn't that disruptive.

> **Origin:** The late Harvard Business School professor Clayton Christensen first introduced the theory of a business being disruptive in a 1995 article, "Disruptive Technologies: Catching the Wave," in the *Harvard Business Review*. In 2003, he published *The Innovator's Solution*, which popularized the term *disruptive innovation* as a business model.

Those who support the concept use the Internet as a classic example of a disruptive innovation. The Internet was a new technology that created unique models for making money that had never existed before. Of course, that created losses for other business models. The big bookselling chains, for example, lost business to Amazon because Amazon could display its inventory without having to own a physical store in every town, and then it shipped the book to the buyer's home.[9]

dog and pony show *n.* An overly rehearsed presentation with more style than substance.

D

BS Definition: Almost any get-rich-quick workshop on real estate.

Origin: Originally used in the United States in the late 19th and early 20th centuries, this term referred to little traveling circuses that toured through small towns and rural areas. From the *Omaha Daily Bee* in 1885: "The dog and pony show of Prof. Morris drew big houses at the matinee and at the evening performance yesterday."[10] The name derives from the common use of dogs and ponies as the main attractions of the events. Among the most notorious was the Prof. Gentry's Famous Dog & Pony Show of 1886, in which teenager Henry Gentry and his brothers toured with their act, originally called "Gentry's Equine and Canine Paradox."[11] Lexicographer and linguist Grant Barrett says that by the 1940s, the phrase had become part of the figurative language of the military and government to denote an activity with more style than substance.[12]

dogfooding/eating your own dog food *v.* **1.** A company using its own workforce to test a product. **2.** Working out the glitches of a new product by testing it with your own people first.

BS Definition: 1. When you're an engineer at Blackberry and you're forced to use the company product, but you'd rather use your iPhone. **2.** C'mon, you can't tell me those executives at Purina never tried the Beggin' Strips?

Origin: Some believe that the origin of the phrase *dogfooding*, or *eating your own dog food*, comes from Microsoft in 1988, when manager Paul Maritz sent another manager at the company an email titled "Eating Our Own Dogfood," challenging his colleague to increase internal usage of the company's product. From there, usage of the term spread through the company. It is believed Maritz's inspiration for the term was Lorne Greene's Alpo dog food TV commercial from the 1970s, in which Greene said his dogs ate Alpo.[13] Others credit the president of Kal Kan Pet Food, Clement L. Hirsch, who was said to eat a can of his company's dog food at shareholders' meetings. He was a thoroughbred racehorse owner and actually has a famous race named after him that is run every year.[14]

dovetail *v.* **1.** To expand upon someone else's idea. **2.** To join or fit together harmoniously.

BS Definition: To hijack someone else's good idea and claim it as your own (see *brainstorm*).

Origin: *Dovetail* is believed to have come from the field of carpentry, specifically the tenon joint, which connects two pieces of wood. The tenon joint is inserted into another piece of wood to join it and is named for the triangle shape of a bird's tail display, which it resembles.[15] These dovetail or tenon joints have actually been around for thousands of years—notably used in the burials of ancient Chinese emperors.

However, the term came into English much later—in the late 1500s, according to etymology sources.[16] One of the early references comes from Thomas Cooper's *Thesaurus Linguae Romanae & Britannicae*, first edition, from 1565: "A swallowe tayle or dooue tayle in carpenters workes, which is a fastning of two peeces of timber or bourdes togither that they can not away." The *OED* says it wasn't until the early 1800s that the term started to be used figuratively to mean joining different thoughts together.

downsize *v.* **1.** To reduce the size of a company or workforce. **2.** To dismiss someone from employment.

BS Definition: To be someone's best friend one minute and then escort them out of the building the next.

Origin: Many sources credit the U.S. auto industry—specifically GM—for coining the term *downsize* in the 1970s. However, our research suggests its original use appears to be in the clothing industry of the 1960s. That's when some manufacturers started labeling their clothing a smaller size, using the word "downsize" to describe the process. The *OED* cites an early reference in the *Phoenix Republic* from June 1, 1968: "The fashion industry in recent years has been down-sizing some of its merchandise, flattering the American woman's ego as her figure . . . has changed its dimensions."

The term then was adopted by the U.S. auto industry, which began to make smaller cars as a response to new Corporate Average Fuel Economy (CAFE) fuel standards enacted in 1975.[17] As mentioned earlier, several sources credit GM with owning the phrase, but this early quote from *The Times Herald-Record* (in Middletown, New York) actually associates it with Ford in May 1975: "By 1981, Markley says, Ford will spend another $2.3 billion . . . to 'downsize' its fleet."

Regardless of who started it, by the mid-1980s, downsizing was synonymous with shedding jobs at various companies, and it began occurring in much greater frequency during the decade.[18] Eastman Kodak, for example, was downsized four times between 1982 and 1992 . . . and now has nearly downsized itself out of existence.[19]

drill down *v.* **1.** To examine something closely (see *deep-dive*). **2.** To move from general information to more detailed information with computer data.

BS Definition: 1. To actually follow the on-screen instructions when trying to figure out why the copier stopped working properly. **2.** What an IT person is doing when they mumble to you, "Have you tried turning it off and on again?"

Origin: *Drill down* had its first citations in military use, where it referred to cadets who competed with one another to follow drill commands the longest. From the *Eau Claire Daily Leader* in August 1889: "At the conclusion of each drill there is considerable excitement as the men drill their best to determine which is the best man . . . There will be a drill down every evening this week."[20] Whether that influenced the eventual business use is unknown, but it wasn't until a century later that *drill down* came to be related to the software/IT industry, where one follows information downward as part of a menu for a database or website. The *OED* documents the year of its first written use in this context as 1987, in an article from *PC Week* magazine: "By selecting directories or folders, you're able to 'drill down' through the directories or folders to access the file you wish to transfer."

drinking the Kool-Aid *v.* **1.** To blindly accept something. **2.** To demonstrate unquestioning obedience or loyalty.

BS Definition: By definition, any employee of Arthur Andersen who worked on the Enron audit.

Origin: The origin of this phrase comes from tragedy. In 1978, several hundred followers of an American cult known as the Peoples Temple, under the leadership of a religious figure named Jim Jones, committed suicide in north Guyana (Jonestown) by ingesting a flavored drink mixed with cyanide.[21] The powdered drink mix used might not have been Kool-Aid, but rather a competing brand called Flavor Aid. However, given Kool-Aid's popularity at the time, it became synonymous with the event. The early negative references to "drinking the Kool-Aid" came soon after in December 1978, when Reverend William Sloane Coffin told a Pax Christi convention that American planning for nuclear war and preparations for civil defense was "the Kool-Aid drill without the cyanide."

One of the other early references to Kool-Aid in the sense of blind obedience came in 1984, when a Ronald Reagan–administration appointee, Clarence M. Pendleton Jr., chairman of the United States Commission on Civil Rights, criticized civil rights leaders Jesse Jackson, Vernon Jordan Jr., and Benjamin Hooks: "We refuse to be led into another political Jonestown as we were led during the Presidential campaign. No more Kool-Aid, Jesse, Vernon and Ben. We want to be free."[22]

D

ducks in a row *n.* **1.** To have everything straight and organized. **2.** To be fully prepared.

BS Definition: The opposite of the guy in charge of putting enough life-boats on the *Titanic* before it set sail (see *due diligence*).

Origin: What's interesting about this phrase is that many people think it comes from sporting events—duck-pin bowling or even billiards (where a *duck* is a pool-hall term for a ball sitting right in front of a pocket)—but most experts believe it alludes to a mother duck leading her ducklings in an orderly single file. Although the *Washington Post* used "economic ducks in a row" in 1932, the first documented use appears to be from the *Daily Progress* of Petersburg, Virginia, in June 1910: "It quite frequently happens that when political parties and even nations think they have 'their ducks in a row' the unexpected happens which knocks their well-laid plans awry."[23]

due diligence *n.* **1.** The time and effort required to make sure everything gets its proper care and attention (see *ducks in a row*). **2.** The process of gathering or disclosing all the relevant information about a prospective deal or business.

BS Definition: The opposite of the guy who let them bring the Trojan horse into Troy.

Origin: According to the *OED*, the first written reference of this BS term happened around 1450 in a document called *The Chastising of God's Children, and The Treatise of Perfection of the Sons of God*: "In loue it is euerlastynglye drawynge yn..who that gyffes dewe dyligence to this indrawynge..into the felthe of dedly synne..maye nought falle." Man, people in the Middle Ages just loved to add a "y" and "e" to every word they wrote, didn't they?

In 1600, English historian Richard Carew was the first to put the modern spelling of due diligence on the page when he wrote "A Herring's Tale" about monarchs who had their commands obeyed "with due diligence." Interestingly, Carew was one of the first to believe in the potential for English to be a world language. *Due diligence* soon found a home in the legal profession after Carew's writing. Indeed, according to author Joanna Bourke-Martignoni, in *Due Diligence and Its Application to Protect Women From Violence*, the writings of several 17th-century jurists—Hugo Grotius, Richard Zouche, and Samuel Pufendorf among them—referenced the concept of due diligence when discussing the responsibility of the sovereign to protect foreign nationals.[25]

dumpster fire *n.* **1.** A complete and utter disaster (a train wreck). **2.** A person or thing that is uncontrollable and no one wants to deal with (a hot mess). **3.** An embarrassing, mishandled mess (a clusterf%#).

BS Definition: The batteries on the Samsung Galaxy Note 7 smartphone. Literally.

Origin: In 1936, a man by the name of George Dempster in Knoxville, Tennessee, invented a new trash-collection system that involved mechanically lifting and emptying large containers of trash into a vehicle. He married the word dump with his own last name and called his creation the "Dempster-Dumpster." Since then, dumpster has been so thoroughly applied as a generic noun that the Associated Press now directs that it be styled in lowercase, and even though fires

D

in waste containers have been around for longer than dumpsters themselves, it's tricky to pin down when *dumpster fire* started to be used as a BS term. The literal definition of a *dumpster fire* has appeared in local newspapers and fire-department training documents as far back as the 1970s. However, it's not until a 2003 review in the *Arizona Republic* of that year's remake of *The Texas Chainsaw Massacre* that we see *dumpster fire* used in print for the first time with a metaphorical reference: "the cinematic equivalent of a dumpster fire—stinky but insignificant."[26] We imagine ol' Leatherface would like to take his chainsaw to that review and throw it in a Dempster-Dumpster.

FYI ON BS ABBREVIATIONS

EQ, FAQ, and *MO* are a few of the BS abbreviations we define in this book. That list is growing, thanks to the popularity of texting and instant messaging in business. For example, *BTW* (by the way), *IMHO* (in my humble opinion), and *BRB* (be right back) are often found in today's business communications. Let's look at some other common ones.[1]

AKA	also known as
DIY	do it yourself
DOB	date of birth
ETA	estimated time of arrival
FYI	for your information
HR	human resources
MD	medical doctor
MIA	missing in action
PC	personal computer
PR	public relations
PS	in Latin, post scriptum; in English, one more thought
RIP	rest in peace
RSVP	in French, répondez s'il vous plaît; in English, to respond or reserve
TBD	to be determined
TGIF	thank God it's Friday

E

EQ *n.* E-Q **1.** Abbreviation for "emotional quotient." **2.** The capacity to recognize and manage your own feelings and those of others in social interactions. **3.** The level of a person's emotional intelligence, sometimes expressed as a score from a standardized psychology test. **4.** The ability to relate to others with compassion and empathy, have well-developed social skills, and direct one's actions and behavior around this emotional awareness.

BS Definition: The ability (or lack thereof) to keep your sh*t together when having a bad day at work.

Origin: This BS term has two origin stories: when it was first used in the English language and when it was first popularized in business speak. Unfortunately, many online sources (we're looking at you, Wikipedia and Psychology Encyclopedia—see *throwing shade*) have confused the two, so let's clarify what's what here.

According to the *OED*, EQ was first described in writing as far back as 1926, in a journal for teaching English-language arts to middle-school and high-school students: "The really gifted student must needs combine with the high I.Q. a high E.Q., or emotion quotient" (*English Journal*).[1] The *OED* cites, in 1934, a different academic journal, *Music Educators Journal*, for using the exact phrase *emotional quotient* this way: "It may be that our schools have overemphasized the intelligence quotient and underestimated the emotional quotient."

In a business sense, the term EQ, or emotional quotient, is often attributed to another phrase popularized in the mid-1990s, *emotional intelligence.* However, even here, online sources need some clarification (sorry again Wikipedia and Psychology Encyclopedia—see *throw under the bus*). Emotional intelligence was first mentioned in writing as far back as 1849, in a book called *Man Primeval*, by minister, author, and college head John Harris: "As an emotional intelligence to whom the creative revelation is made, he contemplates objects." In 1995, psychologist and journalist Daniel Goleman popularized the term (and EQ) for the masses when he published the highly successful *Emotional Intelligence*.[2] The book built on previous research by psychologists Peter Salovey and John Mayer (not the singer) on the idea.[3] However, the term emotional intelligence has since been criticized by some in the scientific world for oversimplifying the concept in leadership and business discussions.[4]

Easter egg *n.* An intentional inside joke, hidden message, or image inside computer software or media.

BS Definition: When your boss says, "You work too hard. Maybe you should take a vacation."

Origin: Vengeance was the driving force behind the origin story for Easter egg. In 1979, Atari employee Warren Robinett was upset that the company had forbidden programmers' names from appearing in game credits. Atari was afraid that competitors would try to steal its employees, and getting their names off a game's credits would make it easier to do so. Robinett objected, so he secretly inserted the message "Created by Warren Robinett" inside *Adventure*, a game he was working on. The message would appear only if play-ers moved their avatar over a specific pixel (the "gray dot") during a certain part of the game. Take that, Atari! Robinett left the company a short time later, but he never told the company about what he did. However, the gray dot and Robinett's message was soon discovered by a player, who told Atari about them. Atari management initially wanted to remove the message and release the game again, but this was deemed too costly. Instead, the director of software development in the Atari consumer division, Steve Wright, suggested they keep the message and encourage similar surprises in future games as a kind of "Easter egg hunt" for players.[5]

E

EBITDA *n.* E-BIT-DA **1.** Abbreviation for "earnings before interest, tax, depreciation, and amortization." **2.** Income before the influence of accounting and financial deductions.

BS Definition: To hear something for the first time and know *instantly* you're going to have to google it to understand what the heck it really means.

Origin: A man nicknamed the "King of Cable" is who's credited with introducing this term into BS lore. John Malone is the largest landowner in America right now, and he acquired his nickname because he made his (first) fortune in the infancy days of the cable business (see *tycoon*). As the story goes, it was during that time, in the 1980s and 1990s, that Malone had a key insight about the cable industry. While Wall Street and most of his peers were obsessed with net income and earnings per share (EPS) in their companies, Malone wanted to *minimize* net income. He figured higher net income meant higher taxes. So, to help him determine what companies to buy or sell, he started to lean on the data point of earnings before interest, tax, depreciation, and amortization, or EBIT-DA for short. Before long, financial analysts started to use EBITDA as a common metric to analyze the profitability of companies: "EBITDA at Macy's is projected at 15.5 percent of sales."[6]

Before we move on, we should acknowledge some other similar-sounding BS terms in the finance world that are sorta, kinda like EBITDA, but aren't. They are:

- **EBIT:** Earnings Before Interest and Taxes. "A company's net income before income tax expense and interest expense have been deducted. EBIT is used to analyze the performance of a company's core operations without tax expenses and the costs of the capital structure influencing profit."[7]
- **EBT:** Earnings Before Tax. "Reflects how much operating profit has been realized before accounting for taxes, while EBIT excludes both taxes and interest payments. EBT is calculated by taking net income and adding taxes back in to calculate a company's profit."[8]
- **EBITA:** Earnings Before Interest, Taxes, and Amortization. It's also a measure of company profitability used by investors.

elephant in the room *idiom* An obvious problem or controversy that is ignored or avoided, usually because it's more comfortable to do so.

BS Definition: Paying your CEO $52 million a year while having to make another round of layoffs in your company.

Origin: Much of the credit for this phrase goes to a poet named Ivan Andreyevich Krylov, who in 1814 wrote a fable, "The Inquisitive Man," in which the title character goes to a museum and notices all sorts of tiny things but fails to notice an elephant. The phrase then became popularized. Fyodor Dostoevsky, in his novel *Demons*, wrote: "Belinsky was just like Krylov's Inquisitive Man, who didn't notice the elephant in the museum." Later, sources credit the *New York Times*'s June 20, 1959, issue as having the first recorded use of this phrase as a simile: "Financing schools has become a problem about equal to having an elephant in the living room. It's so big you just can't ignore it."[9]

elevator pitch *n.* **1.** A succinct and persuasive sales pitch. **2.** A brief, convincing summary of an idea.

BS Definition: Despite best intentions, usually a rambling mess that causes the listener to feel as if they're streaming a show that doesn't allow them to fast-forward through the commercials.

Origin: There are many stories about the origin of *elevator pitch*, but a few stand out. The first comes from former journalist Ilene Rosenzweig, who was dating another journalist, Michael Caruso, during the 1990s. She says Caruso, then a senior editor at *Vanity Fair*, would attempt to pitch story ideas to Editor-in-Chief Tina Brown, but could never get much time to do so, because she was always on the move. So, to pitch her his ideas, Caruso would join Brown during the short free periods of time she had, such as on an elevator ride. Thus, claims Rosenzweig, the elevator pitch was born.[10]

A second story that predates Rosenzweig and Caruso is Philip Crosby, author of *The Art of Getting Your Own Sweet Way*, who wrote in the book's second edition in 1981: "When teaching Quality Management, I always teach my students to learn an 'elevator speech.' This is an all-encompassing, action-producing set of ideas that you pronounce while on the elevator with the big boss for just 1 minute." According to this origin story, Crosby's ideas were picked up by two statisticians—Gerry Hahn from General Electric and Tom Boardman, a professor at the University of Colorado—and they, in turn, started to push the concept onto other statisticians. From there (as the story goes), the elevator pitch caught on to a broader audience.[11]

emerging *adj.* **1.** Coming into existence or view. **2.** Developing.

BS Definition: A modifier usually placed ahead of words like *markets*, *issues*, or *infectious diseases*.

Origin: Arising out of the Latin *ēmergere*, the first use of this word is believed to have occurred in 1646, in the writings of Samuel Bolton, a Church of England clergyman and college head.[12] In "The Arraignment of Error," Bolton wrote, "The power of redressing emerging enormities in a church." Outside of that, no one seems to know exactly when this word *emerged* in the world of business speak. (See what we did there?)

empower *v.* **1.** To make (someone) stronger and more confident in their life or job. **2.** To enable or permit.

BS Definition: **1.** The first word uttered by HR after the employee engagement survey comes back. **2.** A word that's been used so often it's been rendered meaningless—unless it's being uttered by Tony Robbins, who uses it to somehow inspire people to walk on hot coals.[13]

Origin: We think *empower* may be one of the worst words in the BS world because it's overused and so few actually feel empowered when it's used to inspire them. That being said, let's get to the origin.

The word empower is made by combining the Old French prefix *en-*, meaning "in" or "into," and the root *power*, which comes from the early 1300s (meaning "ability" or "strength"). The first known use of *empowerment* was in the mid-1600s, per *Merriam-Webster* and the *OED* (some cite the first use in the 1840s), but it has only recently come back into popular use in the last several decades. In particular, some sources cite the importance of American social psychologist Julian Rappaport, whose seminal work, the 1984 *Studies in Empowerment*, brought the word back into vogue, providing a rethinking of basic approaches to areas such as human services and education.[14]

We hope this information empowers you to never use this word in your business speak again.

end to end *idiom* **1.** Including all the stages of a process. **2.** Providing all the components and resources necessary to meet a customer's requirements and not needing any other supplier to be involved.

BS Definition: A solution marketed as one-stop shopping . . . and priced that way.

Origin: *End* itself has been used in language since before the 10th century, according to etymology sources. But that's not really what we're talking about here. Most recently, the term *end to end* has roots as a design framework in computer networking from the 1960s and 1970s, forming the basis for how the modern Internet works. What would later become the "end-to-end principle" was first articulated by Paul Baran and Donald Davies in their work on packet-switched networks in the 1960s. Louis Pouzin also later pioneered the use of the end-to-end strategy in the CYCLADES network in the 1970s. According to Simson Garfinkel, writing in the *MIT Technology Review*, the end-to-end principle forms the basis for how our current Internet is structured and is sometimes seen as a direct precursor to the principle of net neutrality: "The end-to-end principle asserts that information pushed into one end of the Internet should come out the other without modification."[15]

ergonomic *adj.* Designed to maximize physical comfort or efficiency in a workplace.

BS Definition: Turning your laptop on its side so it matches your eyeline as you lay in bed working.

Origin: That ball you see your co-workers bouncing up and down on? That standing desk that makes you want to sit down and slouch?

These are all part of the field of ergonomics. Derived from the Greek words *ergon* ("work") and *nomos* ("natural law"), the word can be traced to a series of four articles written by Wojciech Jastrzebowski in Poland in 1857. However, the development of preventive measures based on an ergonomic perspective had to wait until the 20th century.

E

In 1921, ergonomic research in Japan began to be pushed by two men, Gito Teruoka, who founded the Kurashiki Institute of Science of Labour, and Kan-ichi Tanaka, who published "Research of Efficiency: Ergonomics" that same year. Later, the name *ergonomics* was officially proposed at a 1949 meeting of the British Admiralty, focusing on the design of the environment in order to optimize human well-being and performance. That event helped lead to the founding of the International Ergonomics Association (IEA) in 1959, helping to spur the organization of ergonomics-related societies or associations in different countries and areas around the world.[16]

LET'S NIP THESE COMMONLY CONFUSED TERMS IN THE BUTT . . . ER . . . BUD

Is it *for all intensive purposes* or for *all intents and purposes*? As a reader of this book, you know the answer. Unfortunately, many people don't and they speak accordingly. The following is a list of other commonly confused BS terms in today's world.[1]

Wrong	Right
shoe-in	shoo-in
I could care less	I couldn't care less
slight of hand	sleight of hand
baited breath	bated breath
honed in	homed in
wet your appetite	whet your appetite
peaked my interest	piqued my interest
tow the line	toe the line
mute point	moot point
nip it in the butt	nip it in the bud

F

FAQ *n.* F-A-Q **1.** Short for "frequently asked questions." **2.** A document that gives answers to a list of typical questions from users.

> **BS Definition:** Answers to everything you'd ever want to know except for the one thing you were actually curious about.

> **Origin:** Let's address the origin of *FAQ* in a FAQ format, shall we?

What are some of the first examples of a question-and-answer format for knowledge-sharing?
The first FAQ may go all the way back to around 400 BC. That's when Plato started to write his dialogues, based loosely on a question-and-answer format. In the second half of the 13th century, Thomas Aquinas wrote *Summa Theologica*, a series of common questions about Christianity to which he wrote a series of replies. In 1647, Matthew Hopkins wrote *The Discovery of Witches* as a list of questions and answers, but he called it "Certain Queries answered,"—CQA, if you will.

When was the acronym of FAQ first officially developed?
In the early 1980s the acronym FAQ was first officially developed due to technical limitations of early mailing lists from NASA.

Why were FAQs developed at NASA?
On ARPANET—a pioneering network for sharing digital resources among geographically separated computers—NASA users tended to post the same kind of questions to the mailing list instead of searching its archives for answers.[1] Repeating the right answers became tedious, so computer-system administrators looked for ways to address the issue.

Who was the first NASA computer-system administrator to post an FAQ?
Eugene Miya developed FAQs between 1982 and 1985 for NASA's SPACE mailing list. The format was then picked up by other mailing lists and Usenet newsgroups. The first person to post a weekly FAQ was Jef Poskanzer, to the Usenet net.graphics/comp.graphics newsgroups.[2]

F

face time *n.* **1.** Time spent visiting with someone in person, as opposed to phone conversations or other means of communication. **2.** The amount of time an employee spends in the workplace.

BS Definition: 1. What the career advice columns always tell you to do with your boss—unless, that is, your boss can't stand you. **2.** The video chat you try to do with your parents, who still can't seem to look directly into the camera.

Origin: No, we're not talking about Face-Time, Apple's famed video and voice service, which was created by engineer Roberto Garcia in June 2010 based on his work in the company's Game Center.[3] *Face time*— the term with two words—has been seen in print since at least the 1970s.

One of the earliest documented references comes from *U.S. News & World Report*, which said this about then-President Jimmy Carter in 1978: "drops by the White House press room . . . guaranteeing himself a few precious seconds of face time on the evening TV news."[4] Later, Major General Perry M. Smith compiled a glossary of the insider lingo at the Department of Defense in his 1989 book *Assignment: Pentagon* that includes: "Face time: time spent near big bosses in attempts to impress them with your diligence and loyalty."[5] Others say the phrase had been used on college campuses for decades, but was taken to mean a slightly different thing: to be seen or be seen.

facilitate *v.* **1.** To assist in the progress of something or someone. **2.** To make an action or process easier.

BS Definition: To be the boss and say things like, "C'mon, people! These widgets aren't going to make themselves!" or "Did you honestly just say that to me?" or "Uh, I write the checks. That's why!"

Origin: According to the *OED*, *facilitate* was probably borrowed from the French word *faciliter* and was combined with an English element to become what we know it as today. In 1599, Jesuit priest Robert Parsons used it for the first time in print when he wrote: "The persons also and qualities of the parties with whome this atonement is or were to be treated, are such as do greatly facilitate the enterprise."[6] This line comes from Parson's work *A Temperate Ward-word to the Turbulent and Seditious Wach-word of Sir Francis Hastinges, Knight, Who Indevoreth to Slander the whole Catholique Cause.* In modern parlance, that title might translate to *A Cool Way to Say Sir Francis Hastings Is a Jack*ss Who Is Throwing Shade on Us Catholics.*

facing *v.* **1.** Interacting with outside clients. **2.** Leading with the customer in your thinking and approach. **3.** Moving your merchandise to the most convenient and appealing location for customers to see it.

BS Definition: Putting your best-looking people out front and hiding the uglies in the back.

Origin: This term comes from the world of retail and, more specifically, grocery stores, where it is considered a driving principle for success. We don't know for sure why it's called *facing*, but our guess is because it involves turning the products you want to sell the most to "face" your customers. Businesses that were the precursor to grocery stores started to appear as early as the 14th century. They dealt in dry goods like spices, sugar, and tea, and because their items were often bought in

F

bulk, they were named after the French word for "wholesaler," *grossier*. The first self-service grocery store was Piggly Wiggly, which opened in 1916 in Memphis, Tennessee. Prior to that, grocery stores were "over the counter," with customers asking the grocer to retrieve items from inventory. This innovation allowed customers to quickly identify items that they wanted to purchase, and also increased the possibility of impulse buying—which led, in turn, to the rise of "facing" products as a business practice.[7] The term has since grown in meaning to encompass larger business ideas.

fake news *n.* **1.** False news stories that are often created or distributed to discredit a public figure, political movement, or company. **2.** Fictitious stories that have enormous popular appeal and are assumed real and truthful by large groups of people.

BS Definition: What you label reports of your bad behavior at office-sponsored functions in order to save your job.

Origin: Given recent headlines, you might think this is a modern term. However, *fake news* has been around for centuries. In the 13th century BC, Ramses the Great spread lies and propaganda that portrayed the Battle of Kadesh as a stunning victory for his Egyptian armies—even though the battle was actually a stalemate. During the first century BC, the first emperor of Rome, Octavian, ran a fake-news campaign of misinformation against his rival Mark Antony, portraying him as a drunkard, a womanizer, and a puppet of the Egyptian queen, Cleopatra VII. And, in the second and third centuries AD, false rumors were spread about Christians claiming that they engaged in ritual cannibalism and incest.[8] (Wait. You mean that "The Top 10 Disgusting Things Christians Do" list I saw on *BuzzFeed* isn't true?!)

According to *Merriam-Webster*, these occurrences were, at first, labeled "false news" starting in the 16th century with 1575's *Familiar Epistles of Sir Anthony of Guevara by Antonio de Guevara* (translated by Edward Hellowes):

> Other thinges are in this Court at a good price, or to say it better, very good cheap: that is to wit, cruel lies, false news, vnhonest women, fayned friendship, continuall enimities, doubled malice, vaine words, and false hopes, of whiche eight things we haue suche abundance in this Courte, that they may set out bouthes, and proclayme faires.

At the end of the 19th century, the descriptions finally switched to "fake news" with this first reference in the *Cincinnati Commercial Tribune* from June 1890: "Secretary Brunnell Declares Fake News About His People is Being Telegraphed Over the Country."[9]

However, it was the 2016 presidential election that made fake news popular in today's BS context. *Entertainment Weekly* reported in July 2017 that Donald Trump started using the phrase in his Twitter account at the end of that year with this tweet: "Reports by @CNN that I will be working on The Apprentice during my Presidency, even part time, are ridiculous & untrue - FAKE NEWS!"[10] Within about six months, he had tweeted about it more than 70 times—often accusing prominent, legitimate media outlets such as the *New York Times*, the *Washington Post*, and CNN of being "fake news."[11]

feeding frenzy *n.* **1.** A period of intense consumer buying. **2.** An insatiable appetite for a news story or information about its protagonists. **3.** An episode of frantic competition or rivalry for something.

BS Definition: 1. What happens when Lonnie leaves a Krispy Kreme box in the employee kitchen. **2.** An annual American tradition when shoppers destroy one another trying to be the first through the door of a Black Friday sale.

Origin: The term, which originally referred to sharks wildly attacking any prey, is believed to have originated around the mid-20th century. One early citation is from *Sports Illustrated* in February 1960: "When sharks are in a feeding frenzy, the man who hangs too close to the surface to grimace,

F

may lose his head—face, grimace and all." Today, the term often refers to the fields of politics and journalism—not that anyone in those professions ever behaves in a predatory manner, right?[12]

first mover *n.* **1.** A service or product that gains competitive advantage by being first to market. **2.** A person or company who makes the first inroads into a new market. **3.** The idea that by acting first you can seize command and conquer all.

BS Definition: Theoretically, the company with the biggest opportunity to succeed. Practically, the company with the biggest opportunity to get copied and made obsolete by those coming behind it (remember Friendster, Netscape, and TiVo?[13]).

Origin: The first recorded citation for *first mover* (as in the person or being that set something in motion), according to the *OED*, comes from Chaucer's *Knight's Tale* from around 1385: "The firste moeuere of the cause aboue." But it wasn't until 600 years later that the term migrated to a business-oriented context, when the term *first-mover advantage* was popularized in a 1988 paper by Stanford Business School professor David Montgomery and co-author Marvin Lieberman. They used it to describe firms that had successfully initiated a product into market, thereby creating an inherent advantage over its competitors, including technological leadership and the preemption of scarce assets.[14]

However, that didn't mean the first mover always succeeded. Indeed, after the paper, evidence suggested that many second movers benefited and thus dominated market share for a particular product or service. Case in point: Netscape invented the browser, but Microsoft's Internet Explorer came to dominate, until eventually it was overtaken by Google's Chrome. Similarly, Amazon was actually not even a second mover in the books market, behind originator Books.com. Perhaps the original paper should've been amended to "first-mover advantage except if facing a monopoly power." By 2000, the concept was hotly debated as *Fast Company* published an article entitled: "He Who Moves First, Finishes Last."[15]

flavor of the month *idiom* **1.** The most recent consumer fad. **2.** The most recent management approach.

BS Definition: 1. Any "pet project" of the CEO. **2.** The most recent company hire. **3.** Caramel chocolate chip.[16]

Origin: As one might guess, the phrase derives from the U.S. ice cream industry—in particular, the advertising slogans of the 1930s. It's not clear who exactly coined the term, but one of the early references could be found in an advertisement in *The Mansfield* (Ohio) *News Journal* in June 1936: "If you haven't tried Sealtest Fresh Strawberry Ice Cream, made by Telling's, you're missing a real treat. It's the flavor of the month for June, selected by the Sealtest Jury." After that, several other U.S. ice cream companies began using the term. By 1946, it had become well-enough established for a state trade association to begin pushing the idea; the September 1946 issue of the *Ice Cream Review*

states: "The Illinois Association of Ice Cream Manufacturers has set up a committee which will give serious study to a suggested flavor and flavor-of-the-month program for 1947."[17]

Today, the term can refer to anything shiny and new, especially in technology. Blockchain, for example, may (ironically) be the new flavor of the month for Ben & Jerry's Ice Cream: "When you pay at the checkout the ice cream brand will pay a penny to counterbalance the carbon in your cone . . . It's the first real-world example of trading carbon credits on the high street, powered by blockchain."[18]

FOMO *n.* FO-MO **1.** Acronym for "fear of missing out." **2.** Anxiety that an exciting or interesting event is happening elsewhere without you, often brought on by posts seen on social media.

BS Definition: 1. Yes, that's you checking out Facebook, Twitter, Instagram, and Snapchat every minute when you're supposed to be working. **2.** A phrase in which you want to make sure you get the syllables in the right order, because MOFO is something *completely* different.

Origin: Since the beginning of human history, there has always been some fear of missing out ("Hey, Grug. Did you notice our cavemen neighbors got a wheel today? Sure wish we had one of those."), but it wasn't until the era of the Internet and social media that this particular form of social anxiety came to be identified as a specific condition.

"Fear of missing out" as a concept was initially identified by Dan Herman, a marketing strategist, who published the first academic paper on the topic in 2000 with the article "Introducing Short-Term Brands: A New Branding Tool for a New Consumer Reality" in the *Journal of Brand Manage-*

ment.[19] The acronym FOMO was popularized by Patrick McGinnis, a Harvard Business School student at the time, who published an article in *The Harbus* in 2004 entitled: "McGinnis' Two FOs: Social Theory at HBS." His other "fear of"? Fear of a better opinion, which didn't seem to catch on.[20] We have an opinion as to why that's the case, but we're concerned you may have a better one, so we'll just keep ours to ourselves.

for all intents and purposes *idiom* 1. One thing that has the same effect or result as something else. 2. In every practical sense.

F

BS Definition: If you thought this phrase was actually "for all intensive purposes," then you may be at a higher risk of saying "I could care less" (instead of the correct "I couldn't care less") as well.[21]

Origin: So often misheard (and misused) as "all intensive purposes," the first recorded use of the term is relatively unambiguous—in an English Act of Parliament under Henry VIII, in 1546: "to all intents, constructions, and purposes," whereby the king was solidifying that, indeed, his proclamations were (for all intents and purposes) the law of the land. Interestingly, the misuse of the term as *all intensive purposes* is not recent, having appeared as early as 1870 in the *Fort Wayne Daily Gazette*, with the reporter stating: "He has never had a representative in Congress nor in the State Legislature nor in any municipal office, and to all intensive purposes, politically speaking, he might have well have been dead." In recent years, *all intensive purposes* was employed commonly in 1980s references, perhaps with the proliferation of intensive care units and intensive treatments and medications at that time.[22]

Fourth Industrial Revolution *n.* 1. The current business environment, in which things such as robotics, virtual reality, and artificial intelligence are changing the way we work. 2. Technical advancements in today's workplace that are blurring the line between the real world and the technological world.

BS Definition: A world where you expect a work colleague to turn to you one day and say, "I need your clothes, your boots, and your motorcycle."[23] (Remember *Terminator?*)

Origin: Ah, if you had to pick *the* BS buzzword for 2020, "Fourth Industrial Revolution" (or "Industry 4.0" or "4IR," as the cool kids say), would definitely be in the running. What exactly is the Fourth Industrial Revolution, and how did I miss the first *three* revolutions, you ask? Well, let's start answering those questions by clarifying things.

The First Industrial Revolution started in the late 1700s and involved the shift from our primary reliance on animals and human effort as sources of energy to the use of fossil fuels and mechanical power. The Second Industrial Revolution occurred between the end of the 19th century and the first two decades of the 20th century. It brought major breakthroughs in electricity, division of labor, wired communication, and mass production. The Third Industrial Revolution was the digital revolution, starting around 1969 with the advent of powerful computing, networks, and automated production.

That brings us to the Fourth Industrial Revolution, a term coined by Klaus Schwab, founder and executive chairman of the World Economic Forum.[24] In a 2015 article in *Foreign Affairs* magazine, Schwab defined the Fourth Industrial Revolution as an era of technologies that combine hardware, software, and biology (cyber-physical systems), as well as advances in communication and connectivity. This period, he says, will be marked by breakthroughs in fields such as robotics, artificial intelligence, nanotechnology, quantum computing, the Internet of Things, fifth-generation wireless technologies (5G), and fully autonomous vehicles.[25]

Overwhelmed yet? Just wait 'till we define the Fifth Industrial Revolution!

funnel, the *n.* **1.** A representation of the customer journey, from aware-ness to action. **2.** The idea that every sale begins with a large number of potential customers and ends with a much smaller number of people who actually make a purchase.

BS Definition: A direct competitor to "the sales cube" and "the market-ing rhombohedron."

Origin: Also referred to as "the purchase funnel," "the marketing funnel," "the sales funnel," and the "customer funnel," the term derives from the volume of users at each step of the buyer journey, which resembles a cone or funnel.

F

The original concept for this dates back to 1898, when advertiser E. St. Elmo Lewis developed a model that mapped a customer journey from the moment a brand attracted a consumer's attention to the point of purchase. St. Elmo Lewis's idea is often referred to as the AIDA model, an acronym that stands for "awareness, interest, desire, and action." The first to actually associate that AIDA concept with a funnel was William Townsend in 1924, who wrote about the structure in the book *Bond Salesmanship*.[26]

G

game plan *n*. **1.** Strategy or approach to achieve a desired result. **2.** A carefully thought-out course of action.

BS Definition: What goes out the window right after your potential client says, "I hate all those ideas. What else you got?"

Origin: *Merriam-Webster* says the first known use of *game plan* was in 1941.[1] However, we couldn't find the exact reference, so we devised a game plan to figure it out. We checked with *Collins Dictionary*, and it gave us a bar chart that suggested the first reference of *game plan* was in 1816, but didn't really start trending upward in usage until around 1970. However, again, no specific citations to work with.[2] We then turned to the Online Etymology Dictionary, which confirmed the year 1941 for the first reference of game plan, from American football.[3] It was only when we subscribed to access the files of the *OED* that we found a specific citation for the first use in print, a 1957 edition of the *Kingsport* (Tennessee) newspaper: "Some years ago you mentioned that you had offered your children $1 for each book in the Bible they would read. And we decided to try that game plan with David."

game changer *n*. **1.** A newly introduced element or factor that changes an existing situation or activity in a significant way. **2.** A shift that alters things.

BS Definition: **1.** Accidentally spilling coffee all over yourself right before a big presentation. **2.** Realizing that the lady you yelled at in traffic outside the office is actually the person you're going to interview with now. **3.** Being told too late that you've been on speakerphone the whole time.

Origin: There is some debate about the origins of the term *game changer*. Some believe (strongly) it was tied to baseball in the 1980s, referring variously to the player who was capable of changing a game's outcome all by himself or a play on which the game hinged. Others credit the first documented reference to playing cards. The *Atlanta Constitution's* "Bridge Forum" of June 29, 1930, looked disparagingly on attempts to improve the game of bridge: "Seldom are the game changers idle." One of the early uses of *game changer* in a figurative sense came from Catherine Hayden in her 1986 book, *The Handbook of Strategic Expertise: Over 450 Key Concepts and Techniques Defined, Illustrated, and Evaluated for the Strategist*:

> Game Changer: an industry event that changes the competitive rules of the game. Game changers are usually evolutionary processes that change the competitive forces in an industry and its intra-industry structure or indications that the competitive forces could be changed by an innovative competitor.[5]

gatekeeper *n.* **1.** Someone preventing unwanted traffic from coming through an entry point. **2.** The person who controls the access or flow of information

BS Definition: 1. Any administrative assistant (see *admin*). **2.** Your voicemail when you get a call from an unknown number.

Origin: The *OED* cites the first written use of gatekeeper (in the sense of one in charge of a gate) in poet John Higgins's *Huloets Dictionary* from 1572, in which Higgins defined it as "gate keeper, or a porter." The first figurative use was in 1867, in an article in *Philosophical Transactions of the Royal Society of London*: "Sabatier speaks of the verumontanum as the gatekeeper of the prostatic portion of the urethra." You may be wondering, like us, what a urethra has to do with a journal on the philosophy of a royal society. Well, it turns out the *Philosophical Transactions* is the world's first and longest-running scientific journal (started in 1665)[5]—with a very odd title used to describe it.

The theory of gatekeeping, as we know it best in the world of business speak, was first introduced by sociologist Kurt Lewin in 1943 in *Forces Behind Food Habits and Methods of Change*, in which he described a wife or mother who decides which foods end up on the family's dinner table.[6] Lewin himself is considered to be the founder of the field of social psychology, having written extensively on the field of group dynamics and the change process. For the latter, his three-step process for making change is still regarded as a foundational model for organizations. After his application of the term *gatekeeping*, Lewin's influence spread to other fields quickly in the 1950s, including media, where *gatekeeper* referred to reporters deciding which sources were chosen to include in a story, as well as editors deciding which stories were printed.[7]

Generation X or **Gen X** *n.* **1.** People born between the early to mid-1960s and the early 1980s. **2.** A generation of people who reached adulthood in the 1980s and 1990s. **3.** A demographic group that followed the Baby Boomers and preceded the Millennials.

BS Definition: A generation of people perceived as directionless, irresponsible, and reluctant to participate in society. You know, the type who grow up to write books about business speak.

Origin: Generation X may have been labeled before it even existed. The *OED* cites the first written use of *Generation X* in a 1952 *Holiday* magazine article: "What, you may well ask, is Generation X? . . . These are the youngsters who have seen and felt the agonies of the past two decades . . . who are trying to keep their balance in the swirling pressures of today, and who will have the biggest say in the course of history for the next 50 years."

Fast-forward to 1991, when author Douglas Coupland famously applied the term to his landmark novel, *Generation X: Tales for an Accelerated Culture*, which characterized the group broadly as slackers and cynical and disaffected youth, because many were latch-key kids who grew up as children of divorced parents or with minimal adult supervision.[8] Although they were also known as the "MTV Generation," *Generation X* became so widely used that it influenced the next generation names of Y and Z.

Interestingly, despite being responsible for popularizing the term, Coupland never quite bought into the idea of a Generation X. He said in 1994:

> This is going to sound heretical coming from me, but I don't think there is a Generation X. What I think a lot of people mistake for this thing that might be Generation X is just the acknowledgment that there exists some other group of people, whatever, whoever they might be, younger than, say, Jane Fonda's baby boom."

In 2017, an article in *Vanity Fair* suggested that this generation—steeped in irony, detachment, and a sense of dread—would prove to be the last best hope of improving America's recent dark days of societal unrest and political instability.[9]

get/keep the ball rolling *idiom* **1.** Start or maintain an undertaking. **2.** To maintain the momentum of an idea or a task (see *strike while the iron is hot*).

BS Definition: A popular thing to say when *brainstorming*, conducting a *hackathon*, or having a *meeting of the minds*.

Origin: According to the *OED*, the phrase *keep the ball rolling* (from which it is believed that *get the ball rolling* descends) goes as far back as the late 18th century. Indeed, in Joseph Chew's *The Papers of Sir William Johnson*, originally published in 1770, the following passage appears: "in Consequence of this a Grand meeting here and a Committee appointed to let the Society in New York know . . . and so the Ball is to be kept rolling."[10] However, most credit U.S. President William Henry Harrison for popularizing this phrase.[11] His 1840 campaign for president used a gimmick known as "victory balls," huge (10 feet in diameter) leather and tin balls that were pushed from one campaign rally to the next as the crowd chanted: "Keep the Harrison ball rolling!" They even inspired a song:

> What has caused this great commotion, motion, motion
> Our country through?
> It is the ball a-rolling on,
> For Tippecanoe and Tyler too,
> Tippecanoe and Tyler too . . .

Harrison went on to defeat Martin Van Buren that year to become the ninth U.S. president, but ironically didn't keep the ball rolling; he died from pneumonia only 31 days into his presidency.[12]

get with the program *idiom* **1.** To conform to the prevailing or accepted way of thinking or behavior (see *toe the line*). **2.** To do what is expected; to follow the rules (see *buy-in*).

BS Definition: Usually said to you when you have to do a task that's completely stupid or counterintuitive to common sense.

Origin: Most experts agree that this is an American colloquialism dating from the 1960s, when, according to Google, usage of the phrase became popular in publications. What's not so clear is the actual origin for it. Some suggest the phrase stems from Alcoholics Anonymous (AA) and its 12-step recovery program. Those who struggled with the 12 steps were allegedly warned to "get with the program" (or they would die from addiction).[13] Meanwhile, William Safire, the late *New York Times* columnist on language, suggested that an early source for *get with the program* was the world of politics—specifically, Sharon Davis, a Republican campaign worker in Santa Barbara, California, who used the phrase frequently during the 1968 presidential campaign.[14]

However, we found an early reference that suggests this phrase may not have come from AA or politics, but rather the military. In the January 1963 publication of *Aerospace Safety*, a journal of the U.S. Air Force, Major Charles H. Metzger writes: "So troops, let's get with the program. Isn't it time to go update that summary again?"[15]

G

ghosting *v.* **1.** Suddenly ending all contact with a person without explanation. **2.** Hiding all comments, threads, or other online content from a specific poster to the public, while keeping the poster unaware of that change.

BS Definition: 1. What your boss does when you ask for a raise. **2.** A popular social media pastime.

Origin: Ghosts (referring to the apparition) have appeared in Egyptian and Greek works dating back thousands of years, including Homer's *Illiad* and *The Odyssey*. Since then, references to "ghosting" have varied but have come to refer to everything from actual haunting to image processing, blurred TV signals, printing mishaps, and even ghost writing for someone else.[16] Most believe the reference to the modern use of ghosting derives from social media in the mid 2000s, but we found one eerily similar reference in 1992's *Geodisic Dreams* by author Gardner Dozois: "She knocked, and opened the door for him, and then left without having said a word, ghosting away predatorily and smiling like a nun."[17]

Perhaps actress Charlize Theron was familiar with Dozois' work when she confessed to ghosting fellow actor Sean Penn in 2015 by ignoring calls and text messages from him. This parting of the former celebrity power couple caused the *New York Times* to write a comprehensive explainer on ghosting at the time.[18]

GIF *n.* pronounced JIF or GIF **1.** A common type of image file found on most computer systems and websites. **2.** An abbreviation that stands for "graphics interchange format." **3.** Usually a looping animation or TV or movie clip that is shared.

BS Definition: 1. What Frank from HR is really looking at on his computer when he closes his office door. **2.** Most likely a video of a dog or cat doing something funny.

Origin: First off, let's address how this BS word is pronounced. The person who invented the GIF, Steve Wilhite, has insisted from its introduction at a computer conference in the late 1980s that the pronunciation is *jif*—as in, the soft *g* of *gelatin* and *giant*—and many computer experts say it that way. However, both pronunciations are commonly in use, and most dictionaries list a hard-*g* and a soft-*g* pronouncer for the term.[19] Now, a little bit more about the GIF's origin . . .

The GIF file format (originally called "87a") was invented—and first mentioned in writing—in 1987. The CompuServe Corporation created the GIF to enable different kinds of computer systems to exchange and display high-quality images. It was unique in that it used encoding technology that allowed data to be downloaded in a reasonably short time, even with very slow modems. In the early 2000s, the popularity of the GIF soared during the Myspace craze, and the rest, as they say, is history.[20]

gig economy *n.* **1.** The production, distribution, and consumption of goods and services based on part-time, temporary, and freelance jobs. **2.** A labor market characterized by the prevalence of short-term contracts and temporary or freelance work as opposed to permanent, full-time jobs.

BS Definition: What you say you're part of when you're interviewing for a job and are actually unemployed.

Origin: *Gig economy* became popular at the height of the financial crisis in early 2009, when the unemployed made a living by gigging, or working several part-time jobs, wherever they could. *Gig* dates to the 1920s, and is said to originate in jazz music as a way to describe the temporary club engagements of musicians. Although today's gig economy has roots in the 1940s—when the staffing industry started to grow in the United States largely as a way to employ housewives for part-time work as office workers—some economists point out that finding work in the gig economy is similar to the employment style prior to the Industrial Revolution of the 19th century. Back then, it was common for one person to take on multiple temporary jobs to piece together livable earnings. The modern "one-person, one-career model" is a relatively recent phenomenon, historically speaking, that the gig economy is disrupting.[21]

give-and-take *n.* **1.** Equal opportunity to exchange thoughts or criticisms between parties. **2.** Granting mutual adjustments or compromises.

BS Definition: What you invite a potential business partner to do when it's clear you've said something to upset them.

Origin: It's amazing to think that one sport can deliver so many expressions that are now common in the English language. And no, we're not talking about baseball (although that has certainly provided its fair share). We're talking, once again, about horse racing. (See sidebar on page 153).

According to the *OED*, the origin of this term dates as far back as 1769, to something known as a "give-and-take plate," which was a prize for a race in which taller horses had to take on more weight in the race than shorter horses. From the *St. James's Chronicle* in August of that year: "Will be run for on Huish Downs . . . A Free Plate of 50l.

Give and Take, by any Horse, Mare, or Gelding." Today, such races are popularly known as "handicaps," where many older or more successful horses carry more weight than their younger, often less successful adversaries. By 1778, that phrase came to be used metaphorically to mean "the practice of mutual yielding." The earliest citation comes from Frances Burney, in her novel from that year, *Evelina*: "Give and take is fair in all nations."[22]

P.S. This phrase is not to be confused with *give or take*, which means that something is approximate or estimated. (See sidebar on page 74.)

G

glad-handing *v.* **1.** To shake hands with everyone present in an effort to win favor. **2.** To greet or welcome with a phony appearance of warmth.

BS Definition: To spread the flu in your office in a very effective way.

Origin: Thought to have originated in the United States in the late 19th century and shortened from the expression *give a glad hand to*, this term is now used quite extensively to describe a politician's behavior when greeting crowds in an energetic, but perhaps insincere, way. If we could pinpoint the individual who actually coined the term, we would certainly glad-hand that person, but alas, we cannot. The best we can do is tell you when *glad-hand* was first used in print. According to the *OED*, it was 1895, in a literary magazine called the *Inlander*, published by students at the University of Michigan: "Give the glad hand, to welcome."[23]

go-to guy *n.* **1.** A person who can be relied upon, especially in a difficult situation. **2.** Someone sought out for expert knowledge, advice, or performance in a crucial time.

BS Definition: The opposite of the person in charge of talent scouting for Decca Records in 1962, who famously said, "The Beatles have no future in show business."[24]

Origin: The origin of this term is believed to come from basketball, where it was popularly used in the mid-1980s. One of the first documented references comes from Los Angeles Clippers coach Don Chaney in April 1985 talking about one of his players, Derek Smith: "Derek is one of my go-to guys—players who want the ball in crucial situations." Smith played for five teams over nine years in the NBA, with a field-goal percentage of 49.9 by the end of his career.[25] So, in addition to being the "go-to guy," one could say Smith's shot was closer to being "good 24 hours a day, seven days a week, 365 days a year" then, say, Jerry Reynolds's (see *24/365*).

GOAT *n.* **1.** Abbreviation for "greatest of all time." **2.** The person considered the best ever at a certain activity or occupation.

BS Definition: What you call your office-supply person when they replenish the coffee machine in the break room.

Origin: If you weren't alive during the days when boxing reigned supreme around the world, it's hard to describe a figure like boxer Muhammad Ali in the 1960s and 1970s. Called the "Louisville Lip" (remember "float like a butterfly, sting like a bee"?), he was bold, brash, loud, and, yes, self-proclaimed "the greatest of all time," from which this acronym originates.

It was 1964 when Ali (then known as Cassius Clay) predicted ahead of a fight with Sonny Liston that he would knock out the then–heavyweight champion, saying to reporters: "I am the greatest!" After he stopped Liston, who wouldn't come out for the seventh round, Ali also

G

repeated his claim, shouting that he was "the greatest" to critics and media in attendance. In subsequent interviews, after changing his name to Muhammad Ali in the mid-1960s, he began frequently referring to himself as "the greatest of all time." However, the key date in the origin of this acronym came in June 1992, when Lonnie Ali, Muhammad Ali's wife, submitted papers to incorporate G.O.A.T. Inc.—a company that would be used as an umbrella for all of the former boxer's intellectual properties being used for commercial purposes.

With that said, *Merriam-Webster* says it wasn't until 1996 that the first evidence of GOAT being pronounced like "goat" would appear—in an Orlando Magic forum referencing Penny Hardaway. "The sentence," says *Merriam-Webster* editor at large Peter Sokolowski, "is simply, 'Penny is the GOAT (Greatest of All Time).' "[26] But the person credited with really bringing the "goat" pronunciation of G.O.A.T. into the mainstream is none other than rapper LL Cool J, who released the album *G.O.A.T. (Greatest of All Time)* in September 2000. In 2016, the rapper gave Ali credit for the origin of the number 1 album in a *Rolling Stone* interview, saying "Without Muhammad Ali, there would be no 'Mama Said Knock You Out,' and the term G.O.A.T. would have never been coined."[27]

golden parachute/golden handshake/golden umbrella

n. **1.** A generous severance package, usually given to members of upper management. **2.** A large payment or other financial compensation guaranteed to a company executive should that person be dismissed as a result of a merger or takeover.

BS Definition: An obscene amount of money given to a deposed company leader amid allegations of incompetence, sexual harassment, or both.

Origin: What term you use to describe this idea may depend on where you live. Golden parachute has its roots in the United States, while golden handshake is considered to be U.K.-born. Who knows where golden umbrella came from? Spain?[28]

While both *golden parachute* and *golden handshake* first appeared in the early-to-mid-1960s, the former's origin story is probably the more interesting of the two. *Golden parachute* derives from the 1961 battle by creditors to wrest controlling interest of Trans World Airlines (TWA) from eccentric billionaire Howard Hughes.[29] TWA's legal status was shaky, so when Charles C. Tillinghast Jr. came on board as chairman of the company, his employment contract guaranteed him a large sum of money in the event that he lost his job. Tillinghast left TWA in 1976 to become vice chairman of an investment bank that was later acquired by Merrill Lynch, so his golden parachute never opened.[30] That's probably a good thing, based on the fact that using a parachute made of gold would certainly not land you safely anywhere.

guerrilla marketing *n.* **1.** Unconventional methods of advertising that avoid traditional media. **2.** Innovative and low-cost marketing techniques for maximum exposure of a product.

BS Definition: The guy dressed up in a Statue of Liberty costume, spinning a big arrow sign on a busy street corner.

Origin: *Guerrilla* derives from Spanish in the early 1800s, and was adopted into English during the Peninsular War (1808–1814), when bands of Spanish peasants and shepherds annoyed the occupying French. Instead of just calling them "irregular," these combatants came to be known as "guerrilla fighters."

Guerrilla marketing was first mentioned in print in 1971 in the *London Magazine*: "Cooking up of slogans and angles . . . and incentives to pep up my guerilla marketing strategy." However, the term became much more widespread when Jay Conrad Levinson published his book *Guerrilla Marketing* in 1984. Levinson's original guerrilla-marketing concept involved simply making the maximum amount of people aware of a product or service (usually in public) on a minimum budget. However, now the term can be interpreted to be all nontraditional tactics—including those designed to annoy customers—so, much closer to the original definition of guerrilla.[31]

BS REPORTING FOR DUTY, SIR!

Guerrilla marketing is just one of the terms you'll find in *The BS Dictionary* with a military connection. There are many more. Matter of fact, as you turn these pages you'll find entry after entry with ties to the armed forces in one way or another. Here are a few military-inspired BS terms that didn't make the cut in this volume, but are used on a regular basis in the business world.[1]

ASAP	as soon as possible
Benedict Arnold	a traitor
blockbuster	a giant success
deadline	the time by which something must be complete
face the music	own up to your mistakes
good to go	ready to act
hotshot	a particularly important person or one with exceptional skill
I heard it through the grapevine	news passed through rumors and hearsay
Murphy's Law	if anything can go wrong, it will
not on my watch	something that will not happen while you're in charge
on standby	ready to act when needed
skimming off the top	taking cash out of a fund without reporting or paying taxes on it
slush fund	monies set aside for illicit or corrupt purposes.

H

hackathon *n.* **1.** An event typically lasting several days in which a large number of people meet to engage in collaborative computer programming (also known as a hackfest or codefest). **2.** An event where computer programmers get together to work intensely on software projects (also known as a hack day).

BS Definition: An event that computer programmers typically travel to attend (and have to adjust to the light of being outside for the first time in years as a result).

Origin: What linguists would call a "portmanteau" (meaning "a blending"), *hackathon* is derived from the words *hack* and *marathon*.[1] According to the *OED*, the first written reference to a hackathon happened in a newsgroup on one of the world's oldest computer-network communications systems, called Usenet, in 1990.[2] A user posted, "Just after the Hack-A-Thon. A little tired, but it's still early, just after 3 a.m. I log onto the Vax and find that two of the people from the Hack-A-Thon are already on." Although this may be evidence of a "Hack-A-Thon" having just taken place in that time and space, it wasn't until June 1999 in Calgary, Canada, that the first (widely recorded, at least) hackathon was held. It was at a somewhat obscure conference and was attended by about 10 developers using OpenBSD, a free and open-source operating system. In the 2000s, hackathons became significantly more widespread, and now it seems like everyone's doing one.[3] For instance, there are now reality-show hackathons, marijuana hackathons, NBA hackathons, and even a Vatican City hackathon.[4]

halo effect *n.* **1.** The transfer of positive feelings about one product, company, or brand to an associated product, company, or brand. **2.** When the positive experience with a particular item is extended to the broader brand. **3.** Any desirable side effect that a brand gets by associating itself with another brand.

> **BS Definition:** The reason the Fyre Festival paid Kendall Jenner $250,000 for a single Instagram post.[5]

> **Origin:** This term was first coined by psychologist Edward Thorndike in 1920, when his research suggested that the more attractive you found an individual, the more likely you were to think they were a good person. Thorndike wrote about this halo effect in an article, "A Constant Error in Psychological Ratings." Since then, researchers have studied more about the power of attractiveness and its bearing on the judicial and educational systems, as well as expanded its definition to include business and brand marketing.[6]

hammer out *v.* **1.** To work toward agreement. **2.** To produce or bring about as if by repeated blows.

> **BS Definition:** **1.** What MC Hammer said to pop-music stardom after scoring his last hit, "2 Legit 2 Quit." **2.** Often used dramatically by lawyers to explain their value in finalizing a difficult deal contract (which, in reality, probably did involve a lot of repeated blows by each side).

> **Origin:** The first actual tool resembling a hammer dates to 3.3 million years ago, found by archaeologists excavating a site near Kenya's Lake Turkana. *Hammer* first appeared in Old English, having been appropriated from Germanic tribes, meaning "stone weapon" or "tool with a stone head" used to pound things. Experts suggest that almost as soon as *hammer* began to be used in a literal sense, it also developed a wide range of figurative uses for both the noun form and as a verb. In the 14th

century, for example, a hammer was "a person or agency that beats down or crushes opposition."[7] According to *Merriam-Webster*, the first use of "hammer out," occurred much later, however, in 1632.[8]

handle *n.* **1.** A public username. **2.** An identifying nickname used in online forums.

BS Definition: If you put the name Kardashian anywhere in one, you're guaranteed at least a million followers.

Origin: 10-4, good buddy. The 1970s craze of CB radio is often credited as the origin of *handle* associated with usernames online. That's because, just like online communication, using a nickname on CB radio allows people to get to know one another in a quasi-anonymous way. For example, Betty Ford, the former first lady of the United States, used the CB handle "First Mama."

However, the *OED* says the first written reference to a handle as a personal nickname predates CB radio, which originated in the 1940s. In 1838, Joseph Clay Neal wrote in *Charcoal Sketches; or, Scenes in a Metropolis*: "They were satisfied that a sonorous handle to one's patronymic acts like a balloon to its owner." (Don't worry. We had to look up *patronymic* as well. It means "derived from the name of your father.")

So, how did *handle* become synonymous with a public nickname in these situations? One online user who dedicated himself to the origin of the word says, "The term handle is an old slang term for name that goes back to the cowboys of the Old West. Telegraphers picked it up and the ham radio operators got it from them. CB operators copied the hams. I can vouch for the use of 'handle' long before the CB craze by amateur radio operators ("hams") after WWII." Roger that, Bubba. We got a Smokey on our back door, so we're going to hammer down to the next entry now.[9]

hands-down *adj.* **1.** Easy. **2.** Certain.

BS Definition: The kind of success the makers of New Coke probably thought their product would have before it hit the market.

Origin: Score another one here for the "sport of kings." (See the sidebar on page 153.) Yes, the origin of this phrase comes from none other than horse racing, specifically a jockey's hand position to control the animal's speed. For example, if a horse is going so fast that it might burn itself out before the end of the race, the jockey puts their hands up, pulling the reins to slow the animal down and control pace of the race better. On the other hand, if the horse is cruising easily, and the jockey doesn't need to do a whole lot, they might be "hands down" with the reins or the whip.

According to the *OED*, the earliest written reference to this phrase was in 1832 in the newspaper *Bell's Life in London and Sporting Chronicle*. Josh Chetwynd, in his book *The Field Guide to Sports Metaphors*, says that same paper gave us this horse race description in 1852:

> The Cup on the second day gave us . . . a race between the winning Storyteller and Kate. . . . The latter might have done better had the [jockey] been permitted to allow the mare to go in front with his hands down instead of pulling and hauling the animal as he did, by which much ground was lost.[10]

The phrase became so popular in the mid-1800s that it became a wider synonym for ease or minimal effort required in anything.

hardball *n.* **1.** Aggressively playing any kind of game, including real life, in the toughest possible way. **2.** Uncompromising and ruthless methods or dealings.

BS Definition: What you have to play when a crowded subway train pulls up at rush hour in New York City.

Origin: To explore the origins of this word, we must first play hardball with the belief that baseball was invented by Abner Doubleday in 1839 in Cooperstown, New York.[11] The reality is, it wasn't, and most modern baseball historians now acknowledge that. Most likely, American baseball developed as a variation of rounders, a game played in Great Britain and Ireland as early as the 1700s.[12]

Hardball was commonly used to describe the actual ball used in the game of baseball because, well, it was hard. Before long, the word started to be used as a metaphor for "tough, uncompromising behavior."[13] The *OED* says 1889 was the first time the word appeared in print with this meaning, in a write-up from the *Cleveland Leader* newspaper: "Cleveland has the pitchers, too, and if they keep up as they are now they will make Boston, New York, and Philadelphia play hard ball to win."

has legs *idiom* **1.** Has staying power. **2.** Has potential to endure, stay relevant, maintain interest, or even grow in popularity.

BS Definition: An idea that's usually followed by a maniacal "Muahaha-hahahaha!" laugh of evil and greed in the business world.

Origin: You thought baseball and horse racing gave us a lot of idioms? Wait until you get a load of the word *leg!* In no particular order, the word factors into the following business speak phrases: *shake a leg, pulling your leg, leg work, sea legs, not having a leg to stand on, a leg up*, and, of course, *it has legs.*[15]

According to the *OED*, the phrase in question here was first used in writing in 1930 by a publication from the Texas Folklore Society: "His stuff was much copied and when he wrote something that went the rounds he would say that 'it had legs.' " The idea of the phrase is that, by having or growing legs, something can move sort of creepy-crawly-like into other things. Journalists often use it when describing a story that has multiple follow-up angles to pursue. Used in a sentence: "The Kardashian family story has legs that just keep growing . . . and changing sexual orientation . . . and making X-rated videos . . . and . . ."

P.S. Another place this phrase might come up in the business world is over dinner with colleagues. Wine, as you may know, also "has legs." They are the streaks of liquid that form on the inside of a wineglass when drinking. The more legs, the more alcohol in your wine (three sheets to the wind, anyone?).

hashtag *n.* **1.** A word or phrase preceded by a hash sign and used to identify messages relating to a specific topic on social-media websites and applications. **2.** A hash mark (#) used within a social-media post to identify a keyword or topic of interest and facilitate a search for it.

H

BS Definition: 1. Putting a hash mark in front of words that you hope the public will use to search your company, but probably won't because they're too busy searching for #giveaway or #cats. **2.** Because asking someone to "octothorpe" your wedding could lead to some awkward responses.

Origin: What does this symbol (#) stand for? If you answered, "the pound sign," you're right, because it pertains to a keypad on phones, but chances are you're over 30 and a bit out of touch. Today, the # symbol is a sign for the beginning of a hashtag, which was initially created to label a group on the social-media site Twitter, but then spread to other social media.[16]

The big moment came on August 23, 2007, at 12:25 p.m., when Chris Messina, an open-source-software advocate, made the following tweet: "How do you feel about using # (pound) for groups. As in #barcamp [msg]?"[17] After some initial back-and-forth with other Twitter users to explain how it worked, Messina went on to say two days later: "To join a channel, simply add a tag hash (#) like this: #barcamp The grid is open!" And thus, the pound sign became the hashtag! "The very ephemerality of hashtags is what makes them easy and compelling to use in a fast-moving communication medium like Twitter," Messina said.

Right. . . . Maybe too fast-moving for some companies. In 2012, the company Research in Motion, which owned Blackberry and was promoting a jobs announcement at the company, created the hashtag #RIMjobs. If you don't know what a "rim job" is, two thoughts: 1. No worries. Apparently, the social media team at Research in Motion didn't either. 2. Don't google it at work (it's #NSFW).[18]

heavy hitter *n.* **1.** A very important or influential person or brand. **2.** An extremely successful person or company.

BS Definition: Usually said about a celebrity spokesperson (who also charges like one).

Origin: There is some dispute not only about the origin of this term, but also the timeframe surrounding its first use. What the various sources agree on is that the term definitely came from sports, though which sport is the subject of some debate. Some believe the term came from boxing (someone who hits hard), though others suggest the origin is more closely related to baseball—an individual who gets extra base hits or home runs (also known as a power hitter).

In terms of the date, sources such as *Merriam-Webster* cite the earliest reference as 1922.[19] However, in *God Bless America: The Origins of Over 1,500 Patriotic Words and Phrases*, author Robert Hendrickson suggests the first use of the term came in 1887, and the *OED* has it as 1874 in the *Chicago Tribune*: "It [sc. a livelier ball] would give their heavy hitters a better opportunity to display their strength."[20] Which source is correct? We'll leave that to the heavy hitters in etymology research to decide.

heavy lifting *n.* **1.** Hard work. **2.** A demanding duty that requires great effort.

BS Definition: 1. All the back-breaking, nonstop work you do to make that new initiative successful. You know, the same work your boss refers to as "the easy part." **2.** Getting yourself up from the all-you-can eat buffet at your out-of-town conference.

Origin: According to the *OED*, the first known use in print of *heavy lifting* in a metaphorical sense (not the actual lifting of heavy objects) occurred in 1934 in the *New York Times*:

> Gordon Stanley Cochrane (Mickey himself) has been added as catcher and manager . . . Cochrane is the boss now and he can do the brain work and let his hired men do the heavy lifting if he feels so inclined. But he says he will catch 125 games. He never was afraid of work.

Gordon Stanley "Mickey" Cochrane was, as you may have guessed, an American professional baseball player, manager, and coach who is considered one of the best catchers in the game's history.[21] With this reference, you can now add heavy lifting to the long list of business speak terms with a baseball connection.[22] (See the sidebar on page 251).

hedge your bet *v.* **1.** To leave yourself a means of retreat. **2.** To take an action that allows you to compensate for a potential future loss. **3.** Betting on both sides to ensure you make a profit, regardless of outcome.

BS Definition: When you apply to Harvard for school but also the local community college, just in case.

Origin: According to the U.K. Phrase Finder website, *hedge* can be found in the English language as a verb as early as the 16th century, with the meaning of "equivocate or avoid commitment."[23] One example comes from Shakespeare's play *The Merry Wives of Windsor*, in 1600: "I, I, I myself sometimes, leaving the fear of God on the left hand and hiding mine honour in my necessity, am fain to shuffle, to hedge and to lurch." The full term, hedge (one's) bets, first appears decades later with the meaning of "laying off of a bet by taking out smaller bets with other lenders." It was first used by George Villiers, the second duke of Buckingham, in his satirical 1672 play, *The Rehearsal*: "Now, Criticks, do your worst, that here are met; For, like a Rook, I have hedg'd in my Bet."[24]

herding cats/squirrels *v.* **1.** To manage a difficult and chaotic situation (read: juggling hand grenades). **2.** To organize a group of people who are distracted by something else (aka coaching a soccer team of five-year-olds).

BS Definition: What it's like to have an all-hands meeting in the office while the local basketball team is playing a March Madness day game.

Origin: Getting to the true origin of this term is hard. There are so many different opinions swirling around all at once. It's like, what's the phrase? Herding cats![25] Some suggest the origin of this term is *Monty Python's Life of Brian*, the 1979 film in which Michael Palin's character, a shepherd, suggests: "Can you imagine a herd of cats waiting to be sheared? Meow! Meow! Woo hoo hoo." Meanwhile, the *OED* says the first print citation comes from the *National Journal* in 1986: "Yerxa will have to continue to juggle the divergent views of the subcommittee members, a task he said 'can be like trying to herd cats.'" However, Google Answers suggests it comes from a year earlier, in the *Washington Post Magazine*, from writer Brad Lemley: "At Group L,

[David] Stoffel oversees six first-rate programmers, a managerial challenge roughly comparable to herding cats."[26]

Regardless of its actual beginnings, herding cats can be added to a long list of feline-inspired business speak that gives baseball some competition in the origin category (see the sidebar on page 251).[27] Alas, squirrels are less represented in this category, with *squirrel away* being the only other major squirrel-related business speak idiom we could find.[28] Nuts!

hired gun *n.* **1.** An outside person hired to resolve difficult problems or disputes. **2.** A consultant who comes in to do the dirty work of management.

> **BS Definition:** The college buddy of one of your bosses who comes in to pillage your workplace . . . before letting you go.

> **Origin:** We could tell you the origin of hired gun, but then we'd have to kill you. Seriously, the term's etymology, as we word-nerds call it, suggests it came into being in the literal sense as early as the 1820s. One reference came from 1828 in England, from the *Second Report From the Select Committee on the Public Income and Expenditure of the United Kingdom* (a report commissioned by the House of Commons), which lists in a table an expenditure for "Pay of the Crew of 1 Hired Gun, Hoy at Plymouth, (being Ordnance Men)" with a total cost of 116 pounds. Interestingly, author Truman Capote also used the phrase in his famed book *In Cold Blood* in 1965: "He was always talking about making his living as a hired gun." Sources suggest the term became popular around that time but it's unclear when it began being used in a non-gun-wielding business context.[29]

honcho (as in "the head honcho" or "big honcho") *n.* **1.** The person in charge. **2.** The boss of all bosses.

> **BS Definition:** When the honcho is not present, it is usually said sarcastically and with air quotes around it.

Origin: Borrowed from the Japanese *hanchō*, which means section chief, the term was brought back to the U.S. by servicemen stationed overseas in Japan during World War II. The *OED* says its first written mention was in a photo caption in 1945 in the *Coshocton* (Ohio) *Tribune*: "This prisoner is the 'honcho,' or group headman, in the POW stockade." The Japanese called British or Australian officers in charge of work parties in prisoner-of-war camps *hanchō* during the war. By the 1960s, the word had become part of conversational American jargon—though we Romanized it with an *o* instead of an *a* at the beginning, the pronunciation is the same.[30]

H

honeypot *n.* A decoy computer system designed to engage and track hackers or spammers.

BS Definition: More like a decoy computer system that your IT group doesn't have the resources or wherewithal to execute.

Origin: The earliest honeypot techniques are described in Clifford Stoll's 1989 book, *The Cuckoo's Egg: Tracking a Spy Through the Maze of Computer Espionage*.[31] It is Stoll's first-person account of the hunt for a computer hacker who broke into a computer at the Lawrence Berkeley National Laboratory (LBNL) in California. Stoll found that the intrusion was coming from West Germany via satellite. In order to entice the hacker to reveal himself, Stoll set up an elaborate hoax—a honeypot to trap the bear (aka the hacker)—inventing a fictitious department at LBNL that had supposedly been formed by a (fake) contract for a real missile defense system called SDI. When Stoll realized the hacker was particularly interested in the fake SDI entity, he filled the "SDInet" account (operated by an imaginary secretary named Barbara Sherwin) with large files full of impressive-sounding bureaucratese. The ploy worked, and authorities located the hacker at his home in Hanover, Germany. The hacker's name was Markus Hess, and he had been engaged for several years in selling the results of his hacking to the Soviet KGB.[32]

hump day *n.* **1.** Wednesday. **2.** The middle of the workweek.

BS Definition: A little, tiny glimmer of hope in the black-hole vortex that is your workweek (#WhyMommyAndDaddyDrink).

Origin: While hump day's connection to Wednesday is clear—from the Old English *Wōdnesdæg*, or "Wooden's Day," and the Middle English *Wednesdei*, "day of Woden"—its beginnings are less certain.[33] Some suggest that hump day first appeared in print in the *Dictionary of American Regional English* in 1965, referencing summer-camp counselors who used the term instead of Wednesday. Others suggest it had been used long before that, in the 1950s or even the 1940s, when it referred to any targeted milestone after which things got easier. One example: 1959's *Long Beach* (California) *Press Telegram*: "The highlight of any patrol is Hump Day . . . 'That's the day the patrol is half over, when the rest of the way is downhill.'" What we know for certain is that it did *not* come from the camel in Geico's TV commercials, so you can dispel that thought right now.[34]

"CATS AND DOGS LIVING TOGETHER! MASS HYSTERIA!"

The lines above come from the 1984 movie *Ghostbusters* and were delivered by the hilarious Bill Murray. The thought of all cats and dogs living together peacefully does suggest that the world as we know it is coming undone. The same can be said in the world of BS. Only the words *raining cats and dogs* actually bring these two animals together in one phrase. Other than that, they live two completely separate lives in our world, albeit busy ones.

Besides the canine- and feline-inspired entries listed elsewhere in this book (see *herding cats* and *screw the pooch*), here's a list of other cat and dog idioms that litter our business speak from time to time:

Cats	
cat got your tongue	a momentary inability to speak
cat out of the bag	a secret revealed
copy cat	to mimic the behavior or performance of someone else
fat cat	wealthy or powerful person
look what the cat dragged in	an arrival that is untidy or disheveled
nine lives	immunity to being hurt or killed
playing cat and mouse	alternating between provoking and threatening an opponent

Dogs

barking up the wrong tree	to pick the wrong course of action or person to talk to
bite the hand that feeds you	To treat poorly the person you rely on for your survival
call off the dogs	to stop doing what you're doing
dog-eat-dog	to have to fight others to get what you want
every dog has his day	everyone gets what they deserve eventually
top dog	the boss or victor
turn tail	to retreat
work like a dog	to labor very hard
you can't teach an old dog new tricks	it's hard for older people to learn new things

I

ideation *n.* **1.** The process of forming ideas or images. **2.** The creation of new ideas (see *brainstorm*).

> **BS Definition:** Used when "let's come up with some ideas here" just doesn't sound cool enough.

> **Origin:** Contrary to popular belief that *ideation* is somehow related to more recent phenomena, such as the movement toward design thinking, the word has been around for almost two centuries.[1] According to the *OED*, it first appeared in the written form in one of the notebooks of poet and philosopher Samuel Taylor Coleridge in 1818: "Reality, as a primary Self-revelation or Idea having itself for its Object or Ideation." Interestingly enough, Coleridge's notebooks were never written with the intention of making them public. They were basically his personal diaries until he decided they might be a good legacy to pass down to his disciples, so he published them.

in a nutshell *adj.*, *adv.* **1.** In a few words. **2.** Concise, condensed.

> **BS Definition:** What you may think your boss's brain could fit into.

> **Origin:** The phrase, as it was originally constructed, actually referred to anything that could be written in so few words that it would fit inside a nutshell. Most scholars credit that origin to Pliny the Elder, who in AD 77 said in his book *Natural History* that Cicero recorded *The Iliad*, by Homer, on parchment and enclosed it within a nutshell. (*The Iliad* is hundreds of pages long, by the way, when written in a standard text

font). Shakespeare, who often alluded to the classics, also gave Hamlet the line in 1603: "I could be bounded in a nutshell, and count myself a king of infinite space, were it not that I have bad dreams."[2]

in the weeds *adj.* **1.** Immersed or entangled in details. **2.** To be completely overwhelmed and unable to keep up the pace. **3.** Struggling with problems, troubles, or difficulties.

> **BS Definition:** **1.** A lot like what managing employees feels like. **2.** A lot like what parenting kids feels like.

> **Origin:** We're in the weeds about the origin of *in the weeds*. Some believe it comes from the U.S. military; it meant you were in a place where you'd likely get killed due to the exposed nature of lying "in the weeds." Others say it originates in agriculture; if you harvested too close to the ground, you were likely picking up weeds along the way. Another group suggests roots in prohibition; hiding liquor in the back (literally, "in the weeds") would shield it from authorities who might come looking for it. Then there are those who believe it's a golf term, in that driving your ball off the fairway and "into the weeds" can make for a trickier shot to the hole. Finally, some believe it's a restaurant term; being "in the weeds" means your staff is overrun with customers.[3] The one thing we can say with *certainty* about *in the weeds* is that it is the title of a 2000 movie starring Molly Ringwald.[4] You're welcome.

incentivize *v.* **1.** To offer or give reward for increased productivity. **2.** To provide (someone) with an incentive for doing something.

> **BS Definition:** Why free food is provided at almost any meeting that requires full attendance.

> **Origin:** The *OED* traces the first use of *incentivize* to 1968 in Britain, where it followed British spelling in the *Guardian* newspaper: "You have

got to appeal to people's greed. The most successful station operators incentivise their forecourt staff." Its first American use was not until 1980, however, in *Time* magazine: "Americans were not conserving gasoline because they were 'not sufficiently incentivized.'"

In case you're wondering, the main difference between British and American spellings of such words is that British English has kept the spelling of words it absorbed from other languages, mainly French and German, while American English spellings are based mostly on how the word sounds when it is spoken. These differences were cemented when Samuel Johnson published an authoritative text on British word spellings, *A Dictionary of the English Language*, in 1755. In America, Noah Webster's *A Compendious Dictionary of the English Language*, first printed in 1806, popularized the American spellings of words that were being used instead of the British versions, such as *color* instead of *colour*.[6]

influencer *n.* A person who has the power to lead others toward similar tastes or opinions on products, usually through a large amount of followers on social-media posts.

BS Definition: A person you've never heard of, but your kids look up to and admire.

Origin: Research by the *OED* suggests that the use of *influencer* (as in one who influences others) dates back to 1660, when Henry More was referred to as "the head and influencer of the whole Church [of England]." More, an English philosopher of the Cambridge Platonist school, "attempted to use the details of 17th-century mechanical philosophy—as developed by René Descartes—to establish the existence of immaterial substance," according to his Wikipedia entry.[7] We guess that kind of stuff made you an influencer back then. Of course, the most recent usage of the term influencer is tied to social-media marketing tactics using individuals who aren't necessarily philosophers, and, frankly, may have a hard time spelling the word *philosophy*. In 2019, Kylie Jenner (of the Kardashian family) became the world's youngest self-made billionaire (taking the spot from Facebook's Mark Zuckerberg) thanks in large part to her status as an influencer.[8]

Internet of Things (IoT) *n.* **1.** Everyday objects embedded with microchips that give them network connectivity. **2.** A network of devices, appliances, and other objects equipped with computer chips that can collect and transmit data through the Internet.

BS Definition: The reason a robot may be doing your job one day.

Origin: The origin of this term starts with a guy who was just trying to think of a catchy title for his PowerPoint presentation. Kevin Ashton was working at Procter & Gamble when, as he tells it, one day he:

> had to make a PowerPoint presentation in the 1990s to convince the senior management of the company . . . that we should put an RFID tag, a tiny microchip, in everything that Procter & Gamble made. They had no idea what I was going to tell them, but they knew the Internet was a big deal. So if I could get the word *Internet* into the title of my presentation, I could get their attention. So I very hastily called the presentation the Internet of Things because we had things that we wanted to track around the Procter & Gamble supply chain. And the presentation was successful [and it] went with me. I never changed the title.[9]

Where Ashton went was MIT, where he co-founded a research center that made his "Internet of Things" concept an area of focus. Ashton says it's not unusual for people to misunderstand IoT and think it's about a refrigerator talking to a toaster. It's not. Ashton says the easiest real-world example of the Internet of Things is your smartphone: "It has about 10 sensors in it. They're all connected to the network. You can take a picture and upload it and have algorithms identify the faces in the picture. You wouldn't go anywhere now without your GPS, which is network location sensing. That's the Internet of Things."[10]

IT *n.* I-T **1.** An abbreviation for "information technology." **2.** The use of computer devices to handle electronic data.

BS Definition: All the computer stuff at your workplace that keeps failing on you at the most inopportune time.

Origin: Common wisdom would hold that the reference to one's IT department is relatively new—with the advent of more personalized computing in the 1980s. However, the term information technology, or IT for short, was first written about in 1952 and started becoming popular in 1958 after Thomas L. Whisler and Harold J. Leavitt used it in an article published in the *Harvard Business Review*.[11] At the time, few organizations had anything resembling an "IT department"—primarily just banks and hospitals that needed to store data. IT was used only to describe the process of storing information. Today, computer programming and software development (at one point handled by mathematicians and computer scientists because they were so complex) are now included in the IT department, as well as all those random services that seem to fail on you when you need them most and take forever to fix.

it is what it is *idiom* **1.** Something that can't be changed or altered. **2.** A circumstance that must be accepted or dealt with as it exists (aka *que será será*).

BS Definition: The equivalent of saying "I have no responsibility for all the bad things that are happening and hope this inane phrase ends the debate."

Origin: William Safire, speechwriter and *New York Times* columnist on language, suggested that the phrase first appeared in print in J.E. Lawrence's column in the *Nebraska State Journal* in 1949 about the way pioneer life molded character: "New land is harsh, and vigorous, and sturdy. It scorns evidence of weakness. There is nothing of sham or hypocrisy in it. It is what it is, without apology." Safire also noted the increasing use of the phrase near the end of the 20th century and into the 21st century.[12] To that end, a flurry of activity around *it is what it is* followed Billy Frolick's 2001 movie with that title, and the jam band The String Cheese Incident used the words a year later as the title for one of its more popular songs.[13] Some say it makes sense that *it is what it is* would be popular right now in business speak since we, as a people, love anything that absolves us of responsibility in an outcome.[14] I'm sorry if you disagree with that statement. It is what it is, after all.

I

J

jet lag *n.* **1.** A feeling of tiredness after flying through several time zones. **2.** A temporary condition of fatigue and irritability due to the disruption of circadian rhythms in the body following a long flight.

BS Definition: 1. When you operate just on instincts and unleash your inner ugly on the world. **2.** A nice way of saying "I'm a hot mess right now."

Origin: News sources point to the first use of the term *jet lag* in a 1966 *Los Angeles Times* article: "If you're going to be a member of the Jet Set and fly off to Katmandu for coffee with King Mahendra," wrote Horace Sutton, "you can count on contracting Jet Lag, a debility not unakin to a hangover. Jet Lag derives from the simple fact that jets travel so fast they leave your body rhythms behind." However, the *OED* points to an even earlier news reference, a 1965 *New York Herald Tribune* piece: "Jet lag strikes suddenly. The victim disembarks from the . . . plane feeling gay as a sprite, dashes through customs, checks into home or a hotel . . . greets friends and in the course of the next few hours falls into a light coma."

Some speculate that, like other BS terms, *jet lag* had been used for a while (as early as the 1950s) before appearing in print. At that time, jet lag only really affected the "jet set"—those who could afford the luxury and privilege of being served fine food and wine while they traveled across time zones. Today, those same kind of people are similarly affected by jet lag, but the fine airline cuisine has been replaced by a pack of pretzels and a can of soda.[1]

jockey for position *v.* **1.** To compete for an advantage. **2.** Using whatever means necessary to get into a better position than your rival.

BS Definition: 1. What managers do when it's announced the CEO is retiring. **2.** What a 12-year-old girl does at a Justin Bieber concert.

Origin: This term comes from horse racing, specifically a jockey's attempt to maneuver a racehorse into a better position for winning as the race progresses. Although the *OED* says 1835 was the first year a variation of this phrase was used in print, it wasn't until the mid-1900s that it became used in a business context to refer to individuals who lined up for consideration for a prize, reward, or promotion: "In Alberta when there was no jury, congestion was caused by lawyers jockeying for position in order to appear before the right judge."[2]

John Hancock *n.* **1.** American statesman who was the first signer of the Declaration of Independence. **2.** Your signature.

BS Definition: 1. The phrase a salesperson uses instead of saying, "Sign your life away right here, sucker." **2.** The name of someone other than you . . . unless your real name is John Hancock—which, really, what are the odds? C'mon—we're sure there are several John Hancocks in the world and maybe there are a couple of people that, as a joke, give it as their Starbucks name, but how many of those people  are going to get this book? One or two maybe, tops. And of those people, how many are actually reading this passage right now? Zero. Absolutely none of them (see *it is what it is*).

Origin: As president of the Second Continental Congress, John Hancock was the first to sign the Declaration of Independence after it was ratified on July 4, 1776, and sent to the printer. He did so with such a flourish—making his signature big and bold to make sure that King George would see it—that his name has become synonymous in the United States with signing any document.[3] According to the *OED*, as early as 1834 Hancock's signature started to become a metaphor for signing your name on paper, as evidence in the *Letters of J. Downing, Major Downingville Militia, Second Brigade, to his old friend, Mr. Dwight, of the New-York Daily Advertiser*: "I got the Gravers to copy one of his Signatures . . . and it is as much like the original handwritin of Major Downing, as old John Hancock's is of hisen to the Declaration of Independence."

jump (or beat) the gun *idiom* **1.** To begin before an approved or authorized time. **2.** To act hastily; to start prematurely.

BS Definition: To start eating the buffet lunch brought in for the out-of-town guests before they are finished with it.

Origin: As one might expect, the origins of this term come from track and field, in which a gun is used to signal the start of a race. According to the *OED*, the earliest citations are for "beating the pistol" and come from the 1905 book *Rowing and Track Athletics*, by Samuel Crowther (rowing) and Arthur Ruhl (track athletics): "False starts were rarely penalized . . . and so shiftless were the starters and officials that 'beating the pistol' was one of the tricks which less sportsmanlike runners constantly practised." In modern parlance, one early reference we found comes from *Boy's Life* (published by the Boy Scouts) magazine in May 1932: "But the competition had his goat; with men to beat his nerves went haywire. He'd jump the gun, the starter'd set him back twice, three times, maybe. By then, he was out of the race."[4] In addition, a source for the phrase's popularity in modern times may lie in The Beatles' *White Album*. The song, "Happiness Is a Warm Gun," has a well-known refrain of "Mother Superior jump the gun."[5]

ROOTED IN THE BIBLE

According to the *OED*, no other written source has given us as many new words in the English language as the Bible. (William Shakespeare is second, by the way.) That probably goes for BS terms as well. Besides the terms already defined in this book, here are some other Bible-inspired BS phrases.[1]

bite the dust	to fail or die (Psalms 72:9)
blind leading the blind	someone who lacks skill or knowledge being led by someone else who is just as inept (Matthew 15:13-14)
by the skin of your teeth	to barely accomplish something (Job 19:20)
drop in the bucket	a small, inadequate quantity (Isaiah 40:15)
fly in the ointment	a problem that may prevent success (Ecclesiastes 10:1)
go the extra mile	to do more than is expected (Matthew 5:41)
good Samaritan	someone who unselfishly helps others (especially strangers) in need (Luke 10:30-37)
live by the sword, die by the sword	if you use force against others, you can expect to have it used against you (Matthew 26:52)
money is the root of all evil	a focus only on financial gains eventually leads to no good (1 Timothy 6:10)

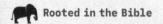

no rest for the wicked	you have to work hard to be wicked (Isaiah 57: 20-21)
put words in someone's mouth	to say what you think someone else means (2 Samuel 14:3)
scapegoat	someone who is held responsible for others' actions (Leviticus 16: 9-10)
see eye to eye	to be in agreement (Isaiah 52:8)
thorn in your side	a constant source of irritation (2 Corinthians 12:7)
wash your hands of	to distance yourself from any responsibility (Matthew 27:24)
wit's end	no patience left (Psalm 107:27)

K

KISS *acronym* **1.** Stands for "Keep it simple stupid." **2.** Stands for "Keep it super simple."

> **BS Definition:** Keep it simple (in-such-a-rudimentary-way-that-even-a-moron-who-was-genetically-engineered-to-be-an-even-bigger-moron-and-forced-to-spin-around-a-bat-10-times-really-fast-after-drinking-a-bunch-of-Hurricanes-during-Mardi-Gras-followed-by-a-lobotomy-could-understand-it) stupid.

> **Origin:** This acronym was reportedly coined in 1960 by Kelly Johnson, lead engineer at the Lockheed Skunk Works (which created the Lockheed U-2 and SR-71 Blackbird spy planes, among others). According to the story, the term arose as Johnson handed a team of design engineers a handful of tools, with the challenge that they design an aircraft that could be repairable by an average mechanic in combat conditions with only those tools. While popular usage has transcribed it for decades as "Keep it simple, stupid," Johnson transcribed it more simply, without the comma: "Keep it simple stupid."[1]

KOL *acronym* K-O-L Abbreviation for "key opinion leader(s)."

> **BS Definition:** Any individual with a phone willing to film himself or herself doing something completely inane and/or naked (see *influencer*).

> **Origin:** Some have suggested a difference between a KOL and an influencer, from a marketing standpoint, is that key opinion leaders influence a particular segment or sector of an audience while an influencer's impact is on the audience as a whole. That may just be a different kind of BS

created by a bored blogger, but what we do know is that the popularity in today's business speak for KOLs is generally credited to Paul Lazarsfeld and Elihu Katz. They wrote a book in 1955 called *Personal Influence*, which reported the results of a pioneering study that suggested messages from the media may be further influenced by informal "opinion leaders" who intercept, interpret, and share what they see and hear with their own personal networks.[2] And while the term influencer dates back to 1660, it is Lazarsfeld and Katz's work in 1955 that really put KOL on the BS map.

kid gloves *n.* **1.** To treat with delicacy and sensitivity. **2.** To treat with extreme tact or gentleness.

BS Definition: Often, the individual being treated with kid gloves deserves to be treated with gloves of the boxing variety.

Origin: Kid gloves were actual, real gloves made primarily of lambskin. Given their delicate nature, they were never intended for hard labor; hence, wearing them was the equivalent of, say, having pale white skin, in that it indicated the wearer was rich enough to indulge in a life of indoor idleness. According to the *OED*, the earliest known reference comes from a listing in a French-English dictionary by Guy Miege in 1677, where kid gloves is simply translated into French (*gans de chevre*)—literally "goose of goats." (It doesn't have to make sense—it's French, just go with it.) The term is also used in *The Old Bachelor*, a play from 1693 by William Congreve:

> Why, the father bought a Powder-Horn, and an Almanack, and a
> Comb-Case; the Mother, a great Fruz-Tovr, and a Fat-Amber-Necklace;
> the daughters only tore two Pair of Kid-Gloves, with trying 'em on. O
> Gad, here comes the fool that din'd at my Lady Free-love's t'other Day.[3]

By the 1800s, the term had begun to take on negative connotations in Britain—associated with a lack of manliness. As it crossed into the United States, *kid gloves* became more known for its current-day definition of "handling delicately or carefully." The New York monthly magazine, *Knick-erbocker*, has the first example of the term in print with that meaning, from 1849: "Belligerent topics are not our forte and never was; neither do we handle them with kid gloves, when they fairly come in the way."[4]

kill the goose that lays the golden egg *idiom* **1.** To destroy a source of repetitive success, profit, or wealth. **2.** To destroy a source of income or livelihood for shortsighted reasons.

BS Definition: To make a reference that causes at least one or two people in the room to think of the movie *Willy Wonka and the Chocolate Factory.*[5]

Origin: This idiom comes from *Aesop's Fables*, the collection of tales credited to Aesop, a slave and storyteller believed to have lived in ancient Greece between 620 and 564 BC. In "The Goose That Laid the Golden Eggs," Aesop tells the story of a greedy couple (a farmer and his wife) who killed their goose, which laid one golden egg a day. They had thought that they would find more gold inside, but instead found the goose to be just like other geese and, in the end, lost their means of livelihood.[6]

Business case in point: Anyone remember AltaVista, the search engine? It used to be Google before Google, but then decided it wanted to be more like Yahoo. Now, it survives only as a pop culture reference to the mid-1990s in the film *Captain Marvel.*[7] (It's a Marvel world folks; we just live in it.)

kill two birds with one stone *idiom* To accomplish two different things through one action.

BS Definition: 1. When your business trip allows you to get away from the family and buy them souvenir trinkets they don't need at the same time. **2.** To forward an email chain about a project to your boss—

forgetting that the chain includes you and co-workers complaining about how big of an idiot he is.[8]

Origin: This phrase is believed to have first appeared in English in a 1632 book, *Complete History of the Present Seat of War in Africa Between the Spaniards and Algerines* by an author identified as "J. Morgan Gent." Gent wrote that a military chief "came resolved to kill two Birds with one Stone, return the Spaniards their Compliments, and conduct his insolent Turks, where he was certain at least some of them would be knocked on the head." There has been much debate about whether the phrase actually has origins in other languages, but nothing conclusive has been shown. Some have pointed to the story of Daedalus and Icarus, who escaped from the labyrinth by making wings and flying out, according to the myth. And according to the Grammar-phobia blog, Daedalus supposedly got the feathers to make the wings by killing two birds with one stone. But neither of the principal sources of the myth, details anything about Daedalus's acquisition of the feathers.[9]

knockoff *n.* **1.** A cheaper copy or reproduction of a popular product. **2.** An unlicensed, and usually low-quality, copy of a more expensive item.

BS Definition: That $20 Rolex you bought off a street vendor during a trip to New York City that stopped working properly a week later.

Origin: In the 1800s, this term could have referred to a number of things: working quickly; falling asleep; beating someone up. In August 1919, the first use of *knock off* to mean stealing something may have come in the publication *The Athenaeum*: "A curious term used by a Tommy [British soldier], in 'explaining' his deficiencies of kit, is 'Someone knocked it off' for 'Someone pinched (or made away with) it.'"

Eventually, the word *knockoff* came to be used as a noun as a way to imply a cheap or otherwise deficient duplicate of something.[10]

For Bob Wiltfong, the words *knock* and *off* were part of a go-to refrain in his childhood home whenever his dad wanted the kids to stop doing something immediately: "Knock [it] off!" he would say. As far as that version of knock [it] off goes, the origin appears to be from the world of auctioneers. In the 1800s, if nobody bid on an item, an auctioneer would command "knock it off" as a way of saying, "Let's dispose of this quickly."[11]

knowledge economy *n.* **1.** An economy in which the acquisition, distribution, and use of information drives growth rather than traditional means of production. **2.** A line of work where a large number of jobs require the ability to create new knowledge rather than manual labor (for example, software developers creating tools to organize and explore data).

BS Definition: 1. Another way of saying: "Our economy doesn't produce anything anymore." **2.** A workplace where there are a lot of people sitting in bean bags, playing foosball, or riding scooters into meditation rooms.

Origin: Popular wisdom (which is almost never right, it seems) has it that *knowledge economy* has really only come into being in the last several years with the confluence of the Internet, social media, mobile computing, and a wave of smart devices. However, the term actually stems back to the 1960s. The *OED* says the first written reference to it was in 1967, in an issue of the weekly *Saturday Review*: "From an industrial economy . . . we shall . . . more and more become . . . a knowledge economy, with 50 per cent or more of our work force involved in the production of information." Author and authority on business management Peter Drucker popularized the term in 1969 when he used it as a title of a chapter in his book *The Age of Discontinuity*. Drucker was writing about the transition from an industrial economy to a more knowledge-based or information economy, where knowledge resources such as trade secrets and expertise would be as critical as other economic resources. Even before then, Drucker had been anticipating a large shift to the age when people would generate more value with their minds than with their muscle. In 1959, he described the rise of "knowledge work" in his book *Landmarks of Tomorrow*.[12]

kudos *n.* **1.** Congratulations. **2.** Honor, glory, or acclaim.

BS Definition: I don't have anything of real value to give you—like money or a cool gift like *The BS Dictionary*—so maybe just saying this silly little word to you will suffice?

Origin: Coming from the ancient Greek word *kydos* (glory), its crossing into English was said to be somewhat of a joke, according to the *OED*. In 1799, the romantic poet Robert Southey, writing about the installation of William Cavendish-Bentinck, duke of Portland, as the chancellor of Oxford, said that the duke's fur robe was "kudos'd egregiously in heathen Greek."

Despite that beginning, the word gradually gained favor in Britain in the 1800s and became more synonymous as a slang word for praise by the 20th century, particularly by journalists.[13]

L

lawyer up *v.* **1.** To put together a team of attorneys (usually preceded with "you better . . ."). **2.** To obtain legal services, especially while being investigated for possible wrongdoing.

> **BS Definition:** Something anyone running for higher office has to do these days (see *new normal*).

> **Origin:** You can thank the TV show *NYPD Blue* for popularizing this term in our modern business lexicon. During the 1990s, *NYPD Blue* used it so much that it became the subject of a drinking game: Every time you hear a character say "lawyer up," you have to drink.[1] With that said, it makes sense that the *OED* records the first written reference to *lawyer up* being in a 1995 *New York Times* article about *NYPD Blue*: "What really spooks the detectives on '*N.Y.P.D. Blue*' is the prospect of a suspect 'lawyering up.'"[2]

lean in *v.* **1.** To actively participate in the conversation or activity at hand. **2.** To be assertive in the workplace.

> **BS Definition:** To look like you actually care when the boss drones on about third-quarter results.

> **Origin:** Facebook COO Sheryl Sandberg's landmark 2013 book of the same name popularized this phrase in the BS world.[3] Sandberg promotes the idea that women need to "lean in" to have their voice heard more in the workplace rather than "leaning out." However, after it was revealed that a right-wing political consulting agency Cambridge Analytica had obtained data on millions of Facebook users without their knowledge,

some alleged that Sandberg was consciously "leaning out" of the conversation to avoid blame.[4]

leave-behind *n.* 1. A handout. 2. Any item that you give to a client after a meeting or other networking event.

BS Definition: The first thing clients leave behind (often in the trashcan) after a presenter exits.

Origin: Originally referring to people, the term the *left-behind* had its origins in the mid-1800s, according to the *OED*. Somewhere between there and the present day, the phrase has evolved to a "leave-behind"—a sales and marketing term for a pamphlet or brochure that is left after a visit.[5]

left holding the bag *idiom* 1. To have blame or burden thrust upon you. 2. To be put in a situation in which you are responsible and deserted.

BS Definition: To have all your colleagues come down with the flu the night before you're scheduled to present disappointing project findings to the boss.

Origin: A practical joke and the world of crime are the two most likely origins of this phrase, both dating from at least the 1700s. The practical joke origin has to do with a "snipe hunt," in which an unsuspecting newcomer is led to the woods and instructed to hold a lantern over an open burlap bag waiting for a wild "snipe" to come—which it never does, because the "snipes" in question are imaginary.[6] The other origin comes from organized crime in Britain when a person was left holding a bag of stolen goods for police to discover, while the rest of the gang slipped away. The original version of this idea was "to give somebody the bag to hold," which has evolved into "left holding the bag." One source quotes Thomas Jefferson making this reference when he wrote in 1793, "if the bankruptcies of England proceed . . . she will leave Spain the bag to hold."[7]

long in the tooth *adj.* **1.** Old or aging. **2.** An unkind or humorous way to say someone is getting old.

> **BS Definition:** You know you're it when you have to explain to a co-worker what the world was like before email (#OneFootInTheGrave).

> **Origin:** This expression alludes to a horse's gums receding with age and making the teeth appear longer.[8] The *OED* dates the first written use of this term to 1834 in the book *Angler in Wales or Days and Nights of Sportsmen*, by Thomas Medwin: "A brown gawky leggy Rozinante, very long in the tooth, and showing every bone in his skin, was generally ridden by his courier."

> That quote is *straight from the horse's mouth* (definition: from the most reliable source). If you're like us, you're probably *champing at the bit* (definition: excited; anxious) to share it with your colleagues, but, remember, *you can lead a horse to water, but you can't make it drink* (definition: you can't force someone to accept an opportunity). *Don't look a gift horse in the mouth* (definition: don't be critical or show a lack of appreciation for something that was given to you in good faith) here by finding fault with that. Just *hold your horses* (definition: calm down), and maybe look for a moment of *horseplay* (definition: rough play) in the office to slip it in somewhere.[9]

long shot *n.* **1.** An effort that has little chance of succeeding. **2.** A person or team with a very small probability of winning.

> **BS Definition:** **1.** What the boss says instead of directly replying "no way in hell" to your new idea. **2.** A genetically engineered life form from another dimension who joins the X-Men.[10] **3.** The Washington Generals.[11]

> **Origin:** The *OED* cites 1796 as the first year *long shot* appeared in writing (in a document titled "Original Letters, etc. of Sir John Falstaff") with

this meaning. Some sources say it derives from shooting at a target from a great distance, thus making it difficult to hit. However, most sources say *long shot* truly found its meaning in horse racing, which dominated sporting life and news coverage in the 19th and 20th centuries. Indeed, by the mid-1800s, a *long shot* referred primarily to a horse that had little chance of winning a particular race.[12] (See the sidebar on page 153.)

lots of moving parts *n.* **1.** The presence of many different elements for one project. **2.** To have many working components to manage all at one time.

BS Definition: Said when you want to blame something other than your own ineptitude for things not going well.

Origin: Congratulations to this phrase for being voted one of the "most annoying business jargon" terms by *Forbes* magazine in 2012![13] To help celebrate, we organized an elaborate gala complete with a dog and pony show, Kool-Aid to drink, and all the bells and whistles!

Seriously, one of the earliest references we could find for this BS term was actually literal, coming from the *Elevator Constructor*, a journal of the International Union of Elevator Constructors, in 1947: "but you know, elevators have lots of moving parts, and moving parts will wear out, much to the owners dislike."[14] We couldn't find any evidence of how and when it started to be used figuratively. However, to be honest, we had a lot of moving parts going on at the time (what with the gala planning for the *Forbes* listing and all), so we had to abandon our search. Don't blame our ineptitude (see *it is what it is*).

lowball *v.* **1.** To put in a low offer or bid. **2.** To deliberately give a lower price for a service or product than you intend to eventually charge.

BS Definition: **1.** To get paid your current salary. **2.** The opposite of highball (which is a term no businessperson ever uses, except when ordering at a bar).

Origin: As long as there have been individuals or businesses desperate to sell, there have been people using lowball techniques against them. In 1978, researchers led by Robert Cialdini defined why lowballing works in a study published in the *Journal of Personality and Social Psychology*.[15] The psychological concept of "cognitive dissonance" is at play, which refers to the mental comfort of a person who struggles to understand two disharmonious elements. Cialdini's experiments showed why cognitive dissonance causes a person who already wants to buy (or sell) a product, and is already anticipating the future benefits of doing so, will not be motivated to back out of the deal, even if they're not thrilled about the initial price offer (high or low).

As far as who labeled this technique lowballing and when, we defer to the experts at the *OED*, who suggest it may have come from the game of baseball. In 1917, the *New-York Tribune* reported on a baseball pitcher who may have been making balls look like strikes through "lowballing": "Williams was lowballing the Yanks while Faber used some of his justly celebrated speed and a few of his not so celebrated curves." How this reference led to the BS use of lowball is still unknown, but we're open to paying one of you to investigate it further for us. We'll start the negotiation with a lowball offer of one penny. Any counteroffers?

low-hanging fruit *n.* **1.** Tasks that are easy to address. **2.** A thing or person that can be won, obtained, or persuaded with little effort.

BS Definition: Usually much higher than anyone anticipated—but it's not like you can go around saying, "Let's go after the *high*-hanging fruit!" and expect people to get on board with you.

Origin: The literal sense of low-hanging fruit has been used for hundreds of years. Some scholars pinpoint its first written mention as 1628 in Henry Reynolds's translation of Torquato Tasso's *Aminta*:

> Being but a Lad, so young as yet scarse able
> To reach the fruit from the low-hanging boughs
> Of new growne trees; Inward I grew to bee
> With a young mayde, fullest of loue and sweetnesse,
> That ere display'd pure gold tresse to the winde;

However, the use of low-hanging fruit as an idiom is more recent. Although some scholars cite evidence of it being used in the early 1900s, the *OED* says its first written use was 1968, from the U.K.'s *Guardian* newspaper: "His rare images are picked aptly, easily, like low-hanging fruit." A study of the *New York Times* by University of Pennsylvania researchers says the mention of low-hanging fruit started to increase in the mid-1990s. Today, it is a well-known expression in business and marketing, especially in sales.[16]

L

lunch & learn *n.* **1.** A meeting held while people eat lunch (aka grub club). **2.** A seminar offered during a free lunch (aka the learning trough).

BS Definition: 1. Let's face it; the lunch part is usually pizza—and only two types—pepperoni and plain. If it had more variety—veggie, sausage, maybe even throw in a roasted red pepper—we would go more often. **2.** Not getting a break for lunch, but instead having to suffer through a "voluntary" presentation while eating crappy food.

Origin: As it turns out, this phrase may actually have origins outside the business world in the realm of 1970s housewives. Indeed, our crack *BS Dictionary* research team found that the Department of Agriculture's *Extension Review* journal from 1973 appears to unlock the mystery around who started the first lunch & learn: "So they looked for a time when homemakers did have time to spare. Their solution: the noon hour—a time when these women could 'lunch' and 'learn' at the same time."[17] The journal suggests that the two women with the idea—Sandra Stockall and Jeanette Grantham of Nebraska—went on to move the concept of a "lunch & learn" to two local industrial plants, employing some 600 people, where it was enthusiastically received.[18] So now you know. And we didn't even have to serve you pizza!

L

REPORTS OF LATIN'S DEATH ARE GREATLY EXAGGERATED

No one speaks Latin as their first language anymore. As a result, it's considered "dead." But don't tell that to anyone who speaks BS. Business speak is littered with Latin words and phrases.[1] Here are some examples.

ad hoc	for a specific subject, purpose, or end
bona fide	real or genuine
carpe diem	seize the day
de facto	someone who holds a position, usually without the right to do so
e.g.	for example
ergo	therefore
et cetera	further items matching this list could be included
i.e.	to say something in a different way or to give a more specific example; literally translates to "that is," and commonly mistaken for the same meaning as e.g.
impromptu	spontaneous; without any prior planning
per se	emphasizes the stand-alone importance or connection of something
pro bono	done for free

quid pro quo	a favor or advantage given in return for something of equal value
re	about; commonly used in email replies
status quo	an existing state of things
verbatim	repeating something word-for-word from the original
versus	against
vice versa	things that are interchangeable

M

MO/modus operandi *n.* M-O **1.** Mode of operating. **2.** The way in which a person or business works.

> **BS Definition:** Almost always used as a way to explain a negative event or behavior (for example, "He led her to believe that she was doing great. Then he fired her without cause. But that's his MO").

> **Origin:** Coming from the Latin words for "mode of operating," this BS term traces its origin back to the 1600s. The *OED* notes its first written use in 1654 from Ζωοτομία, or, *Observations on the Present Manners of the English*, by Richard Whitlock: "Because their Causes, or their modus operandi (which is but the Application of the Cause to the Effect) doth not fall under Demonstration."[1] The abbreviation of "MO" is more recent, with the *OED* citing 1915 as its first written occurrence. In today's business world, it's often used when examining a person's pattern of behavior on the job.

magic bullet *n.* **1.** A solution that takes care of a previously unsolvable problem without causing harmful side effects. **2.** A solution that addresses simultaneous problems in a way that defies logic.

> **BS Definition:** Something Kodak, Palm, and Blackberry could've used to fend off the iPhone.

> **Origin:** This term derives from medicine, specifically German Nobel laureate Paul Ehrlich, who coined the term in 1900 to describe the possibility of killing specific microbes (like bacteria) without harming the body itself. Ehrlich envisioned a hypothetical agent called *zauberkugel*

("magic bullet"), that would hit a specific target—like a bullet fired from a gun. Eventually, he and colleague Sahachiro Hata tried this concept on the microbes causing syphilis and, in 1909, discovered one compound, number 606 (later called "Salvarsan"), that worked with no adverse effects on the patient.[2]

A secondary meaning of *magic bullet* came from the assassination of U.S. President John F. Kennedy in 1963. In the aftermath, a government commission (known unofficially as the Warren Commission) issued a finding that concluded Kennedy and Texas Governor John Connally were struck by the same bullet—even though evidence (for example, the Zapruder film) suggested a single bullet causing that kind of damage is unlikely. This "magic bullet theory" fueled a conspiracy theory that someone other than Lee Harvey Oswald was involved in the shooting.[3] Do yourself a favor and go on YouTube to see how all of this inspired the "magic loogie" story line from a famous episode of the TV show *Seinfeld.*[4]

master(s) of the universe *n.* **1.** An extremely powerful, successful, or wealthy person, especially someone working in the financial industry (see *tycoon*). **2.** A highly successful businessperson (see *anointed*).

BS Definition: A title that is usually self-proclaimed and applies to the type of person who gives their home a name—like Xanadu 2.0 (ahem, Bill Gates) or Kensington Palace Gardens (looking at you, Lakshmi Mittal).[5]

Origin: The author Tom Wolfe made this phrase a BS term when he described arrogant Wall Street bankers in *The Bonfire of the Vanities*, published in 1987: "The world was upside down. What was he, a Master of the Universe, doing down here on the floor, reduced to ransacking his brain for white lies to circumvent the sweet logic of his wife?" The term is an allusion to a phrase describing God that has been mentioned in writing since the 17th century, and possibly to a series of superhero action figures by the same name that preceded Wolfe's book by a few years in the 1980s.[6] Those "masters of the universe" included He-Man and Skeletor.[7]

meeting of the minds *n.* **1.** An understanding or agreement between people. **2.** A concept used to describe the intentions of parties forming a contract. **3.** A gathering of business leaders.

> **BS Definition:** A business assembly that, ironically, may display very little brain activity.

> **Origin:** This term originally derives from the Latin phrase *consensus ad idem*, which has been used in the world of law

since the 1700s. The phrase translates to "agreement to the [same] thing," which is actually a little different from what meeting of the minds means in BS terms, and some legal authorities, including U.S. Supreme Court Justice Oliver Wendell Holmes, have argued that the idea behind meeting of the minds is pretty much fiction.[8] Regardless, as time has continued, the term has begun to take on other meanings, such as when business leaders (see *honcho*) get together to discuss matters of importance (like at Sun Valley, Google Zeitgeist, World Economic Forum, or Bilderberg[9]).

meme *n.* **1.** An image, video, piece of text, or so forth that is copied and spread via the Internet, often in creative and humorous variations. **2.** An image that depicts a certain cultural concept or behavior and is spread rapidly from person to person on the Internet.

> **BS Definition:** Grumpy cat.

Origin: First, let's define the difference between a meme and a GIF. A meme is typically static (though it can move on occasion), typically uses a big font, and makes some kind of topical or cultural reference. A GIF, meanwhile, generally takes a clip from a movie or television show and animates it (a Phoebe eye roll from *Friends*, for example). Now that that's situated, let's look at the origin of meme, shall we?

The word was coined by British biologist Richard Dawkins in his 1976 book, *The Selfish Gene*. Dawkins suggested the possibility that cultural entities—like song melodies or fashion trends—were subject to the same pressures of evolution as biological attributes. He wanted to label these units of imitation and replication, and did so by saying:

> The new soup is the soup of human culture. We need a name for the new replicator, a noun which conveys the idea of a unit of cultural transmission, or a unit of imitation. "Mimeme" comes from a suitable Greek root, but I want a monosyllable that sounds a bit like "gene." I hope my classicist friends will forgive me if I abbreviate mimeme to meme. . . . It should be pronounced to rhyme with "cream." Examples of memes are tunes, ideas, catch-phrases, clothes fashions, ways of making pots or of building arches.[10]

Using this definition, the "Kilroy was here" graffiti phenomenon of the 1940s was an early meme.[11] However, according to the *OED*, it wasn't until a January 1998 broadcast of the CNN show *Science and Technology Week* that *meme* was used in its current BS context of the Internet: "The next thing you know, his friends have forwarded it [an animation of a dancing baby] on and it's become a net meme."

Millennial *n.* **1.** People (especially North Americans) born between 1981 to 1996. **2.** A generation of people who are reaching adulthood in the 2000s. **3.** A demographic group sometimes called "Generation Y," "Generation Next," or "Generation Me."

BS Definition: A generation of people labeled as lazy, entitled, and narcissistic by older people—because we older people aren't guilty of being any of those things, right? Nah!

Origin: Authors William Strauss and Neil Howe are widely credited with naming the Millennial generation in their 1991 book, *Generations: The History of America's Future, 1584 to 2069*. It came out around the time children born in 1982 were in early grade school, and the media was first identifying their prospective link to the impending new millennium as the high-school graduating class of 2000. Other attempts to label this generation have included Generation Y (first proposed by *Advertising Age* magazine), Generation Me (described in a book by psychologist Jean Twenge), and Generation 9/11 (from *Newsweek* magazine).[12]

mindshare *n.* **1.** Consumer awareness of a product or brand compared with those of competitors. **2.** Public awareness of a phenomenon.

BS Definition: When you decide to share your thoughts about politics on Facebook . . . then have a person you went to high school with tell you how big of an idiot you are for having those thoughts.

Origin: According to the *Encyclopedia of Public Relations*, it was Cornelius Dubois, president of the market research firm Cornelius DuBois & Company in New York, who coined the term *mindshare* in the late 1940s or early 1950s.[13] Dubois believed that mindshare would predict a company's market share and would foretell a key aspect of a company's success. Later, in 1955, Edward Bernays expanded the definition to suggest mindshare was related to the share of the consumer's mind relative to competing ideas, not just products. While Dubois was first with the term, Bernays himself perhaps has the greater mindshare—as he is considered to be one of the pioneers in the field of public relations.[14]

miss the boat/bus *idiom* **1.** To fail to take advantage of an opportunity. **2.** To miss the point.[15]

BS Definition: To show up to work on a day that it was announced the building would be closed.

Origin: This origin story is one that involves a teacher and his student in 1840s England. The tale begins with John Henry Newman, an evangelical Oxford University academic and priest in the Church of England, who was a leader in the Oxford Movement—an influential group of Anglicans who wanted the Church of England to return to Catholic beliefs and rituals.[16] In 1845, Newman decided to leave the Church of England—and his teaching post at Oxford—to convert to Catholicism and be ordained a priest. It was a big deal and, as the story goes, one of Newman's followers, Mark Pattison, wanted to approach Newman the day of his decision. However, whether due to lack of nerve or some other reason, he literally missed the bus (and his opportunity to go to Rome). The event was later chronicled in John Morley's *Critical miscellanies*, published in 1886: "Though he [Pattison] appeared for all intents and purposes as much a Catholic at heart as Newman or any of them, it was probably his constitutional incapacity for heroic and decisive courses that made him, according to the Oxford legend, miss the omnibus."

Later, the idea was adapted to "missing the boat" by Americans. In 1930, the *Aberdeen Press and Journal* had this to say about a George Bernard Shaw play: "As a medium for a dull debut, 'A Devil's Disciple' by Bernard Shaw . . . to use an Americanism, missed the boat by twenty years."[17]

mission critical *adj.* **1.** Vital for success. **2.** Absolutely necessary for a business or operation to function properly.

BS Definition: **1.** An appropriate phrase for NASA to use when sending astronauts into space. Not so much when sending interns into Panera for your lunch. **2.** What a sense of humor is when annual budgets are due.

Origin: Originally a military term, *mission critical* has morphed into a business phrase, used commonly in the world of computer software or hardware systems whose failure could potentially jeopardize a company's well-being. The term's first written mention, in 1976, reflects its origins in the military. The *OED* says it comes from *Aviation Week* magazine: "Hardening of mission-critical government-furnished avionics for the USAF/Rockwell International B-1 bomber is being negotiated by USAF and Boeing Aerospace Co."[18]

mom-and-pop *adj.* **1.** Not part of a bigger chain. **2.** Stand-alone, small. **3.** Denotes a lack of sophistication.

BS Definition: **1.** Wait. There are still mom-and-pop stores?! **2.** The people you're convinced have no sense of humor when you're a teenager.

Origin: The buying and selling of goods goes back as far as 17,000 BC, and our guess is some of those people buying and selling things were couples we might refer to as a "mom and pop" in today's world.[19] You know, the mom probably knew where all the fire-making material was, while the pop grumbled to himself getting a wheel out of the cave. However, according to the book *The Mom and Pop Store*, the first retail mom-and-pop shops were created around 650 BC in Turkey.[20] It took thousands of years for the label mom-and-pop to appear, though, as a way of distinguishing smaller business establishments from larger corporate entities or chains.[21] The *OED* says one of the earliest written references was in 1951 from a study by sociologist C. Wright Mills called *White Collar: The American Middle Classes*: "The hole-in-the-wall business, also known as a Mom-and-Pop store."

Monday-morning quarterback *n.* **1.** A person who unfairly critiques something after it has happened. **2.** A person who assumes wisdom about something after the fact.

BS Definition: A saying that gets all screwed up when your NFL team plays on Monday night . . . or on a Thursday night . . . or in one of those weird Saturday games late in December . . . or overseas, where who knows what day it is when they kick off.

Origin: This phrase first came to national attention in the 1930s. The *OED* says its first written use was in the *Macon* (Georgia) *Telegraph*, but it was at a meeting of the New England Association of Colleges and Secondary Schools in Boston on December 4, 1931, that Monday-morning quarterback was launched into the BS term we know today. At that meeting was  Harvard's star quarterback, Barry Wood, one of the most prominent football players of his day. He once graced the cover of *Time* magazine and went on to become a prominent physician, medical researcher, and hospital administrator at Washington University and Johns Hopkins. On that day, Wood was listening to audience members criticizing the day's recruiting scandals and overemphasis on winning in college football. When Wood spoke, he chided these critics by saying the answer to the overemphasis on winning in the game was to be found not on the field, but in the stands, where sit what Wood called "the Monday morning quarterbacks."[22] We assume, if there was a microphone at this event, that Wood dropped it on the floor at that point and walked out (read: mic drop).

move the needle *v.* **1.** Make a significant difference or generate a reaction. **2.** To change a situation in a noticeable direction (see *mindshare*).

BS Definition: What would have happened to Excite.com if it had bought Google for $750,000 in 1999.[23]

Origin: There are two different theories of origin for this one:
- » It comes from the indicator needle or speedometer of a car, in which moving the needle meant the vehicle was going faster (before digital speedometers of today).
- » It refers to the needle of a seismograph, which meant that if the needle moved, the Earth would be shaking.[24]

Neither of these origins has enough reliable sources associated with them to say for certain who is correct. Therefore, we suggest supporters of both sides join the Townies and Fermites (see *back of the envelope*) on the playground after school today to settle this debate once and for all.

M

N

net-net *n.* **1.** The main message or bottom line. **2.** A final outcome that has taken into account all the pros and cons associated with it.

BS Definition: Repeating a word needlessly to sound so much more relevant-relevant.

Origin: The original term *net-net* derives from the world of investment.[1] Benjamin Graham, the British-born American investor, economist, and professor known as the "father of value investing," is said to have first coined the term as an investment strategy in which a company is valued based solely on its net current assets.[2] A net-net stock is one that is priced below its current assets minus its total liabilities. Graham wrote two of the founding texts on investing: *Security Analysis* (1934) with David Dodd, and *The Intelligent Investor* (1949). Warren Buffet, the famed investor and billionaire, was said to have used net-net investing in the 1950s for many of his early gains. In common parlance, the term has morphed over the years to be more of a synonym for a true value or result.[3] And that, my friends, is the net-net of this term in today's BS world.

new normal *n.* **1.** Something that was previously abnormal that has become commonplace. **2.** The financial conditions following the economic crisis of 2007–2008 and its aftermath.

BS Definition: Your life after your co-workers find embarrassing images of you online.

Origin: The term *new normal* has been around for at least 100 years or so, according to the *OED*. However, its origin in its current BS meaning stems from the financial crisis of 2007–2008 and its immediate after-math. In 2009, Mohamed A. El-Erian, the co-CEO and co-CIO of American investment management firm PIMCO, wrote investors about the prolonged slow-growth recovery that was happening: "Indeed some of you may have already heard us argue that the world is traveling on a bumpy road to its new destination—or what PIMCO has labeled 'the new normal.'" Media outlets popularized the term by using it in their reporting on the economy. A few years later, in 2016, El-Erian penned an article asking if this "new normal" was already over.[4] Seven years seems like a short amount of time for a period in history to be over, but maybe that's the new normal of things, right?

nip in the bud *idiom* **1.** To stop something at the beginning of its devel-opment. **2.** To suppress or halt at an early stage.

BS Definition: Something you wish you could have done to those office rumors of impending layoffs.

Origin: If you're the type of person who believes that the lyrics to the Credence Clearwater Revival song "Bad Moon Rising" includes the phrase "there's a bathroom on the right," then you may have been using this phrase wrong as well. Often misinterpreted as "nip in the butt" (because that would certainly hurt), the origin of this one comes, as you might guess, from agriculture. If you literally nip (squeeze or pinch) a plant bud you are potentially stopping its growth at an early stage of development.

Depending on the source you believe, the first citation came in the late 1500s in the usage of "nip in the bloom" or "nip in the blade." The *OED* suggests that "nip in the blade" came first in 1590 in *Rosalynde, or Euphues golden legacie* by Thomas Lodge, an English physician and author: "Nature hath prodigally inricht thee with her fauours . . . and now . . . to haue all these good partes nipped in the blade, and blemisht by the inconstancie of Fortune."

In 1595, "nip in the bloom" followed, appearing in Henry Chettle's romantic play, *Piers Plainnes Seaven Yeres Prentiship*: "Extinguish these fond loues with minds labour, and nip thy affections in the bloome, that they may neuer bee of power to budde."[5] The first citation for "nip in the bud" came a few years later in 1607 with Francis Beaumont and John Fletcher's comedic play, *The Woman Hater*: "Yet I can frowne and nip a passion Euen in the bud."[6] Interestingly, this same play has a number of first uses of words cited in the English language, according to the *OED*, including *earshot* and *prostitute*.[7]

not my first rodeo *idiom* **1.** To have experienced a situation before and have a deep understanding of it. **2.** Not naive or inexperienced.

BS Definition: Another way of saying, "I know everything there is to know here already, kid, so shut your mouth."

Origin: At first glance, you might think this phrase originated with someone like American cowboy humorist Will Rogers, but, according to *Forbes*, the first documented use of the term (or near equivalent) comes from the 1981 film *Mommie Dearest*. In a scene where the lead character, Joan Crawford (played by Faye Dunaway), is addressing the board of directors at Pepsi-Cola, she says, "Don't f*ck with me fellas! This ain't my first time at the rodeo!"[8] Lines from the movie like that and others—including "No wire hangers!"—were so disturbingly memorable that they quickly became part of the pop culture lexicon of the time. According to *Forbes*, the book by Crawford's daughter, Christina Crawford, on which the film was based, didn't have the rodeo line in it, so perhaps credit for it belongs to late screenwriter Frank Yablans, who was also a former president at Paramount Pictures.[9]

Oh, and in case you've never been to a rodeo personally . . . it's an exhibition or competition demonstrating traditional cowboy skills, such as bull riding, calf roping, and steer wrestling.

N

AND THE WINNER IS . . . HORSE RACING!

If you study the area of language long enough (and we think writing this book earns us an opinion) one of the fascinating things about business speak is the creativity that has gone into coining some of the terms (*yak shaving*, for example) or the history involved (such as *running amok*). What's also interesting is that BS origins are indiscriminate. They draw from everywhere: religion, technology, military, law, the arts, literature, agriculture, and so on. However, no one source proves as significant a background for these words and phrases as sports, where metaphors of winning, losing, and tying apply easily to business circumstances. Baseball may the biggest sports influence on our BS words of today, but there's another sport that's hugely influential that you may not think of right away: horse racing.

For many of us, horse racing's impact may be limited to drinking a mint julep every once in a while or perhaps putting on a fancy hat for the Kentucky Derby. You definitely get the impression that it's a dying sport. Track patrons, at least in the United States, have aged in a way that makes the portable oxygen tank industry drool. But that wasn't always the case. At one time, horse racing was one of the biggest sports in the world, both in Europe and the United States. That's demonstrated in the amount of BS terms it has given us (or popularized).[1] Here are just a few:

- across-the-board
- also-ran
- bad actor[2]
- by a nose
- caught flat-footed
- dark horse
- dead ringer
- down to the wire
- first out of the gate
- front-runner
- give-and-take
- hands down
- home stretch
- in the money

- inside track
- jockey for position
- leg up
- neck and neck
- off to the races
- playing the field
- photo finish
- running mate

- shoo-in
- straight from the horse's mouth
- stud (as in "he's a stud")
- trifecta
- under the wire
- upset (not mad, but when an underdog beats a favorite).[3]

At one time, it was not uncommon for the masses to tune in on the radio or show up at the track to follow horse racing on a regular basis. In the book *Seabiscuit*, author Laura Hillenbrand makes the claim that in 1938, the famed underdog horse received more press than Franklin Delano Roosevelt or Hitler that year.[4] Indeed, in the legendary match-up of Seabiscuit and War Admiral, some 40 million people tuned in to listen to the race, including FDR himself.[5]

Of all the sports around today, horse racing is also one of the oldest. Archaeological records suggest that societies in ancient Greece, Babylon, and Egypt raced horses, and horse racing was a part of the events at the ancient Greek Olympics as early as 648 BC.[6] In Britain, horse racing has been recorded as early as the 12th century, after the English knights returned from the Crusades with Arab horses, which were, in turn, bred to English horses to produce the modern-day thoroughbred. However, it wasn't until the mid-to-late-1600s reign of King Charles II, an avid fan, that horse racing came to play a more prominent role in European society.

In the United States, the first recorded racetrack opened in Salisbury, New York (a section of what is now Long Island), in 1655. From there, other tracks opened in Virginia and beyond. *The American Stud Book* was started in 1868, prompting the beginning of organized horse racing in the United States, and by 1890, there were more than 300 tracks operating in the U.S.

alone. According to the book *The History of Thoroughbred Racing in America* by William H.P. Robertson, horse racing was the most popular spectator sport in the country in the 1960s.

Josh Chetwynd, author of *The Field Guide to Sports Metaphors*, says that three factors really pushed horse-racing terms into the public consciousness.[7] First, as noted previously, the sport was established in the English-speaking world long before others, many of which didn't make their debut until the Victorian era (1837–1901). Second, horse racing's gambling component provided compelling storylines of risk and reward, and—as we've noted in other parts of *The BS Dictionary*—gambling terms have long held the public's fascination. Finally, he says, horse racing (along with baseball and boxing) truly came of age during the golden period of sports literature and sports journalism in the early 20th century, when many great writers such as Ring Lardner and Damon Runyon penned their columns about sports: "They [the sportswriters] turned metaphors into idioms and that's when you get into the popular culture."

O

offline *adj.* **1.** Meeting at a later time to disucss something that is outside what's currently being addressed (see *parking lot*). **2.** When a computer is disconnected from other computers or a communication system.

> **BS Definition: 1.** What you say to delay a person's realization that you don't really give a rat's a** about their problems. **2.** Thanks to Steve Jobs, what you never are.

> **Origin:** Surprise! The origination of offline (and its opposite, online) didn't arrive with the development of the World Wide Web. The earliest references actually go back as far as the 19th century, to the railroad and telegraph industries. In particular, the term *online* was often used in the context of a signal box that would send messages, via telegraph line, to linemen indicating the railroad track's status: "Train on line" or "line clear."[1]

> Interestingly, pig farming also played a hand in making online the BS term we know today. In the early 1900s, some groups dedicated to keeping track of breed numbers and purity—like the American Poland-China Record Association, for example—recorded new piglets in their published records as "online" (for example, "Lady Online 366450" or "Model Online 366454"). We assume when a pig died, it was listed as "Lady Offline 366450." Regardless . . .

The arrival of the Internet is when today's definition of offline really started to take shape. The Internet was first invented in the 1960s, and *online* began to communicate being connected electronically to the World Wide Web through email, text, or other messaging means.[2] Offline, by contrast, referred to not being connected or reachable via electronic means. However, in today's world, that meaning is evolving, because you're never really "offline" these days, right? Your boss can always reach you.

on point *adj.* **1.** Relevant; accurate (aka spot on). **2.** Good. **3.** Compliant with rules and regulations.

BS Definition: The opposite of the 24-hour filibuster U.S. Senator Strom Thurmond gave in 1957.[3]

Origin: The year 1937 is the first time, according to the *OED*, that *on point* appeared in writing, in the *Atlantic Reporter*: "We have no decisions in our state directly on point." As to who, exactly, created this phrase and why, we don't know. However, our guess is that it's someone who wanted to acknowledge when things were communicated accurately.

on the ball *idiom* **1.** Alert; quick to take action. **2.** Competent; knowledgeable.

BS Definition: What you try to look like when your out-of-town boss visits the office.

Origin: According to *The Field Guide for Sports Metaphors*, an early reference to this phrase comes from baseball in the 1860 book, *Ernest Bracebridge, or, Schoolboy Days*, with the following passage about a player who "kept his eye on the ball and hit it so fairly that he sent it flying away to a considerable distance" during a game of rounders (a baseball precursor).[4] Hence, any batter "on the ball" in baseball was someone with focus and attention. Applying those same qualities to a business conversation started to happen in 1939, when the *OED* says "on the ball" appeared in writing in selected letters from poet and physician William Carlos Williams: "The novella by Quevedo . . . [is] right on the ball."

onboarding *n.* **1.** The process by which new employees get the necessary knowledge, skills, and behaviors to become effective members of the organization. **2.** Integrating a new employee into an organization by familiarizing them with the company's products, services, and policies.

BS Definition: In theory, a yearlong process steadily integrating the new employee into the culture of the company and aligning their individual goals to the overall company goals. In practice, tossing a laptop and W-4 at that person and saying, "Welcome to the job. Now get working."

Origin: This management jargon started to become common in the 1970s, but its origins likely date back centuries, where *on board* could potentially describe passengers or crewmembers boarding a vessel, those who were already on a vessel, coming alongside a vessel (as in another ship), transferring into a train or a ship, or even drinking.[5] Indeed, the earliest references where *on* appears next to *board* come in the early 1500s, according to the *OED*.

Regardless, the BS use of this word was likely inspired by the thoughts of boarding a ship, plane, train, or bus. From 1991's *Management Live: The Video Book* by Robert D. Marx, Todd Jick, and Peter J. Frost, an illustrative reference follows: "Proctor & Gamble implemented an 'Onboarding' program after a company study found that white men were quick to adjust to the corporate culture while minorities, particularly women, were slower."[6] We trust that this conclusion acknowledged that it was easier for white men to adjust because the corporate culture in question was probably invented by white men? Regardless, onboarding programs today vary at different companies. Some can last up to a year, whereas others are far less than that.[7]

once in a blue moon *idiom* **1.** To do something very rarely. **2.** Very seldom.

BS Definition: When your boss calls you in front of the room to acknowledge a job well done.

Origin: One of the stranger phrases in our lexicon is once in a blue moon—especially given that there is no such thing as a moon colored blue in our night sky. Speculation is that *blue* may have come from the now obsolete *belewe*, which meant "to betray." A "betrayer moon" is an additional spring full moon, which means people have to fast for an extra month during Lent. There's also a theory that we have a "blue moon" because the Maine *Farmers' Almanac* used to list the date of the first moon of a month in red text and the second full moon of a month (which only happens every two or three years) in blue.[8]

The first use of the phrase varies widely depending on what source you trust. One early cited example comes from a pamphlet published in 1528 by William Barlow, the bishop of Chichester, called the *Treatyse of the Buryall of the Masse*. In a conversation between two characters, one says, "Yf they say the mone is blewe/We must believe that it is true." The expression was apparently used in situations to imply that gullible people will believe just about anything. Others suggest the saying in its present meaning was first recorded in 1821 in the publication of *Real Life in London*, by Pierce Egan: "How's Harry and Ben?—haven't seen you this blue moon." Meanwhile, the *OED* reports its first use as 1833 in a publication called *Athenæum*: "We are no advocates for the eternal system of producing foreign operas to the exclusion of the works of English composers, but once in a blue moon such a thing may be allowed."

one smart cookie *n.* **1.** A clever, smart person. **2.** An intelligent person who makes good decisions.

BS Definition: If you use this term on a regular basis today, we will assume you were born before 1950.

Origin: In the 1920s, *cookie* became a slang term for an attractive girl. Over the next 20 years it started to lose its feminine connotation and become attached to words like *tough* and *smart*. Cookie had a good run in the idiom world in the mid-1900s, with several other cookie sayings appearing in written form for the first time as well, like *cookie cutter* (1922) and *that's the way the cookie crumbles* (1957). We tried to find out when the phrase *caught with your hand in the cookie jar* first appeared, too, but our search results were half-baked.[9]

one-two punch *n.* **1.** An action followed immediately by another (aka double trouble). **2.** Any strong combination of two people or things (aka double dose).

BS Definition: Getting flayed alive after saying something dumb in social media, then losing your job because of it.[10]

Origin: This phrase comes from the sport of boxing, where the "old one-two" referred to a quick combination of punches. The *OED* says the first written allusion to this idea was in 1811 in *The Sporting Magazine*: "He had no difficulty at getting at his man when he chose with a one, two." By 1919, it had become the phrase we know today, as seen in this listing from the *Oakland Tribune*: "The fans will see a big difference in Frankie. He is far stronger than he was before going to France, and he is hitting much harder. He has the old one-two punch down to perfection and he stings every time he lands."[11]

Over time, *one-two punch* began to represent things or people that are considered a strong combination. From *TechCrunch* in April 2019:

You can think of this as the Amazon one-two punch: The company's vast power in e-commerce is only the initial, quick jab to an opponent's face. Data-focused innovations in offline retail will be Amazon's second, much heavier cross. Traditional retailers too focused on the jab aren't seeing the cross coming.[12]

open the kimono *v.* **1.** To reveal confidential information. **2.** To share your secrets, as in a Japanese wife showing her husband her naked body by opening her silk robe or kimono.

BS Definition: A good phrase to use when "drop your pants" doesn't quite work.

Origin: The more you learn about the term *open the kimono*, the more you sense the sexist and racist overtones in using it as an idiom, especially in the Western world.[13] Regardless, open the kimono gained popularity in the 1980s during a wave of Japanese acquisitions of American enterprises. In particular, many point to Microsoft, where the phrase was said to be widely used throughout the decade. However, it hardly started with the tech giant. Indeed, Sonia Jarvis, a lecturer at Baruch College School of Public Affairs, has suggested that the term originated in feudal Japanese times and referred to the practice of "proving that no weapons were hidden within the folds of clothing." Jamie Dimon, the CEO of JP Morgan Chase, said his company was "open kimono" with regulators in 2012. And even *Marie Claire* used the phrase in 2014 when writing about demographic numbers at Netflix.[14] However, *open the kimono* has become so reviled in some quarters that, in a 2015 *Fast Company* poll, it was voted the worst of the worst 32 business phrases.[15]

org chart *n.* **1.** A document that shows a company's management hierarchy. **2.** A visual representation of an organization's structure and chain of command.

BS Definition: The document that still shows Phil in a role he left in 1997.

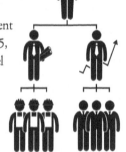

Origin: Though you might think org chart is a recent corporate phenomenon, it actually dates back to 1855, when a Scottish American engineer named Daniel McCallum developed what is now considered to be the first diagram representing an organization's structure. Working as the general manager of the New York and Erie Railroad, McCallum didn't call it an organizational chart at the time, but he used it to define a division of roles and responsibilities. By diagramming those things with designer George Holt Henshaw, he believed work relationships could be better understood and more transparent.

The term *organizational chart* didn't come into vogue until much later in the 20th century. In particular, one big milestone came in 1917, when IBM (then known as the Computing-Tabulating-Recording Company, or CTR[16]) needed a way to visualize the relationships and relative ranks of its job positions. Rather than the treelike figure of the earlier railroad system, CTR drew its structure in a more symmetrical, pyramid-like form and included more detailed information.[17] So now when you look at your own org chart and realize how far you are from the top, you have two sources you can blame.

organic growth *n.* **1.** Expansion of a firm's operations from its own (internally generated) resources, without resorting to borrowing or acquiring other firms. **2.** The growth rate a company can achieve outside of takeovers, acquisitions, and mergers.

BS Definition: 1. The best way to avoid the bitterness of employees from a just-merged business. **2.** How you might describe what's been growing in the bottom drawer of your break-room refrigerator.

Origin: The word *organic* stems from the Greek word *organon*, meaning "instrument, tool, or organ." It's also the name given to Aristotle's collection of six works on logic (in the sense of *organon* being the instrument of all reasoning). In the 18th century, *organic* became an adjective with the meaning "of or pertaining to the bodily organs," and eventually evolved to mean anything that had organs, or any living thing.[18]

The first use of the term *organic growth* (implying natural growth) has not quite been pinpointed with any great accuracy, though some have cited an early reference of the term in Inazo Nitobe's 1900 book *Bushido: The Soul of Japan*, which explored the way of the samurai. Finally, in 1958, Edith Penrose took on the subject of organic growth extensively in her book *The Theory of the Growth of the Firm*, which discussed how internal constraints often limited the speed at which companies could grow.[19]

out-of-pocket *adj.* **1.** Out of reach; unavailable. **2.** Paying expenses with your own money (as opposed to being reimbursed by the company).

BS Definition: What your boss usually is when you have urgent business.

Origin: To us, this might be the one example of the English language at its most maddening: myriad meanings for the same phrase.[20] From our experience, the most common meaning of out-of-pocket these days is to lay out one's own money for a business expense (it comes directly out of your pockets, ergo out-of-pocket). The first citation with this meaning, according to the *OED*, comes from an 1885 law journal: "The plaintiffs . . . incurred various out-of-pocket expenses." However, by the early 20th century, out-of-pocket also came to have another meaning—out of reach or unavailable—thanks to writer O. Henry, who used it in this

way in 1908's "Buried Treasure," published in *Ainslee's* magazine in July of that year: "Just now she is out of pocket. And I shall find her as soon as I can." Ironically, O. Henry was out-of-pocket several times in his colorful life when he was on the run from the law, which wanted him in jail for allegedly embezzling funds from the First National Bank of Austin. Interestingly, while on the run in Honduras, O. Henry also coined the term *banana republic*, which came to describe any small, unstable tropical nation in Latin America.[21]

outside the box *idiom* **1.** To come up with a creative solution that avoids traditional or common approaches. **2.** In an innovative or unorthodox manner; with a fresh perspective.

BS Definition: Asking Siri what happened to your stapler after losing it for the millionth time in your office.

Origin: According to the Phrase Finder, a U.K.-based website that does original research focusing on word etymology, the term *outside the box* comes from the management-consulting world of the 1960s and 1970s, where experts exhorted their trainees to think differently to solve a problem.[22] Many of these consultants used a specific image from *Sam Loyd's Cyclopedia of 5000 Puzzles, Tricks, and Conundrums (With Answers)*, published in 1914, known as the "Nine Dots Puzzle." This nine-dot, two-dimensional square formed the shape of a box with (sloppy) instructions to: "Draw a continuous line through the center of all the eggs so as to mark them off in the fewest number of strokes." The consultants encouraged their clients to "think outside the box" to solve the puzzle—leading them to a successful solution that was accomplished after your pencil went outside the box of dots to create your lines.[23]

Different people claim ownership of popularizing this phrase. John Adair, a British academic and theorist, claims to have introduced the concept in 1969.[24] Alternatively, management consultant Mike Vance suggests that the use of the nine-dot puzzle in consultancy circles stems from the corporate culture of the Walt Disney Company, where the puzzle was used in-house.[25] However, the *OED* says the first document-ed reference to the idea comes from an Alberta, Canada, newspaper in 1970: "The problem . . . is to think 'outside the dots' about the questions of how to feed a hungry world."

over a barrel *idiom* **1.** In a position of weakness or difficulty. **2.** Left without a choice. **3.** In someone else's power; vulnerable.

BS Definition: What you are when your boss invites you out for drinks with everyone, but all you want to do is go home and relax.

Origin: The Spanish Inquisition and college fraternity hazing are the two most common sources cited for the origin of this phrase. What-ever side you sit on, one thing is for certain: *Over a barrel* has a strong history of pain, suffering, and humiliation. During the Spanish Inqui-sition (1478–1834), one supposed form of torture was to suspend someone over a "barrel," or cauldron of boiling oil, with the threat of being dropped in. Yikes.

The other origin possibility—fraternity hazing—wasn't much better. This one has an American birth dating as far back as the 1740s, and it involves putting a nearly drowned or unconscious person over a barrel and flogging them to either clear their lungs of water or to haze them. One early citation of this meaning comes from the Delaware newspa-per *The Daily Republican* in July 1886, which reported the initiation ceremony of a college fraternity: "He was bound hand and foot and rolled over a barrel. Next he was stripped naked and placed upon a cake of ice . . . and branded on his back with the fraternity emblem."[26]

P

POV *n.* P-O-V Acronym for "point of view."

BS Definition: To increase your job security, an opinion that matches that of your boss.

Origin: *Point of view* was derived in the early 1700s from the French phrase *point de vue*, which described the position from which something was viewed. The acronym POV started to appear in the 20th century with the advent of cameras and motion pictures. That's because point-of-view shots were helpful in storytelling.[1] For example, in making 1927's *Napoléon*, director Abel Gance wrapped a camera in padding so that the actors could punch it, portraying the leading character's perspective during a fight. Legendary filmmaker Alfred Hitchcock would use POV shots, as they became to be known, extensively—most notably in famous scenes in *Psycho* and *Rear Window*.[2] This knowledge has little overall effect on the use of this term in the business world, but it does make you kind of cool for knowing it.

paint the town red *idiom* 1. To celebrate in a flashy way, especially by making a round of stops at bars and nightclubs. 2. To enjoy yourself in a boisterous and flamboyant way.

BS Definition: To do what you do every night while attending a business conference in New Orleans.

Origin: Even though the *OED* says this phrase originated in the U.S., the town of Melton Mowbray, England, begs to differ. Indeed, this small enclave north of Leicester says the phrase *paint the town red* comes from one of its natives, the marquis of Waterford, who was a known drunkard, and in 1837, led a group of revelers through Melton Mowbray, knocking over flowerpots and generally vandalizing the town's buildings. The night culminated with the marquis and his friends painting the tollgate, and doors of several homes, with red paint—ergo the phrase *paint the town red*. This depiction fits with the biography of the marquis, a hooligan whose misdeeds included fighting, stealing, breaking windows, and literally upsetting apple carts (an idiom of its own).

Skeptics of this origin story point to the fact that *paint the town red* didn't actually appear in print until almost 50 years later and only in the United States (not the U.K.) at first. They say it's much more likely that it was actually born out of the brothels of the American West, and referred to men behaving as though their whole town were a red-light district.[3] Either way, the first written reference of the term dates to July 1883 in the *New York Times*: "Mr. James Hennessy offered a resolution that the entire body proceed forthwith to Newark and get drunk. . . . Then the Democrats charged upon the street cars, and being wafted into Newark proceeded, to use their own metaphor, to 'paint the town red.' "[4]

P

parachute in *v.* **1.** To be suddenly placed on a task or in an organization (usually when things are not going well). **2.** To unexpectedly send an outside person in to deal with an emergency or undesirable situation.

BS Definition: The heroic action you envision yourself doing when you swoop in at the last minute to save a project—only to be told you are "divorced from reality" during your review later.

Origin: The word *parachute* comes from the French words *para* (an imperative form of *parare*, which means "to avert, defend, resist, guard, shield, or shroud") and *chute* (meaning "fall"). It was coined by Louis-Sebastien Lenormand, the person credited with inventing the first modern parachute out of two umbrellas and jumping from a tree with it in 1783.[5] However, it should be noted that some 4,000 years before Lenormand's jump, Chinese author Sima Qian wrote a fictional account of a parachute-like device in his book *Historical Records*. In the story, a Chinese emperor runs away from his murderous father by climbing onto the top of a high granary. Seeing nowhere else to go, he grabs two bamboo hats, leaps, and glides down to safety.[6]

Sources cited by the *OED* suggest *parachute in*, as a business-friendly term, started in the U.S. around the mid-1900s and then migrated to other parts of the English-speaking world. One of the earliest references comes from the *Listener* magazine in the U.K. in 1968: "Too many of the existing hierarchy are civil servants 'parachuted' in from outside."

paradigm shift *n.* **1.** A significant change in how things are done. **2.** A fundamental change in approach or underlying assumptions.

BS Definition: 1. Blockchain and cryptocurrency . . . or not. **2.** What happened when you realized exactly what your parents had to do to make you.

Origin: Thomas Kuhn, a University of California professor, published his landmark book, *The Structure of Scientific Revolutions*, in 1962. Kuhn argued that scientific progress was driven by revolutionary events, rather than being built incrementally on accepted knowledge. He said these anomalies could lead to a change in the existing paradigm, or a "paradigm shift." The book, which Kuhn originally described as more of a "sketch," moved slowly at first but then eventually took off, and by 1987 had sold 650,000 copies.[7]

One influential piece that helped popularize the concept beyond science—and into the business world in general—was British philosopher Margaret Masterson's influential 1970 paper, "The Nature of a Paradigm." Masterson argued that Kuhn's paradigm could refer to any special kind of achievement that causes the existing establishment to adjust. Since then, *paradigm shift* has been applied to all kinds of events, including the introduction of personal computers, Lebron James's arrival in the NBA, and even pixie haircuts for women.[8] This has caused some critics to say *paradigm shift* has been abused and overused to the point of becoming meaningless.[9]

paralysis through analysis/analysis paralysis

n. **1.** The state of overthinking something so much that you never take action on it. **2.** A condition in which research, study, or meetings lead to even more of the same.

BS Definition: **1.** A phrase used when you need to encourage action (or participate in a rap battle in the break room). **2.** The reason you have chips from the vending machine for lunch instead of a meal from one of the two restaurants on the first floor of your building.

Origin: Though never expressly stated as such, paralysis through analysis has been a common theme for centuries, appearing within *Aesop's Fables* ("Better one safe way than a hundred on which you cannot reckon"), Shakespeare's *Hamlet* (his youth and vital energy are "sicklied o'er with the pale cast of thought"), and the writings of Voltaire ("The perfect is the enemy of the good"). One early instance of the words *paralysis* and *analysis* appearing together occurred in 1803, in a dictionary that didn't tie the words together into any combined meaning, but rather only noted that they rhymed. The first use of the term that we could find was in 1928 at the General Convention of the Episcopal Church, when Reverend C. Leslie Glenn said that the religious collegiate climate was at risk of "paralysis by analysis" from being too speculative. Later, during World War II, Winston Churchill, after hearing that the landing-craft designers were spending the majority of their time arguing over design changes, sent this message: "The maxim 'Nothing avails but perfection' may be spelt shorter: 'Paralysis.'"

For it's introduction in the business context, some point to the year 1956, when the concept began to take more of a foothold in commerce. That year, Charles R. Schwartz wrote the article "The Return-on-Investment Concept as a Tool for Decision Making" in *Changing Patterns and Concepts in Management*, stating: "We will do less guessing; avoid the danger of becoming extinct by instinct; and, by the adoption of one uniform evaluation guide, escape succumbing to paralysis by analysis."[10] We will take Schwartz's advice by leaving further analysis of this entry's origin alone now and moving on.

parking lot *v.* **1.** To postpone the discussion of an important but non-agenda item that arises during the course of your meeting (see *back burner*). **2.** To save a question until the end of a presentation (see *put a pin in it*).

> **BS Definition:** To hope, as a presenter, that someone will forget their pain-in-the-neck question by promising that you'll come back to it later.

> **Origin:** From the "I've got too much time on my hands so I'm going to write about the history of parking lots" department: According to the Parking Network, an online community of professionals in the park-

ing industry, the first so-called transportation "lots" for automobiles appeared in the early 1900s, when the first multi-story parking garage was built for the now demolished La Salle Hotel in Chicago (northwest corner of La Salle Street and Madison Street) in 1918. Surely a parking lot fan or two has visited this location and taken pictures, right? We get chills just thinking of what it must be like to stand near that kind of history. Anyway. . . . Designed by Holabird and Roche, the concept at the time was revolutionary—providing customers with a convenient place to park their cars as streets became crowded with vehicles.[11]

How and when *parking lot* got applied to today's common meeting practice of moving non-agenda items to the end of the discussion, we don't know.[12] There are no available, credible sources that we can find that provide those answers. Perhaps a meeting of linguists somewhere put that to-do in a parking lot at some point, and then, like most parking lot items, forgot about it later?

pass the buck *idiom* 1. To shift responsibility or blame to another person. 2. To make someone else suffer the consequences of your actions.

BS Definition: The amazing ability that has allowed your boss to stay in power for far too long.

Origin: Poker is the most likely origin for this phrase—even though there are theories that it might come from alternative activities like passing money (bucks) or plates of venison—but exactly how is up for debate. The two main definitions of what "the buck" was in 19th-century American poker playing are:

» A marker—usually a knife with a handle made of buck horn (referred to simply as "the buck")—that was placed on the table in front of the player who was dealing the cards. If a player did not wish to deal, he could shift the responsibility by passing the "buck" to the next player.

» According to the 1887 book, *The Game of Draw Poker*, by J.W. Keller, "The 'buck' is any inanimate object, usually knife or pencil, which is thrown into a jack pot and temporarily taken by the winner of the pot. Whenever the deal reaches the holder of the 'buck,' a new jack pot must be made."

The earliest written reference to "passing the buck" in poker came in July 1865 in the *Weekly New Mexican*: "They draw at the commissary, and at poker after they have passed the 'buck.' " Famous writers of the day also used the phrase. Mark Twain wrote in 1872 in *Roughing It*: "I reckon I can't call that hand. Ante and pass the buck." By the turn of the century, "passing the buck" in the United States came to mean shifting responsibility from one person to another. In a famous variation of the phrase, President Harry Truman had a sign in his Oval Office that said "The buck stops here," meaning he would ultimately accept the responsibility of running the government.[13]

pass with flying colors *idiom* 1. To achieve with great distinction. 2. Overwhelming success.

BS Definition: A status enjoyed by few who have to undergo mandatory drug testing in Denver. #milehighcity

Origin: This phrase comes from the nautical world of the 1600s and early 1700s.[14] With no modern communication devices, the best way for a ship's crew to tell people on land how they fared at sea in battle would be to fly their flags (colors) on their mastheads. Ships that were victorious would sail into port with their flags flying. Those that were defeated would take their flags down to signify the loss. Christine Ammer, author of *Fighting Words: From War, Rebellion, and Other Combative Capers*, says by 1700 or so, the phrase with flying colors was being used figuratively, "signifying any kind of triumph."[15] One early often-cited reference comes from George Farquar's play from 1707,

The Beaux's Stratagem: "Our friends, indeed, began to suspect that our pockets were low, but we came off with flying colours, showed no signs of want either in word or deed."[16]

peeps *n.* **1.** People. **2.** Close friends or associates.

BS Definition: If you say this word in the office, it pretty much guarantees you are not on the short list for next company CEO.

Origin: No, in this case, we're not talking about the popular marshmallow candies sold in the United States and Canada that are shaped into chicks, bunnies, and other animals. We're talking about the shorthand for people that, according to various sources, first came into popular use in the United States in the 1800s. One early reference comes from the December 29, 1847, issue of the *Janesville Gazette* in Wisconsin, in which a French chaplain is quoted as offering this prayer in the Michigan Legislature: "O Lor! Bless de peeps and their servant de representatives. May dey make laws for de peeps and not for demselves—amen."

After a bit of a dormant period, usage of *peeps* started to come back in the 1950s. This quote also comes from December 29, but 1951, in an issue of the *Chicago Daily Tribune*: "Around the country, high schoolers are greeting each other with 'Hi, peeps' (short for 'hello, people,' of course)."[17] In 21st-century America, *peeps* skews as a word more likely to be used by someone under 30 than over it.

phone it in *v.* **1.** To do something with minimal effort or attention (read: half-ass). **2.** To work or perform in a superficial or unenthusiastic manner (read: lazy-ass).

BS Definition: What most people do with work on a beautiful Friday afternoon.

Origin: Shortly after Alexander Graham Bell invented the telephone in 1876, he began using the name of the device as a verb (OK, you linguists, yes, this is an anthimeria). In describing his invention to the *Telegraphic Journal* of 1877, he said: "I telephoned the leader of the band and requested him to place the higher cornets

nearer the instrument." As Bell's device became more popular, both the noun and verb forms were shortened to "phone." An early example highlighted by the *OED* comes from 1910 in the adventure story "Boy Aviators on Secret Service": "Wait a minute while I go to 'phone my resignation."

According to Ben Zimmer, a linguist and a contributor to the *Wall Street Journal* and the *Atlantic*, the convenience of having a telephone to transmit a message long distance rather than show up in person led to a number of jokes about "phoning it in." One example Zimmer highlights is a February 1938 syndicated newspaper column called "Senator Soaper Says." The column includes a sarcastic comment about Thornton Wilder's *Our Town*, which was then a controversial new play, referencing Wilder's supposed stage instructions: "No curtain. No scenery." Senator Soaper then suggested: "Now that a Broadway drama has attained hit proportions with no scenery, the next step is to have the actors phone it in."[18]

piggyback *v.* **1.** To add to a previously stated idea. **2.** To take advantage of or build on the work of someone else.

BS Definition: **1.** What almost every big idea in business has done with the ideas before it. **2.** What the kids of Will Smith are doing with his career in Hollywood.

Origin: What's fascinating about the origin of *piggyback* is that it has absolutely nothing to do with pigs.[19] The earliest forms of this construction are rooted in the terms *pick pack* and *pick back*. The first documented citation is from an essay in 1564 on religious themes. John Rastell's "A Confutation of a Sermon Pronounced by Mr. Juell" states: "What a tale is this, that the oblation of the church should be borne vpon an Angell (on pick pack perchaunce)." Similarly, James Calfhill's "An Aunswere to (John Martiall's) Treatise of the Crosse," published in 1565, says: "To easy . . . is that way to heauen, whereto we may be caried a pickbacke on a Roode [horse]." Pick, in this case, refers to pitching—as in "pitching a tent"—and pack means load, while back means, literally, your back or shoulders.

How did such phrases become *piggyback* then? Apparently, it was a mere misstating of the original phrase! The earliest citation with pig and back comes in 1736, in Robert Ainsworth's *Thesaurus Linguae Latinae Compendiarius*: "Back, To carry on pig back." Then, *piggyback* itself comes in 1843 in Baynard Rush Hall's book, *The New Purchase: Or, Early Years in the Far West*: "Meanwhile, two thus doing piggy-back in reverse order, had gradually advanced to the door." It wasn't until the mid-1900s that *piggyback* started to cross over into its metaphorical meaning in the business world. The earliest written citation with that meaning is from the *Atchison* (Kansas) *Daily Globe* newspaper in February 1946: "That story should be pasted in the hats of all Democrats who piggy-backed into office!"

ping *v.* **1.** To send someone an email or text. **2.** To make contact by electronic communication.

> **BS Definition:** To text colleagues that you're looking forward to "sleeping" with them rather than "speaking" with them. Curse you, autocorrect!!!

> **Origin:** Because of its onomatopoetic nature, the word *ping* has been used over the years in a variety of contexts, including as a way to describe the firing of a gun, the ringing of a bell, and the sound

of a submarine's sonar. Matter of fact, during World War II, sonar operators were sometimes called "ping jockeys."

However, it was in the 1980s that *ping* started to take on the BS meaning we associate with it today. During the infant stages of the Internet, *ping* was used to describe when one computer would connect to a second (say, a network server). From there, the word evolved to include human communication as well. One citation noting this evolution: In a newsletter from the American Dialect Society, in 2000, "one member observed that 'a computer science person I work with' sometimes said ping to mean 'get in touch with or send a reminder to a person.' "[20]

pipeline *n.* **1.** A salesperson's collection of leads. **2.** An activity or a product that is at some point between starting and completion.

BS Definition: Something you make up on the spot when your boss comes to you asking what the heck you've been doing the last six months.

Origin: The American Petroleum Institute hosts a website, Pipeline 101, that gives the history of pipelines.[21] After Edwin Drake struck oil at a well in Titusville, Pennsylvania, in 1859, it didn't take long to realize the commercial potential of this new energy source. The need to bring the product to cities became evident, and initially oil was transported by the Teamsters to train stations using converted whiskey barrels and horses. However, due to costs, eventually the oil companies bypassed them altogether by building the first wooden "pipeline" in 1862. By 1905, crude-oil pipelines were crossing the nation. By the mid-1940s, the word pipeline started to be applied to a business-related context. In September 1945, the *Times* of London reported: "I also directed the Administrator . . . to enter into immediate negotiations with the receiving Governments for the purchases of all goods in the pipeline or in storage."[22]

pivot *v.* **1.** To turn your attention to a related item. **2.** To make a fundamental change to your business after determining your current focus isn't working.

BS Definition: To use a term that makes you optimistic about the future of your startup rather than facing the reality that it is a complete and utter disaster (see *dumpster fire*).

Origin: The first known use of pivot as a noun—that is, a shaft or pin around which something turns—occurred in the 14th century, according to *Merriam-Webster*. The *OED* says it transitioned into a verb as early as 1841 in *The Irish Dragoon* by Charles James Lever: "The 7th took up their ground at Frenada pivoting upon the 1st Division." Considering its heavy use in startups and Silicon Valley, many might believe use of *pivot* today far exceeds anything in the past.[23]

However, according to a Google analysis of printed books, use of *pivot* actually peaked in 1865. Still, that doesn't stop people from saying they coined this BS term for adapting products or changing a business direction. Blogger and author Eric Ries, says his June 2009 blog post, "Pivot, Don't Jump," was a watershed moment, after which Silicon Valley companies began regularly using the term. *Fast Company* bestowed the honor upon Ries as well as suggesting he "coined" pivot as a business term.[24] That may be an overstatement, but we are talking about Silicon Valley here, where overstatement appears to be part of doing business. The list of businesses there that have successfully pivoted in their history is impressive. Consider:

» Odeo (network where people could find and subscribe to podcasts) pivots into Twitter
» Burbn (check-in app that included gaming elements from Mafia Wars) pivots into Instagram
» The Point (website devoted to "social good" fundraising) pivots into Groupon
» Tote (website that let people browse and shop their favorite retailers) pivots into Pinterest.[25]

play it by ear *v.* **1.** To do something by instinct rather than according to rules or a plan. **2.** To act according to the given circumstances.

> **BS Definition:** To say something that you hope excuses your lack of planning and preparation with colleagues.

> **Origin:** Taken literally, this is kind of a ridiculous phrase. Imagine using your ear to play something! Regardless, given its origin, it makes sense.[26] It comes from the world of music, where starting in the mid-1600s people started to use it as a way to describe playing an instrument without the aid of written music: "To learn to play by rote or ear without book," according to 1658's *A Breefe Introduction to the Skill of Musick for Song & Violl* by John Playford. Almost 200 years later, the phrase started to appear in its current BS meaning in the writings of Ralph Waldo Emerson. This example from *Essays* in 1841: "I knew an amiable and accomplished person who undertook a practical reform, yet I was never able to find in him the enterprise of love he took in hand. He adopted it by ear and by the understanding, from the books he had been reading."

postmortem *n.* **1.** The meeting or report given at the end of a project. **2.** The examination of a failed project after the fact.

> **BS Definition:** The time in which everyone tries to separate themselves from the stink that was this crappy idea.

> **Origin:** First derived from Latin in the early 1700s—with *post* meaning after and *mortem* meaning death—postmortem was naturally linked to autopsies to find out the cause of someone's passing.[27] Eventually, the morbid reference came to carry a business context in which organizations began analyzing events after they occurred. The *OED* says the earliest reference to this meaning came in 1850 in Henry Theodor Cheever's book . . . wait for it . . . *The Whale and His Captors: or, The Whaleman's*

Adventures, and the Whale's Biography, as Gathered on the Homeward Cruise of the Commodore Preble: "To report a full and accurate, leisurely post-mortem of the subjects we have discussed."[28]

Postmortems became hugely popular in business in the 1980s and 1990s, and by 2007, a new idea started to take hold as well. The "premortem" concept was developed by Gary Klein, the chief scientist at Klein Associates, and it defined the way businesses can imagine an event before it happens to better identify the risks involved.[29] In other words, a premortem can help you kill an event before a postmortem shows you how you messed it up.

pot calling the kettle black *idiom* **1.** Those who criticize others for having the same characteristics they have. **2.** Being critical of others while failing to acknowledge similar faults in yourself.

BS Definition: When your boss calls you from the golf course to tell you that you need to work harder.

Origin: The earliest appearance of this phrase comes from Thomas Shelton's 1620 translation of the classic novel by Miguel de Cervantes, *Don Quixote*.[30] In a scene where the protagonist, Alonso Quixano (who becomes Don Quixote de la Mancha), bristles at the criticisms of his servant Sancho Panza, Quixano says: "You are like what is said that the frying-pan said to the kettle, 'Avant, black-browes.'" The actual Spanish text is: "*Dijo la sartén a la caldera, Quítate allá ojinegra*," which translates as, "Said the pan to the pot, 'Get out of there, black-eyes.'"

In 1682, William Penn, the founder of Pennsylvania, provided a closer version to the current phrase in his collection *Some Fruits of Solitude in Reflections and Maxims*: "If thou hast not conquer'd thy self in that which is thy own particular Weakness, thou hast no Title to Virtue, tho' thou art free of other Men's. For a Covetous Man to inveigh against Prodigality, an Atheist against Idolatry, a Tyrant against Rebellion, or a Lyer against Forgery, and a Drunkard against Intemperance, is for the Pot to call the Kettle black."[31] Not sure all of William Penn's analogies make complete sense here, but, then again, look at Pennsylvania itself. It's the same state that gave us the Philly Phanatic after all, and that thing makes *no* sense (see *throwing shade*).[32]

preaching to the choir *v.* **1.** To convince the people who are already convinced. **2.** To advocate for something your audience already supports.

BS Definition: 1. When you show up at the first big event of the company's Fun Times Committee, and the only people you see are the fellow members of said Fun Times Committee. **2.** To tell a convention of atheists that God doesn't exist.

Origin: In the U.K., this phrase may be better known as "preaching to the converted," and that variation of the theme appeared in print far before the U.S. version ("preaching to the choir") did.[33] In November 1857, the *Times* newspaper reported: "It is an old saying that to preach to the converted is a useless office, and I may add that to preach to the unconvertible is a thankless office."

It wasn't until 1970 that the *OED* says the American phrase *preaching to the choir* appeared in print in the U.S., in the *Washington Post* in September that year: "Foster spoke yesterday before a packed Air Force Association seminar . . . Admitting that this was like 'preaching to the choir,' he nevertheless went on to detail a rather gloomy view of declining U.S. defense capabilities."

pull out all the stops *idiom* **1.** To use all means possible. **2.** To do everything you can to achieve something.

BS Definition: At an auto show convention, it's putting every available employee (men and women) in a bikini at your booth.

Origin: The pipe organ at your local church is the source of this idiom. A pipe organ has components called "stops" that control the airflow through the pipes. When you pull out the stops, it increases the musical volume of the instrument.[34] According to the *OED*, the earliest reference to this maneuver comes from George Gascoigne's 1576 satire *The Steele Glass*: "But sweeter soundes, of concorde, peace, and loue, Are out of tune, and iarre in euery stoppe." That may seem a bit of a stretch for the phrase *pull out all the stops*, but in 1865, Matthew Arnold connected us more completely with the BS meaning of the idiom with this commentary from his *Essays in Criticism*: "Knowing how unpopular a task one is undertaking when one tries to pull out a few more stops in that . . . somewhat narrow-toned organ, the modern Englishman."

pulling your leg *idiom* **1.** To joke, fool, or trick someone. **2.** To deceive a person by lying in a joking manner.

BS Definition: Usually something you find way funnier when it's not done to you.

Origin: The Phrase Finder website out of the U.K. calls this idiom "one of the holy grails of etymology," with which we agree. There are two main theories on where this phrase came from, but neither has any substantiated proof to confirm them. The first origin story is that in old-time England, thieves used to pull at people's legs to trip them and then rob them.[35] The problem with this theory is there is no historical evidence to back it up. Same situation with the second main theory. In that one, people who attended public hangings in the English town of Tyburn were allegedly hired to hang on to the victim's legs to give them a quick end. There are two problems with this theory. First, having your leg pulled in order to be killed doesn't exactly sound like a funny trick, and, secondly, even though these executions were reported in minute detail, there is no mention of leg pulling.

The one thing experts seem to know for certain with this phrase is that its first written mention happened not in the U.K., but in the U.S. Phrase Finder discounts the earliest source (J. Gallatin's *Diary*) as bogus, and says it happened in 1883 in Ohio's *Newark Daily Advocate* newspaper—"It is now the correct thing to say that a man who has been telling you preposterous lies has been 'pulling your leg.'" The *OED* has an 1883 source as well, but it's the *Wellsboro* (Pennsylvania) *Agitator*: "The Chinese giant once told me he had half a dozen wives at home, but I think he was pulling my leg."

With these conflicting origin stories and citations, we think it's only fitting that at least some of the information on pulling your leg has to be false. The joke, it appears, is indeed on us.

push the envelope *idiom* **1.** To go beyond what is considered possible at the time. **2.** To innovate in ways that are pioneering and extend boundaries.

BS Definition: Usually said before you do something really stupid—like paying $1 million for your mobile app (see *screw the pooch*).

Origin: Author Tom Wolfe didn't invent this phrase (it's been around since World War II[36]), but he's certainly responsible for making it popular through his landmark 1979 book, *The Right Stuff*, which told the story of the U.S. *Mercury* space program.[37] *Push the envelope* appears for the first time early in the book:

> The young men in Group 20 and their wives were Pete's and Jane's entire social world. . . . In a way, they could not have associated with anyone else, at least not easily, because the boys could talk only about one thing: their flying. One of the phrases that kept running through the conversation was "pushing the outside of the envelope."

Wolfe goes on to explain that the "envelope" is a flight-test term referring to the limits of a particular aircraft's performance: the tightness of the turns it could make at particular speeds. The pilots weren't referencing a letter envelope, but rather were focused on the mathematical concept of an envelope—similar to the curve or slope at which the center of a ladder might fall down a wall. This envelope is represented by an advanced mathematical equation that, frankly, tests the boundaries of our brain-power trying to understand it, so we won't push the envelope with you by publishing it here.[38]

put a pin in it *v.* To hold a thought for later.

BS Definition: **1.** A way to sidestep an issue and hope it never gets brought up again (see *parking lot*). **2.** A more socially acceptable way to say, "Shut your piehole."

Origin: The leading theory for where *put a pin in it* comes from is World War II, when soldiers were encouraged to put a pin back into an active hand grenade so it wouldn't go off.[39] However, we have no credible sources to back that up, so let's just put a pin in this origin story for now, shall we? Thank you.

put lipstick on a pig *v.* **1.** To put a positive spin on a negative situation. **2.** To try desperately to make something that is unappealing or unattractive appear to be just the opposite.

BS Definition: Saying, "I needed to pursue other opportunities" when asked why you were fired from your last job.

Origin: Throughout history, pigs have rarely been considered pretty. Perhaps it's the wrinkled snout; the small, erect ears; the large jowls in proportion to the head; or even its willingness to wade in mud and filth. The idiom that "you can't make a silk purse from a sow's ear" dates back to the mid-1500s, and references to unattractive, "pig-faced" women (the result of witchcraft according to the narrative at the time) exist in legends told throughout England, Holland, and France during the 1630s.[40]

However, because lipstick wasn't invented until 1884, it would be a while before the two words showed up together. One of the early references came in 1926 from Charles F. Lummis, writing in the *Los Angeles Times*: "Most of us know as much of history as a pig does of lipsticks." But the exact wording of "putting lipstick on a pig (or hog)" didn't actually show up until much later in the century. In 1985, the *Washington Post* quoted a San Francisco radio host on plans for renovating Candlestick Park (instead of building a new downtown stadium for the Giants): "That," replied KNBR personality Ron Lyons, "would be like putting lipstick on a pig."[41]

put to bed *v.* 1. To conclude. 2. To complete something and either set it aside or move on to the next step.

BS Definition: What you need to do to any of your social-media posts that might have captured unflattering images from your college days.

Origin: In the 20th century, *put to bed* was often used to refer to the act of finishing the final edits on a print publication. In the 21st century, publications are usually digital, and updates can be ongoing, so things aren't "put to bed" as much as "put to nap" these days. Regardless, the first written mentions of the phrase *put to bed*, as you can imagine, involve human beings—not business tasks—and because human beings have been sleeping for as long as they've been around, the language involved in the citations is pretty old-fashioned. For example, the *OED* gives us this selection from 1654's, *Mercurius Fumigosus*, a newsbook published by journalist John Crouch: "Hee that is the Conqueror, shall that Night have a warm Clowt, lay'd to his Breech by the Lady that was fought for, and so to be put to Bed together."[42]

BS BEYOND OUR BORDERS— PART I

When you look at some BS terms in their literal sense, it's hard to imagine how they became business speak. (We're looking at you, *raining cats and dogs*, *drinking the Kool-Aid*, and *yak shaving*.) However, weird business idioms are not unique to the English language. Indeed, there is odd BS beyond our borders too.

Consider these BS terms from the English language and how the same ideas are expressed in other countries.

the boonies	• Australia: *the wop-wops* • Germany: *where the fox and hare say goodnight to one another*
broke	• Australia: *on the wallaby track* • Italy: *to be at the green* • Spain: *to be without white*
kill two birds with one stone	• Germany: *kill two flies with one swat* • Brazil: *kill two rabbits with just one shot*
nuts	• Australia: *mad as a cut snake* • France: *being in the West* • Spain: *to be like a goat*
piece of cake	• Japan: *I'll do it before I eat breakfast* • New Zealand: *Bob's your uncle* • Spain: *to be bread eaten*
tell it like it is	• France: *calling a cat a cat* • Spain: *not having hairs on your tongue*
when pigs fly	• The Netherlands: *when the cows are dancing on the ice* • France: *when hens have teeth* • Russia: *when a lobster whistles on top of a mountain*

Q

quality assurance *n.* **1.** Administrative and procedural activities implemented in an organization so that requirements and goals for a product, service, or activity will be fulfilled. **2.** A way of preventing mistakes and defects in manufactured products and avoiding problems when delivering products or services to customers.

BS Definition: What you wish more companies had in place for their public restrooms.

Origin: Although simple concepts of quality assurance (sometimes referred to simply as "QA")—like establishing membership in guilds and military training—can be traced back to the Middle Ages, the ideas behind QA became more important in the United States during World War II, when high volumes of munitions had to be inspected. In 1947, the first International Organization for Standardization (ISO) was established in Geneva, Switzerland, and, since then, ISO's published standards have become a driving force behind most quality-assurance programs. These standards change over time; the latest is the ISO 9000 series. Initially popular just in Europe, ISO 9000 certification began to increase in the U.S. in the early 1990s.

The first written mention of the term *quality assurance* happened in 1940, according to the *OED*. It comes from the membership directory of the *Journal of the American Statistical Association*: "Dodge, Harold F., Quality Results Engineer, Quality Assurance Department, Bell Telephone Laboratories, Inc." In the healthcare industry, some have labeled Dr. Avedis Donabedian the "father of quality assurance." Donabedian published a three-volume series, *Explorations in Quality Assessment and Monitoring*, that established seven pillars of quality healthcare and is viewed by some as the industry QA standard.[1]

quantum leap *n.* **1.** Any sudden and large change or increase. **2.** An abrupt and dramatic advance or improvement.

BS Definition: A phrase that—along with the words *game changer, cutting-edge*, and *revolutionary*—doesn't apply to 99.9 percent of product advertisements.

Origin: In the beginning, there were no quantum leaps, only quantum *jumps*. Originating in physics, a *quantum jump* referred to the change of an electron from one energy level to another within an atom. It's called this because the electron appears to "jump" from one energy level to another, typically in a few nanoseconds or less.[2]

This term began to be used in and around the 1920s following the discoveries that were being made by many notable scientists of the time—particularly Neils Bohr and Albert Einstein. One early reference was from the *Proceedings of the National Academy of Science* in March 1924: "The second column gives the quantum numbers designating the quantum jump under consideration." In 1930, the first use of quantum leap appeared in print in the *Journal of Philosophy*: "We may refer the arbitrary character of a single ultimate physical event, such as a quantum leap, to the arbitrary character of the whole universe of which the single event is a part."

By the 1950s, *quantum leap* started to acquire its BS meaning outside of physics. Case in point, a 1956 report about Soviet-American relations and how American policy was addressing the challenge of Communism, called *Russia and America: Dangers and Prospects*, written by Henry L. Roberts:

Q

"The enormous multiplication of power, the 'quantum leap' to a new order of magnitude of destruction, is something very real and comprehensible."[3]

Finally, no review of the popularity of quantum leap would be complete without acknowledging the influence of the TV show of the same name. NBC's *Quantum Leap* (1989–1993) starred Scott Bakula and Dean Stockwell and centered on a scientist who would "leap" into the bodies of different people throughout history.[4]

quick win *n.* **1.** An improvement that is visible, has immediate benefits, and is swift. **2.** An investment of money, time, or effort that is highly likely to profit in the short term.

BS Definition: Cleaning all the stuff off your work desk (so you can actually work on it).

Origin: We were hoping to give you a quick win here by telling you who coined this term and when. We researched a bunch of sources—including David Allen's book *Getting Things Done* and the *Harvard Business Review*[5]—but no luck. Suffice it to say, *quick* and *win* have been around for quite a while, and understandably, the first references were more literal during the early 1900s to characterize speedy victories in sports or games.

By the 1960s, though, the term morphed into a more figurative use, particularly by the military during the Vietnam War. From the July 1965 *Daily Report, Foreign Radio Broadcasts*: "With the Staley-Taylor plan they attempted to pacify South Vietnam within 18 months by a quick offensive and a quick win."[6] (Of course, that "quick win" didn't really pan out, did it?) Today, the term is used a fair amount to describe any recognizable opportunity or easy-to-achieve triumph in any area of business, especially as it involves the potential to increase revenue. In theory, it's used a lot like the term *low-hanging fruit*. In practice, it's more like finding a *unicorn*.

quid pro quo *n.* **1.** A favor or advantage given in return for something of equal value (used in a similar way as tit for tat). **2.** A Latin phrase that translates, roughly, into "this for that."

BS Definition: Agreeing to give someone a favorable peer review if they'll do the same for you.

Origin: Literally Latin for "what for what" or "something for something," this term is primarily used today in a legal sense, where it can describe any mutual consideration between two parties.[7] However, it is often used in the negative to describe situations such as its context in politics (use of political office for personal benefit) or sexual harassment (a form of sexual blackmail). Quid pro quo played a central role in the impeachment hearings of President Donald Trump in 2020, but it's a concept that pre-dates modern times by hundreds of years.

According to the *OED*, the first known use of the term dates back to 1535 (and a nonlegal context), in the book *Erasmus' Lytle Treatise Maner & Forme of Confession*: "Poticaries and phisions do more greuously offende, than do these persones now rehersed, which haue a prouerbe amonge them, quid pro quo, one thynge for another."

But the reason many business people use the phrase today may be because of the influence of Anthony Hopkins's portrayal of Hannibal "the Cannibal" Lecter in the 1991 film *Silence of the Lambs*.[8] In one memorable, and somewhat harrowing, scene, Lecter tells FBI agent Clarice Starling (played by Jodie Foster): "Quid pro quo. I tell you things, you tell me things. Not about this case, though. About yourself. Quid pro quo. Yes or no? Yes or no, Clarice?" What's interesting is that most people remember the line as "Quid pro quo, Clarice," but Lecter actually never says "Clarice" at the end of "quid pro quo" in the film. It's

Q

a disturbing (but memorable) line and is certainly better to use in a business context than Lecter's other famous line from the movie: "A census taker once tried to test me. I ate his liver with some fava beans and a nice Chianti. *Fuhfuhfuhfuhfuh* [sucking sound]."[9]

QWERTY *adj.* QWER-TY Relating to a standard English-language typewriter keyboard, which has Q W E R T Y as the first six keys on the top left row of letter keys.

BS Definition: A counterintuitive design that, amazingly, most of the world's citizens have adapted to because they had no other choice.

Origin: When you think about it, QWERTY may be one of the greatest examples of a business dictating customer behavior ever. The QWERTY design comes from the mid-1800s and the early days of the typewriter.

The original layout was created by Christopher Latham Sholes in the late 1860s and early 1870s; according to *Merriam-Webster*, Sholes picked the QWERTY design not to help typists go faster, but to actually slow them down. His first typewriters were cumbersome and jammed easily if the keys were pressed too fast, so he picked letter positions that let the typist go faster than a pen, but not fast enough to jam the machine. Sholes's design became popular and was labeled for the first time in writing in 1929 in the *Times Literary Supplement*: "The 'qwerty' keyboard appears first on the Yost in 1887." Even with the advent of the mobile era, designers were conscious of the need for consistency with the QWERTY layout, given the limited keyboard space for today's computers, laptops, and mobile phones.[10] This has allowed today's youth to type at a speed with their thumbs that leaves most parents amazed.

R

raining cats and dogs *idiom* **1.** Raining heavily. **2.** A downpour.

BS Definition: If only we could see out the window from our cubicle, we could tell you what this is like.

Origin: This is one of the more bizarre phrases in the English language and has been around since at least the 17th century. One of the earliest citations comes from British poet Henry Vaughn, who, in his 1651 collection of poems called *Olor Iscanus*, referred to a roof that was secure against "dogs and cats rained in shower." In 1652, writer Richard Brome made reference to the phrase in his comedy *The City Wit or The Woman Wears the Breeches*, "It shall raine . . . Dogs and Polecats," and the first appearance of the modern version of it came from Jonathan Swift's *A Complete Collection of Polite and Ingenious Conversation*, in 1738: "I know Sir John will go, though he was sure it would rain cats and dogs."

There are several theories as to where this idiom originated.[1] A morbid one is that, hundreds of years ago, heavy rains and poor sanitation systems would cause dead animals to be washed through city streets during floods. Yikes. Another theory has a Norse origin, relating to Odin, the god of storms. Odin was often pictured with dogs and wolves, which were symbols of wind. Furthermore, witches, who rode brooms, often took the form of black cats, which became signs of heavy rain for sailors. Therefore, it's speculated that "raining cats and dogs" may refer to a storm with wind and heavy rain. Of course, there may not be a logical explanation at all for this phrase. It may have been used just for its nonsensical, comedic value. The greatest evidence that this may be the case is the fact that several other languages (besides English) have bizarre expressions for heavy rain:

» Afrikaans—ou vrouens met knopkieries reën (It's raining old women with clubs)

» Cantonese—落狗屎 (It's raining dog's poo)

» Dutch—het regent pijpenstelen (It's raining pipe stems or stair rods)

» Finnish—Sataa kuin Esterin perseestä (It's raining like from Esteri's ass)

» German—Es regnet junge Hunde (It's raining young dogs)

» Portuguese (Brazil)—chovem cobras e lagartos (It's raining snakes and lizards)

» Spanish (Colombia)—estan lloviendo maridos (It's raining husbands).[2]

See the "BS Beyond Our Borders" sidebars for more examples of cultural differences in business speak.

ramp up *v., n.* **1.** To increase. **2.** To raise the effort involved in a process.

BS Definition: One letter away from cramp up—which is what you say you're experiencing when your boss tells you to "ramp up" your work production.

Origin: The verb *to ramp* entered the English language in the 14th century, according to *Merriam-Webster*, meaning to stand or act forcefully with arms raised. *Ramp* as a noun, meaning "a sloping plane," entered the lexicon in the early 1700s.[3] However, when *ramp up*, with its current BS meaning (and occasional use as a noun), entered the language is not as clear. Some have suggested it started in the 1960s, with its origins coming from the military use of armored personnel carriers. The carriers were entered and exited through a ramp in the back. The last thing done before moving to engage in combat then was this statement: "We are 'ramp up.' "[4] (OK, it's an awkward construction in today's parlance, but it was the military in the 1960s. Trust us, it was a weird time.) Still others say it comes from the auto industry, used to indicate when a new model was scheduled to ship out, deliver, or "ramp-up" onto auto-vehicle transport trucks.[5]

What makes the origin of *ramp up* even harder to pin down is the fact that the term shows up (in confusing references) as early as the 19th century in various books. In one example, 1816's *The Works of Ben Jonson: In Nine Volumes* by English writer William Gifford, a character named Tibullus is quoted: "Ramp up my genius, be not retrograde; But boldly nominate a spade a spade. What, shall thy lubrical and glibbery muse, Live, as she were defunct, like punk in stews."[6] Yeah. We have no idea what all that means either.

Another example, this one from 1893, gets a little closer to today's business use of the term, we think. It's from *The Textbook of Fortification and Military Engineering*, vol. 2: "It is, therefore, usually necessary to raise the ammunition when it is required for use. It may either be taken up a ramp or raised vertically by means of a lift. A ramp up which shell are to go should not be steeper than Ramps. 1 in 7."[7] Again, we were following that until the last couple of lines. . . .

The written citation of *ramp up* that has the clearest connection to today's business meaning comes from 1980.[8] That's when the *OED* says it was really first used, in *Aviation Week and Space Technology* magazine: "If we get 80 in Fiscal 1981, that will be a ramp up to 96 in 1982."

R

reading the Riot Act *idiom* 1. To give a harsh warning or reprimand. 2. To scold severely for an error or a mistake.

BS Definition: You know that vein on your boss's forehead that starts to protrude when she's really angry? And you know that tendency you have to squirm when you're uncomfortable? If both those conditions are present, you're probably being read the Riot Act.

Origin: The "riot act" that this phrase refers to was a real thing. In 1715, Britain put into effect the Riot Act, which gave the British government the authority to label any group of more than 12 people a threat to the police—and subject to a felony charge, punishable by death.[9] "Reading the Riot Act" used to be a literal event, similar to how the Miranda rights are handled in the United States. Law enforcement in Britain would approach a crowd, read the Riot Act aloud, and then disperse or arrest them.[10] It wasn't until 1967 that this law was officially repealed, but in the meantime, reading the Riot Act became synonymous with someone severely scolding another person, starting in 1784 with this reference from *The Reparation, a Comedy* from English playwright Miles Peter Andrews:

> **Captain Swagger:** Devil burn me, but we'll do as the French do— declare war without saying a syllable of the matter. So come on, Sir Gregory—By St. Patrick, I'll bother both sides of your ears with nothing but war! war!
> *[bellowing]*
> *Enter Colonel Quorum.*
> **Colonel Quorum:** Peace, I say, or I'll read the riot act.

red herring *n.* **1.** Something intended to mislead or divert attention from the central issue. **2.** In finances, a tentative prospectus usually circulated before a company's initial public offering, or IPO, so called because the front cover must carry a special notice printed in red.[11]

BS Definition: A device routinely used by CEOs on earnings calls with analysts.

Origin: Today, red herrings are often used in mystery stories, keeping readers from solving crimes too early, and have been used as a literary device by everyone from Agatha Christie to Sir Arthur Conan Doyle.[12]

The herring itself is a fish, and it only becomes "red" when prepared a specific (and very smelly) way. If you brine and smoke a herring, it will make the fish particularly pungent and turn its flesh a reddish color. The smell of a red herring is so strong, in fact, that legend has it, you can drag it across a trail that hounds are following to throw them off the scent. This is exactly why *red herring* started to be associated with a false or diversionary tactic.

Even though there is written evidence that red herrings have been around as a food source for human beings since the mid-13th century, most experts credit journalist William Cobbett with making red herring a modern BS term.[13] Cobbett's *Weekly Political Register* was an anti-establishment publication during the early 1800s, and in February 1807 Cobbett published a story about how, as a boy, he used a red herring as a decoy to deflect hounds chasing after a rabbit. He used the story as a metaphor to criticize the press, which had apparently been misled by false information about a supposed defeat of Napoleon, and lost focus on important domestic issues. Cobbett wrote: "Alas! It was a mere transitory effect of the political red-herring; for, on the Saturday, the scent became as cold as a stone."

However, let the record show that the use of red herring to distract pursuing scent hounds was tested in the TV show *MythBusters*, and it failed. Although the hound used in the test stopped to eat the fish and lost its target scent temporarily, it eventually backtracked and located it.[14] It turns out, the legend of a red herring may be a red herring itself.

red-flag *v.* **1.** To mark for special attention. **2.** To alert or warn.

> **BS Definition:** To put up a white flag the more you hear how your work is being red-flagged.

Origin: According to the *OED*, the earliest known citation for *red flag* (as a noun) comes from 1585 in reference to the color of the flag that was displayed by military forces as a sign of battle readiness. Throughout history, the color red—and more specifically red flags—has been used for all kinds of alerts and warnings. Recent examples include live-fire exercises by the military, wildfire danger, rough water conditions on the beach, auto-racing stoppages, and raising a red flag on your mailbox to signal that you have outgoing mail that day.[15]

It's not exactly known when *red-flag* switched to being used as a verb to indicate any kind of danger or alert. However, one early citation from 1748 hints at the transition. It is from the book *A Voyage Round the World, in the Years MDCCXL, I, II, III, IV. by George Anson, Esq*, credited to Benjamin Robins and Richard Walter: "A boat a-head of us waved a red flag, and blew a horn. This we considered as a signal . . . either to warn us of some shoal, or to inform us that they would supply us with a Pilot." The *OED* says the first actual use of red-flag in the BS sense was in 1962 in the *Daily Leader* in Pontiac, Illinois: "We'd like to set up a system to red-flag every important transaction which might tip us off to a possible fraud or evasion."

resting on your laurels *idiom* **1.** To stop putting in effort to advance your career or status and instead rely on your past achievements or accolades to remain relevant or successful. **2.** To be so satisfied with what you have already done or achieved that you stop trying to accomplish anything new. **3.** To coast.

R

BS Definition: 1. Homer wrote the *Iliad* and *Odyssey*. Sure, they're both classics, but what did he do after? Nada. **2.** To write "ditto" on a card that everyone is signing for a co-worker.

Origin: Dating back to ancient Greece, the idea of "resting on your laurels" stems from the Hellenic period (507 BC to 323 BC), when leaders and athletes wore laurel leaves that were closely tied to Apollo, the god of music, archery, prophecy, and poetry (among other things).[16] At the time, Apollo was typically depicted with a crown of laurel leaves, and the plant eventually became a symbol of status and achievement. Later, the Romans adopted the practice and presented wreaths to generals who won important battles.

By the 1800s, *resting on your laurels* started to be used to describe people who were overly satisfied with past triumphs.[17] The *OED* cites the first written reference to reposing (aka resting) on laurels from 1859, in *Friends in Council, a Series of Readings and Discourse thereon*, by Arthur Helps: "They might really repose upon their laurels." *Resting on your laurels* was referenced again in 2018, when New England Patriots coach Bill Belichick revealed his five rules of exceptional leadership, one of which included never resting on your laurels.[18] We wonder if another of these rules was drafting Tom Brady?

riding shotgun *idiom* 1. Claiming and then sitting in the front passenger seat of a vehicle on a journey. 2. To guard or keep a watchful eye on something.

BS Definition: 1. If you refer to your role this way, we might suggest you are the same person who "parachutes in" and is a self-titled "master of the universe." 2. Giving the seat to whoever calls for it first (but still screaming for it as you try to beat that person to the car).

Origin: The history of "riding shotgun" goes back to the days of covered wagons and the American Wild West. Traveling across the Plains was dangerous. You were susceptible to sneak attacks from bandits and thieves, so while one member of your party was in charge of holding the reins and driving your team of horses, another member would sit next to the driver with a shotgun and fend off the enemy.[19] We have found no evidence to suggest that this position was referred to as the "shotgun seat" at the time.

R

However, over the years, it has come to be called that. The *OED* says riding shotgun was first referred to in writing in 1940 (in the *Pony Express Courier*). Wikipedia cites an even earlier reference: the 1905 novel *The Sunset Trail*, by Alfred Henry Lewis: "Wyatt and Morgan Earp were in the service of The Express Company. They went often as guards—'riding shotgun,' it was called—when the stage bore unusual treasure." In recent years, "riding shotgun" has expanded to cover a wider metaphorical meaning in the BS world, as in, "riding shotgun over the nation's economy."[20]

right off the bat *idiom* **1.** Instantly and without delay. **2.** The very first thing.

BS Definition: You may think we have *bats in the belfry* (crazy) or we're *blind as a bat* (very bad eyesight), but we think doing something *right off the bat* is similar to being *like a bat out of hell* (acting very quickly). Are we *batty* (insane) for saying that?

Origin: As one might guess, this term originates in baseball, and is related to the actions that occur after a player hits the ball "right off the bat."[21] According to *The Field Guide to Sports Metaphors*, one early reference comes from an 1869 book by George P. Upton called *Letters of Peregrin Pickle*: "The Devil is not only a hard hitter with the bat, but he is a quick fielder, and he will pick a soul right off the bat of one of these soft muscle men."[22]

Other early references date to the 1880s, in particular this one from the *Albion New Era* newspaper from Indiana in 1883: "A person unused to it would net catch one 'fly' out of fifty, and as for stopping and holding a hot liner right off the bat, he might as well attempt to gather in a solid shot fired point blank from a Parrot gun." OK, we're not sure what a "Parrot gun" is, but we do know that starting in 1888, *right off the bat* was referred to outside of a baseball context, as evidenced by Maine's

Biddeford Journal: "Let me hear that kid use slang again, and I'll give it to him right off the bat. I'll wipe up the floor with him."

right up your alley *idiom* **1.** Perfectly suited to your tastes, interests, or abilities (see *wheelhouse*). **2.** The kind of thing you love or know well.

BS Definition: The stuff it takes years for your boss to recognize that you actually like and are really good at.

Origin: Some have speculated that the origin of this phrase is from baseball (the space between outfielders is sometimes referred to as "the alley," and hitting a ball in that space is a great outcome for any batter).[23] However, the best evidence suggests that *right up your alley* has roots in the way we describe the street we live on.

The word alley comes from 14th-century Middle English (with some Middle French influence thrown in there too), meaning "a narrow lane running behind rows of houses." According to the *American Heritage Dictionary of Idioms*, using the term alley to refer to "one's own province" goes all the way back to the 1600s.[24] However, the *OED* says the first reference to this meaning in writing wasn't until 1922, in *The Boy Grew Older*, by Heywood Broun: "I'd like to have him come out with me and do notes of the games. . . . That would be down his alley."[25]

rightsize *v.* **1.** To lay off (see *downsize*). **2.** To adjust to the correct size.

BS Definition: An action initiated by individuals who manage to save their own jobs.

Origin: General Motors may not have coined the term *downsize* (see the origin of *downsize*), but it can certainly lay claim to *rightsize*.[26] Roy Roberts, the vice president of personnel administration for General Motors in 1987, is credited with coining the term when he used it to describe the decision to lay off 25 percent of the automaker's salaried staff that year. The magazine *Black Enterprise* reported on the story, saying, "Roberts bristles when he hears the word downsizing; he dubs the process 'rightsizing.' He plans to 'rightsize' a number of departments by offering white-collar employees salaried separation packages." Roberts's business speak and his company's mismanagement of operations wasn't lost on some. In fact, it inspired Michael Moore to develop the film *Roger & Me*. The documentary—a scathing profile of the GM's treatment of workers—catapulted Moore to fame and devastated the reputation of the once-great automaker.[27]

rings a bell *idiom* 1. To activate a memory. 2. To evoke a vague recollection of something.

BS Definition: What you say to Mike when you want to delay admitting that you were indeed the one who ate his lunch in the break room.

Origin: For whatever reason, a lot of expressions in the English language have *bell* in them. *For whom the bell tolls* (aka a famous Ernest Hemingway novel), *saved by the bell* (aka a not-as-famous U.S. TV show), and *bells and whistles* are just a few examples.

There are two main theories on the origin of the idea of "ringing a bell" to awaken a memory in your brain. The first is, before the days of accurate timepieces, bells were used to signal to people in a town the start of important events, such as a church service, the start of school, or a celebration.[28] Others speculate that the phrase may have been derived from Ivan Pavlov, the Russian physiologist who ran experiments in the early 1900s, in which dogs salivated at the sound of a bell.[29] Both theories make sense, but there is little evidence to support either. The *OED* says the first usage of ring a bell is relatively recent: 1933, in the book *Counterfeit*, by Lee Thayer—"Wait a second, Ray. . . . Why does that name ring a bell with you?" That book title did ring a bell with us (and then made us really hungry for a dog treat, for some reason).

rock star *n.* **1.** A highly regarded person within an organization or industry. **2.** Someone greatly admired for their ability on the job.

> **BS Definition:** In reality, someone who is about as far removed from being a traditional "rock star" as you can be.

> **Origin:** To find out where the term *rock star* comes from, you must first investigate who invented the term that originated it: *rock and roll*. That person happens to be Alan Freed, a deejay who hosted a Cleveland, Ohio, radio show in the 1950s and called the R&B music he was introducing to his white audiences "rock and roll."[30] Dig deeper on what rock and roll means, though, and things start to get a little more interesting. According to the *OED*, starting in the 1920s, the verb *roll* was being used as slang for "sexual intercourse" in the United States, while *rock* was being used as a way to describe dancing music (mainly R&B). Put those two ideas together, and another way to describe rock and roll might be "good dance music to have sex to!"[31]

> The *OED* says the first written use of the term *rock star* was in 1960, in *Billboard* magazine: "Last headliner was a British rock star Emile Ford, but in the last month both Duane Eddy and Johnny Preston have topped weekly bills there." By 1973, the term had evolved into a way to describe anyone who was highly regarded for what they do. In October of that year, *Texas Monthly* described a ballet dancer this way: "And now he's a Christ, a Buddha, a rockstar."[32]

R

roll with the punches *idiom* **1.** To adapt in the moment to adverse circumstances. **2.** To adjust to adversity.

> **BS Definition:** What your department must do every year at budget time.

Origin: In today's world, this is perhaps one of the more useful phrases, given the amount of bad things that seem to happen to good people.[33] As one might expect, the phrase derives from boxing and the technique of moving your head away from an opponent's blows to lessen the impact. The *OED* says the earliest written reference to this is 1910, in the *Washington Post*: "Johnson would allow his head to roll with each punch, one of his ways of lessening the force of the blows."

One of the earliest non-boxing references we could find comes from *Life* magazine in 1938 on an East Asian military conflict: "Since 1931 China's Generalissimo Chiang Kai-shek has hired Germans to train his army. They advised him to avoid Japan's superior military power, to 'roll with the punch.'"[34] By 2009, rolling with the punches was firmly entrenched as a popular BS metaphor for surviving the Great Recession and any other challenging situation. From the *Retirement Income Reporter*, February 9, 2009: "People like him, who have secure jobs and deep-in-the-money mortgages, are rolling with the punches these days."

round-robin *idiom* 1. A tournament format in which each person or team competes against one another at least once. 2. A scheduling process used in computing where the workload is distributed among various computers in alternating fashion.

BS Definition: A format that guarantees your office softball team will spend hours at a park waiting to play its next game.

Origin: The original use of *round-robin* was not even close to what we associate it with today. The *OED* says it was originally a disparaging name for the consecrated Host at the Eucharist in church. Get a load of this Renaissance-era smack-talk from none other than John Calvin (the founder of the Calvinist movement) in his 1546 book, *Faythful Treatise Sacrament*: "Certayne fonde talkers . . . applye to this mooste holye sacramente, names of despitte and reproche, as to call it Jake in the boxe, and round roben, and suche other not onely fond but also blasphemouse names."[35]

OK. First off, we're huge fans of the word *mooste*, and we applaud Calvin for using so many *y*'s and *e*'s, but it's hard to know exactly what he's saying. We're pretty sure he mentions Jack in the Box there, but we're not sure what a fast-food restaurant has to do with this topic. Anyway . . .

Later on, *round-robin* would come to describe several things, including a more plump version of the bird (robin), a small pancake, a person, a fish, and a document (which arranged the names of the signatories in a circle so as to disguise the order in which they signed). It's this document format, often used by sailors, that is the most likely source for the evolution of the term as we know it today.[36] One example comes from the *British High Court of Admiralty Exam & Answers* from 1698: "Some of them drew up a paper commonly called a Round-robin, and signed the same whereby they intimated that if the Captaine would not give them leave to goe a shore, they would take leave."

rule of thumb *n.* **1.** A general method or approach to things based on experience rather than theory or scientific knowledge. **2.** A rough, practical method of action.

BS Definition: 1. Example of a good rule of thumb: Saving 25 percent of your take home pay in a 401k or retirement fund. Example of a bad rule of thumb: Making any rules based on the thickness of one's thumbs. **2.** The first rule of thumb: There is no fight club. Er . . . wait. Sorry. Wrong definition.

Origin: Sometimes a rumor causes bad things to happen (remember what happened to Apple stock prices when people thought Steve Jobs had a heart attack in 2008?).[37] But that's exactly what makes the origin story of *rule of thumb* so fascinating. A rumor started in the 18th century had horrible consequences that stuck with this BS term for centuries! Here's what happened.

In or around 1782, an English judge named Sir Francis Buller allegedly ruled that a man could whip his wife, provided he used a switch no thicker than his thumb.[38] Buller was known to be prejudiced and impulsive, but there's no evidence that he made such a ruling. It didn't matter. The claim was widely circulated and Buller became known as "Judge Thumb" by British caricaturist James Gillray.[39] Later, American court rulings in domestic-abuse cases referred to an "ancient doctrine" that the judges believed had allowed husbands to physically punish their wives using implements no thicker than their thumb—a "rule of thumb," so to speak. That exact phrase, *rule of thumb*, would become associated with domestic-abuse cases in the 1970s, and, despite the shaky legal basis upon which the term derived, was cited as factual in a number of law journals at that time. By 1982, the U.S. Commission on Civil Rights had published a report on domestic abuse titled *Under the Rule of Thumb*.

Thankfully, *rule of thumb* also has a completely different origin story that is based much more on factual findings than rumor. In 1658— long before Judge Buller's supposed ruling—the first written reference to a "rule of thumb" (as an approximate method for doing something) was mentioned in a posthumously published collection of sermons by Scottish preacher James Durham: "Many profest Christians are like to foolish builders, who build by guess, and by rule of thumb." A few years later, in 1692, it also appeared in Sir William Hope's book, *The Compleat Fencing Master*: "What he doth, he doth by rule of Thumb, and not by Art." Historically, the width of the thumb, or "thumb's breadth," was used as the equivalent of an inch in the cloth trade, and the thumb has also been used in brewing beer over the years to gauge the heat of the brewing vat.[40]

run it up the flagpole (and see who salutes) *idiom* **1.** To try something out and see how people respond. **2.** To make a proposal to see how it'll be received (otherwise known by the saying, "Will it play in Peoria?").

BS Definition: Chances are, if you use this phrase in the office, you are 1) a patriot, or 2) someone who also says "Back in my day. . . ."

Origin: A catchphrase that became popular in the 1950s and 1960s America, the origin of this one hasn't quite been pinpointed, though an early influence on its use was most certainly the 1957 film *12 Angry Men*, starring Henry Fonda. During one deliberation of the jury in the film, juror number 12, an advertising executive played by Robert Webber, exclaims: "OK, here's an idea. Let's run it up the flagpole and see if anyone salutes it."[41] Later, in Stan Freberg's 1961 comedy album, *Stan Freberg Presents the United States of America: The Early Years*, the phrase is also used by the character of George Washington, who, having just received the nation's new flag from Betsy Ross, says he'll "run it up the flagpole . . . see if anyone salutes."[42]

running amok *v.* **1.** To haphazardly go around causing mayhem and chaos. **2.** Acting in a wild and uncontrolled manner.

BS Definition: How your department behaves when the vice president in charge gets sacked. Come to think of it, that's how your department behaved before she got sacked, too.

Origin: *Running amok* is commonly used to describe wild or erratic behavior these days, but the phrase actually began as a medical term documenting a condition that involved murder. As early as 1516, European visitors to Malaysia learned of a peculiar mental affliction that caused otherwise normal tribe members to go on brutal and seemingly random killing sprees. They called it "Amuco" at first—after a band of Javanese and Malay warriors who were known for their penchant for indiscriminate violence. The following description comes from the translation of 16th-century manuscripts by the Portuguese trader Duarte Barbosa: "There are some of them [the Javanese] who . . . go out into the streets, and kill as many persons as they meet. . . . These are called Amuco." More than 150 years later, English poet and politician Andrew Marvell continued this morbid fascination by writing in 1672, "Like a raging Indian . . . he runs a mucke (as they cal it there) stabbing every man he meets." Once thought to be the result of possession by evil spirits, the phenomenon later found its way into psychiatric manuals, where it eventually settled into the phrase we currently know, *running amok*. It remains a diagnosable mental condition to this day.[43]

BS BEYOND OUR BORDERS— PART II

A BS term like *running amok* is inspired by a culture that is different than most English-speaking countries. Understanding those cultural nuances can help you appreciate the differences in BS terms around the world. For example, you can recognize the significance of the brainstorming-equivalent phrase *casting a brick to attract jade* in China when you know how valuable jade has been in that country's history. Likewise the Russian phrase *galloping across Europe* (which means "doing something hastily or haphazardly") makes more sense when you know that country's war history. This can be a lot of work, but as the Japanese say, *If you don't enter the tiger's cave, you can't catch its cub*—which basically means "nothing ventured, nothing gained." Consider these other animal-focused BS phrases from around the world.

Australia	
rattle ya dags!	Hurry up! (Dags are parts of the fleece around a sheep's bum that are usually caked in poo and "rattle" when they run.)

Brazil	
to buy a cat thinking it was a rabbit	to be fooled
to swallow frogs	to bite one's tongue

China	
nine cows and one strand of cow hair	a drop in the bucket

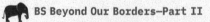

Croatia

you sing like an elephant farted in your ear	you have no ear for music
to talk about the wolf	speak of the devil

France

jumping from the rooster to the donkey	changing subjects with no logic
a rabbit has been put on you	you got stood up

Italy

a chicken waiting to be plucked	someone who can be taken advantage of
a dog in church	an unwelcome guest

Japan

to wear a cat on one's head	you're hiding your claws and pretending to be a nice, harmless person
willing to borrow a cat's paws	you're so busy that you're willing to take help from anyone

Portugal

he who doesn't have a dog hunts with a cat	you make the most of what you've got
pay the duck	to take the blame for something you did not do

South Korea

a dog with feces scolds a dog with husks of grain	people who live in glass houses shouldn't throw stones

Sweden

there's no cow on the ice	there's no need to worry
to slide in on a shrimp sandwich	somebody who didn't have to work to get where they are

Thailand

the hen sees the snake's feet and the snake sees the hen's boobs	two people know each other's secrets

S

SEO *n.* S-E-O **1.** Abbreviation for "search engine optimization." **2.** The process of maximizing the amount of visitors to your website by making sure the site shows up high on the list of results returned by a search engine.

BS Definition: The equivalent of trying to climb to the top of an ever-growing mountain, knocking away your competitors, and screaming, "Hey! Look at me! Look at me!" at the same time.

Origin: Today, SEO is perhaps the holy grail for digital- and content-marketing professionals, and although there's some debate over who exactly coined the term, the rock band Jefferson Starship is (oddly) involved in the most commonly accepted origin story.[1]

In the summer of 1995, Jefferson Starship was the client of an Internet marketing firm called Cybernautics. The band's manager was upset that Starship's website (built by Cybernautics) was only showing up on page 4 of Internet search results. He called one of Cybernautics' co-founders, Bob Heyman, in the middle of the night and laid into him: "Why the #$%$ don't we come up before page 4 on this damned thing? Page #$%$ 4, you #$%$ morons!" The next day, Heyman and Cybernautics' other co-founder, Leland Harden, gathered their team and made some adjustments that focused on mastering search-engine rankings. It was then that Heyman and Harden say they coined the term *search engine optimization* (later shortened to SEO), and soon thereafter hired the first SEOM (search engine optimization manager).[2]

Today, SEO is an $80 billion industry, with some firms charging millions of dollars a year just to focus on improving a company's search results.[3] This activity, of course, is not to be confused with SEM (search engine marketing)—which is the placement of ads in the paid or sponsored-listings area of a search engine, typically at the top or bottom of displayed results.

sacred cow *n.* **1.** Something that cannot be criticized or removed. **2.** An idea, custom, or institution thought to be above criticism.

> **BS Definition:** What comes to be when your boss says, "I've got the best idea ever!"

> **Origin:** This term comes from the Hindu reverence for cows. In Hindu society, cows are honored as maternal figures, symbols of unselfish giving.[4] However, for many Westerners a cow is just a cow, so, starting around the late 18th century, the term *sacred cow* started to appear in writing as a way to define that difference.
>
> The British law journal by Richard Brookes, *The General Gazetteer*, from 1795, is the earliest reference we found that included the term: "and the English had a factory here till 1670, when a bull-dog belonging to the factory, seized and killed a sacred cow, the natives rose and massacred them all."[5] By the mid-1800s, the term started to refer to anything untouchable. According to the *OED*, the earliest known figurative reference comes from the British weekly *Saturday Review of Politics, Literature, Science, and Art*, which published the following in April 1867: "In Mr. Lowe's eyes, the Revised Code is a sort of sacred cow, not to be touched by profane or sacrilegious hands, or, as he puts it more curtly, not to be 'tinkered.'"

sandbag *v.* **1.** To purposely delay or move slow. **2.** To conceal or downplay your strengths. **3.** To underperform in order to gain an unfair advantage.

> **BS Definition:** To linger in the restaurant bathroom longer than needed so you can escape your business dinner as long as possible.

Origin: Put together two words—*sand* and *bag*—and you have the origin of the term itself. Indeed, the noun *sandbag* dates back as far as the late 1500s, per various sources, referring simply to a bag filled with sand that was often used as a weapon or fortification.[6] The noun evolved into a verb in the 19th century, meaning to attack someone with a sand-bag. And, no, we don't really know why someone would choose to attack another person with an unwieldy bag of sand, but that's apparently what they did back then, OK? Check out this report from the *Courier-Journal of Louisville*, Kentucky, in 1887: "The next day Claytor turned up at Central Station with a fairy story that he had been sand-bagged on his way home."

By the 1940s, *sandbagging* had evolved into a poker term, in which a player with a good hand bets somewhat meekly at first, in order to draw other players into continuing to bet. One example of this, according to the *OED*, comes from the 1940 book *Poker* by Oswald Jacoby: "The time to sandbag is when you have three of a kind or better."[7] The modern meaning, to hold back to gain an advantage later, began to take shape around the 1970s and is routinely used these days in the world of sports to describe teams who lose on purpose to increase their draft prospects for the next season (google the Philadelphia 76ers and The Process).[8]

scalable *adj.* **1.** Requires little relative resources to get to market and be competitive. **2.** Capable of being easily expanded or upgraded without using a lot of time or money.

BS Definition: Examples of products that their creators thought this word applied to: the Edsel, New Coke, the AAF.[9]

Origin: *Scalable* is centuries old, first appearing in the late 1500s as a reference to climbing.[10] One early citation comes from 1579–1580's *Plutarch's Lives*, as translated by Sir Thomas North: "Without the wall the height was not so great, but that it was easily scalable with ladders."

Given the upward trajectory of scaling, it fits that the term would evolve (in a broad sense) to refer to the ability to grow output, while managing increased demand.[11]

However, it also could be argued that this business definition of *scalable* (outside its alpine or climbing origins) is more firmly rooted in economics. Specifically, many cite Scottish economist Adam Smith, the famed author of *The Wealth of Nations*, as having played a big role in the eventual development of the microeconomics concept "economies of scale"—which is the proportionate saving in costs gained by an increased level of production.[12] Another Smith idea was the concept of the "invisible hand"—a laissez-faire approach to production in which he argued that society was best served by letting self-interest and freedom of production reign, without government intervention. In a way, Smith's ideas have scaled in their own right, because many of those pillars of economic theory remain today.

screw the pooch *v.* **1.** To mess things up big time (aka snafu). **2.** To make a costly mistake in an embarrassing way (aka Freudian slip).

How did I just blow that deal?

BS Definition: 1. Profane? Absolutely. Appropriate for the level of idiocy you showed in ignoring the boss's warnings? Without a doubt. **2.** Trust us. You don't want to know the literal definition of this one.

Origin: We certainly wouldn't have this phrase in the popular lexicon without Tom Wolfe's *The Right Stuff*, and its film adaptation, about the *Mercury* space program.[13] Wolfe uses the phrase multiple times, including a chapter entitled "The Unscrewable Pooch," where the following passage appears: "Well, there it was, your classic Dear John letter. Even though in his detached moments he realized that he perhaps screwed the pooch here and there, it was hard to believe. He had been left behind."

S

Wolfe most likely picked up the phrase from the test pilots in the *Mercury* program who had been exposed to the military vulgarism "f*ck the dog," which dates as far back as the 1930s. One plausible story of how "f*ck the dog" turned into "screw the pooch" is from a Yale graduate named John Rawlings. Rawlings worked on the *Mercury* program, and said he picked up "screw the pooch" from a friend, deejay Jack May, who softened the old military expression to make it more pleasing to the ear.[14] May shared this origin story with reporter Ben Zimmer in 2014:

> John Rawlings was one of two roommates who were architec-
> ture students. In the spring of 1950 it was time for his project to
> complete the semester. He procrastinated. Apparently, all architec-
> ture students do. He was going to be late even starting his charrette.
> So to be helpful I said the following:
> **Jack:** You're late, John, you're fouling up. You are f*cking the dog.
> **John:** Really, you are so vulgar and coarse, I just don't want to hear it.
> **Jack:** You're still late. Is this better? You are screwing the pooch.
> **John:** (shrill laughter)[15]

show your true colors *idiom* **1.** To reveal your authentic self, especially in a negative way. **2.** To expose who you really are.

BS Definition: To put your headphones on and pretend like you're on a call when you see someone coming to talk to you at work.

Origin: Most scholars believe this term has maritime origins, relating to a practice whereby warships use flags to communicate different things. As far back as the 16th century, writers started to mention ships sailing under "false colors" (flags of different nations or loyalties) in order to elude or deceive enemies. The act behind "showing your true colors" was a warship hailing another ship flying one flag, but then hoisting their own when they got within firing range.[16] Sir Thomas Elyot, an English diplomat and scholar, alluded to the idea in the book *The Boke Named* *the Governour*, published in 1531: "He wyll . . . sette a false colour of lernyng on proper wittes, which wyll be wasshed away with one shoure of raine."[17] The *OED* cites William Shakespeare as one of the first writers to start shaping the idea into the full figurative use we recognize today. He did so in *Henry IV, Part II*, from 1600: "How might we see Falstaffe bestow himself to night in his true colours, and not our selues be seene?"

snail mail *n.* **1.** Messages delivered by post, as opposed to electronically. **2.** Mail sent through physical delivery.

> **BS Definition:** A term invented because *sloth post* and *carrier pigeon express* aren't as catchy.

> **Origin:** The first evidence of *snail mail* in writing took place in 1942 in the *Lowell* (Massachusetts) *Sun* newspaper, in a headline about slow mail delivery, and the term *snail post* (not as memorable, but still . . .) has much earlier usage in 1843's *Fraser's Magazine for Town and Country*.[18] However, it wasn't until 1981 that *snail mail*—to describe conventional mail services versus email (which was created in 1969)—was first used in a BS context by Jim Rutt, the chairman of the influential Santa Fe Institute (a multidisciplinary research organization) and future CEO of Network Solutions (a web services company). Soon after, *snail mail* started to show up more frequently in groups discussing the benefits of electronic delivery for messages. This example from a Usenet group in June 1982—*Reply to: Yacc Wizardry Sought* in *net.unix-wizards*: "Our Unix-Wizard mail is slower than snail mail these days."

spitballing *v.* **1.** To estimate. **2.** To throw out ideas without editing yourself (see *brainstorm*).

> **BS Definition:** Just like its name suggests, a process that results in ideas that are immature, highly disruptive, and more often than not, disgusting.

Origin: Most dictionary sources say that spitball, a piece of paper chewed and rounded into a projectile that schoolkids throw at one another, stems from the 1840s in the United States. By the early 20th century, the term began to be associated with baseball. Pitchers would apply their own saliva (or other liquids, gels, oils, or foreign substances) onto the ball to create more movement on a pitch by changing its aerodynamic properties. Some have speculated that the BS term of spitballing grew out of the saliva-soaked school projectile, while others say it came from baseball with the concept of "tossing" an idea around at the workplace.[19]

Either way, by the 1950s, the term certainly came to be used in the BS context we know today. One early citation comes from 1955, in Harry Kurnitz's book *Invasion of Privacy*: "I'm just thinking out loud. . . . Spitballing we call it in the movie business."[20]

steal one's thunder *idiom* **1.** To use someone's idea for your own benefit before the originator has a chance to use it themselves. **2.** To preempt the anticipated attention or praise someone was going to get by stepping in before it happens. **3.** To take credit for something someone else has done.

BS Definition: To yell "Surprise!" before anyone else does at the office surprise birthday party.

Origin: We found great joy in discovering the origin of this term, which comes from the theater world and the use of fake thunder to mimic the real sound during performances. It all starts with a well-known (and apparently very frustrated) 18th-century theater critic and playwright named John Dennis, who invented a machine that could mimic the crackling, low rumble of thunder in plays.[21] According to history,

Dennis created this "fake thunder" for *Appius and Virginia*—a 1709 production at the famed Drury Lane Theatre in London. After a short run, the theater canceled the production and went on to stage *Macbeth* using the same method for thunder that Dennis invented. Upon hearing this, Dennis was outraged and declared, "That is *my* thunder, by God; the villains will play my thunder, but not my play." Other sources quote Dennis as saying something a little more direct, as in, "Damn them! They will not let my play run, but they steal my thunder."[22] And with that, a *BS Dictionary* star was born!

stick to one's guns *idiom* 1. Keep with your beliefs or actions. 2. Hold steady to your opinion or course of action.

BS Definition: What you do until it's clear that the person who writes your paycheck disagrees with you; then it's, "Yes, whatever you say!"

Origin: According to Dictionary.com, this expression originally alluded to a gunner remaining by his post and was expressed as *stand to one's guns*. Its use dates from the mid-1800s. The *OED* says the earliest reference to *stick to one's guns* comes from the novel *Ten Thousand a Year*, by English barrister (lawyer) Samuel Warren, in 1841: "Titmouse, though greatly alarmed, stood to his gun pretty steadily." Though not the exact construction of the current usage, it's possible the phrase *stick to one's guns* derived from this original usage due to the fact that Warren's novel enjoyed widespread popularity in both Britain and the United States.

However, we found an even earlier reference, coming from *The Life of Samuel Johnson, Volume 1*, by James Boswell, published in 1791: "Mrs. Thrale stood to her gun with great cou'age, in defence of amorous ditties . . ." The earliest mention we could find of this BS phrase in its current figurative form comes from Charlotte Riddell's 1881 novel, *The Mystery in Palace Gardens*: "He stuck to his guns."

S

straight and narrow *idiom* **1.** Acting in a moral and law-abiding way. **2.** Honest and upright.

> **BS Definition:** The opposite of Enron, Lehman Brothers, and Bernie Madoff.[23]

> **Origin:** Given its meaning, it makes sense that this phrase comes from a source known for its own straight-and-narrow approach: the Bible (Matthew 7:14, to be exact[24]). Because we love Lebron James, we'll use the King James version: "Because strait is the gate, and narrow is the way, which leadeth unto life, and few there be that find it." Alternatively, other versions read as follows: "Broad is the way that is the path of destruction but narrow is the gate and straight is the way which leadeth to the house of God." (See the sidebar on page 123 for other BS terms that originated from the Bible.)

> At some point, *straight and narrow* became the shorthand phrase to communicate these thoughts, as evidenced by the 1842 write-up from *Hymns & Scenes of Childhood*, by Jane E. Leeson: "Loving Shepherd, ever near, Teach Thy lamb Thy voice to hear; Suffer not my steps to stray From the straight and narrow way."

> Besides Lebron James, we also love The Who and Pete Townshend, so we would be remiss if we didn't mention them and their classic "Getting in Tune," from 1971's *Who's Next* album.[25] It further cemented straight and narrow into the English lexicon with the following lyrics:

>> I've got it all here in my head
>> There's nothing more needs to be said
>> I'm just bangin' on my old piano
>> I'm getting in tune to the straight and narrow

straight from the horse's mouth *idiom* **1.** From the most reliable source of information. **2.** An authentic and original authority.

BS Definition: Usually a phrase said by a middle manager justifying a dumb decree from up top.

Origin: This phrase started to appear in writing in the 1920s, and its origin appears to have been influenced by two sources: horse racing and the fact that a horse's age can be determined accurately by looking inside its mouth.[26]

As we explain in our entry for *long in the tooth*, a horse's gums recede with age and make the animal's teeth appear longer the older it is. This means, if you really want the authentic age of a horse, you should go straight to its mouth for evidence—or just pull up some records, because we're sure that in today's world, horse people do a better job of keeping track of their animals' ages than just sticking their fingers all up in their mouths, right?

Horse racing factors into this origin because, well, most of us are degenerate gamblers who are always looking for a way to score an advantage at the track, so getting a reliable source of information (like its fitness for the race that day) would be a good thing to have, right? The earliest reference to "straight from the horse's mouth" is clearly horse-racing related and can be found in the *Syracuse Herald*, from May 1913: "I got a tip yesterday, and if it wasn't straight from the horse's mouth it was jolly well the next thing to it."[27]

Given horses' importance to human beings throughout history—for transportation, labor, battles, and so forth—it makes sense that horse-related terms like straight from the horse's mouth would be plentiful in the BS world. We have defined some of them elsewhere in this book, but do you recognize any of these equine-inspired phrases as well?

» *a horse of a different color*—something completely different by comparison

» *back the wrong horse*—to support someone or something that fails
» *cart before the horse*—to do things in the improper order
» *change horses midstream*—to alter your course of action before completing your original task; to get behind a new leader in the middle of doing something
» *dark horse*—someone who unexpectedly wins or succeeds
» *I could eat a horse*—very hungry
» *one's high horse*—an attitude of superiority.

straw man *n.* **1.** A first or early draft that serves as a starting point in the evolution of an idea or a plan. **2.** A brainstormed proposal intended to generate discussion and provoke the generation of new and better proposals.

BS Definition: If proposed by the CEO, the beginnings of a brilliant concept that can't miss. If proposed by a competing peer, perhaps the worst proposal ever put forth!

Origin: As you might have guessed, the actual term *straw man* goes back centuries as a way to describe a figure of a man made of straw. According to the *OED*, the earliest reference to a "straw-man" comes from author Pierre de la Primaudaye's book, *The French academie* (translated by Thomas Bowes), in 1586: "A scarre-crowe to make them afraide, as wee vse to deale with little children and with birdes by puppets and strawe-men."[28] However, it would be hundreds of years before the use of *straw man* as a way to describe the initial plan of something started to present itself.

One researcher suggests it's rooted in this reference from *The Chronicle*, published by the students of the University of Michigan in 1878, in which the idea of propping up an imaginary man of straw as a ridiculous opponent who would be easy to defeat in a debate is addressed: "The average debater knows no finer fun than belaboring a man of straw. How often have we heard that ambitious disputant, in full flush of victory, fashion with his creative tongue that silliest of all fools—the straw man. Into the straw man's mouth are put impossible propositions, and when he has been made to utter them, the speaker proper proceeds to show what an utter ass this straw man is."

However, most sources say the origin of this BS term is actually tied to the 1970s military, more specifically, the U.S. Department of Defense (DoD). Back then, the DoD assigned different names to the building process for developing the computer programming language of Ada.[29] In the stages of development, "straw man" came first, then "wooden-man," then "tinman," then "ironman," and down the line to, finally, "stoneman."[30] We assume every time an ironman proposal was turned in, they jammed to the Black Sabbath classic, no?

strike while the iron is hot *idiom* **1.** To act while circumstances are favorable. **2.** To take advantage of an opportunity while you have the leverage.

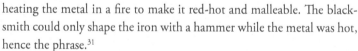

BS Definition: The time to ask for a raise.

Origin: This phrase is centuries old and refers to blacksmiths who worked with iron by hand, heating the metal in a fire to make it red-hot and malleable. The blacksmith could only shape the iron with a hammer while the metal was hot, hence the phrase.[31]

The *OED* says the earliest reference to this idea is from around the year 1400. That's before the discovery of America, folks. We wonder what else is still around from that time?

- » Leeches as a means of medical treatment? Yep.[32]
- » People hunting for unicorns? You bet.[33]
- » A belief that the world is flat? Oh no.[34]

Anyway, here's that first reference for you from 1405's *Melibeus* by Geoffrey Chaucer: "Right so as whil þt Iren is hoot men sholde smyte." Let the record show that *hoot* and *smyte* are officially joining *mooste* on our list of favorite words from the Middle Ages now.

sweat equity *n.* **1.** The amount of hard work put into a project. **2.** Usually refers to start-up companies and the work performed by employees in return for a future share in ownership.

BS Definition: The business ownership plan a start-up company promises you at the beginning of your employment and then inevitably pulls away when things go bust.

Origin: In 1937, a Quaker organization named the American Friends Service Committee (AFSC) began supporting work camps in select areas of the country.[35] They were basically self-help housing and construction projects that involved physical labor on the part of both men and women who participated. In exchange for hard physical work, the campers enjoyed the right to share in the life of the local community. In the 1950s, the AFSC coined the term *sweat equity* to describe this exchange when helping migrant farmers in California to build their own homes.[36]

The business world soon adopted the term for its own use. In the 1990s and early 2000s, sweat equity became a popular way for founders of companies with limited cash to describe their working conditions in comparison with investors who usually got a greater percentage of shares for providing the funding. When most of these companies went belly-up later, some of the workers involved in these endeavors used a different BS term to describe their experience (see *dumpster fire*).

swim lane *n.* **1.** A specific responsibility within a company, process, or flow diagram (aka silo). **2.** A defined role within a business organization.

BS Definition: Something you must never give the appearance of stepping out of—at least to people in power.

Origin: *Swim lane* first appeared as a BS term in the 1940s, when a variation of early flow-process charts, called multicolumn process charts, came on the scene. The swim-lane flowchart differed from other flowcharts in that processes and decisions were grouped visually by placing them in lanes.[37] In the 1990s, Geary Rummler and Alan Brache published a book called *Improving Performance: How to Manage the White Space on the Organization Chart* that highlighted swim-lane diagrams and helped make them popular in today's business world.[38]

Swim lane is unique in the BS world in that it is at least partially credited with spawning yet another BS term: *stay in your lane.* (It should be noted that car racing, basketball, and football also get a nod from some for inspiring this term.) The idea behind the figurative use of these words is to worry about your own job and not take on responsibilities or tasks that are outside your authority. One of the first examples in print (that we could find) of this usage is from a January 1972 sports-page article in the *Advocate* newspaper of Baton Rouge, Louisiana: "'I've got to be sure to stay in my lane and not get faked out,' Waters said. 'It is important that I keep Morris turned inside.'"[39]

SWOT/SWAT team *n.* **1.** A group of experts brought together to solve a problem. **2.** A special unit assembled to address a problem that no one else can fix.

BS Definition: Either way, a sign that you're in deep doo-doo.

Origin: You say "SWOT" and I say "SWAT." (Did anyone else just start singing "you like tomato and I like tomahto"? Or was that just us?[40]). Both

S

versions of this phrase, *SWOT team* and *SWAT team*, are pronounced the same, but they officially stand for different things. *SWOT* stands for "strengths, weaknesses, opportunities, and threats," while *SWAT* is an acronym for "special weapons and tactics."[41] When you use this term in the BS world, generally, you're referring to a SWOT team. However, if you're looking to address a hostage situation with some snipers, then a SWAT team is probably for you. Either way, the phrase *sending in a SWAT team* has become a euphemism for fixing any hard situation. Here are the origins of both SWOT and SWAT teams.

SWOT Team

SWOT was developed in the middle of the last century, born out of business research on strategic planning. It's unclear who exactly developed the SWOT concept, but many credit Albert Humphrey, whose work at Stanford on the Stakeholder Concept—eventually known as TAM or team action management—is often referenced by business leaders, economists, and politicians.[42] Others suggest SWOT should be credited to Harvard Business School Policy Unit professors George Albert Smith Jr., C. Roland Christensen, and Kenneth Andrews, who eventually developed the SWOT usage and application.[43]

SWAT Team

The 1960s saw the beginnings of SWAT. These specialized police units were created to deal with hostage rescue and extreme situations involving dangerous suspects. Some suggest it was first used by the Philadelphia Police Department. However, Daryl Gates, then an inspector with the Los Angeles Police Department, is widely considered the "father" of SWAT. Gates—who would later gain infamy as the chief of police during the L.A. riots and the Rodney King beating—said he developed SWAT in the 1960s to stand for "special weapons attack team," but later went with "special weapons and tactics."[44]

synergy *n.* syn-er-gy **1.** To work with someone to make something better. **2.** To cooperate with others to complete a business task (aka there is no I in team).

BS Definition: To use a word that makes you feel less good about yourself every time you say it.

Origin: If we did a poll of all businesspeople, *synergy* might rank as the number 1 most hated BS term in the world. Overused? Check. Kind of stupid? Oh, yeah. We're just over the term—with variations of it being applied on a regular basis to everything from sports to leadership to mergers.[45] Interestingly, the origin is not as recent as one might think, given the volume of usage these days.

Derived from the Greek word *synergos* (which means "to cooperate or work together"), synergy was introduced into the lexicon through a 1632 theological doctrine from the bishop of Norwich, Edward Reynolds. That doctrine states that individual salvation is achieved through "synergie and co-partnership" with human will and divine grace. By the 19th century, the usage morphed into physiology, and then social psychology. By 1896, French journalist Henri Mazel employed the term *synergy* as part of the title of his book, *La Synergie Sociale*, in which he argued that Charles Darwin failed to account for "social synergy" (or a kind of "social love") when discussing evolution.[46]

Despite those early uses of the word, it wasn't until 1957 that *synergy* became popularized as a business term. That year, British psychologist Raymond Cattell, in his book *Personality and Motivation Structure and Measurement*, repurposed the original meaning in the following way: "Immediate synergy through group membership . . . expresses the energy going into the group life as a result of satisfaction with fellow members."[47] By the 1980s and through the new millennium, *synergy* became a popular buzzword for mergers and acquisitions—because that synergy in the AOL–Time Warner deal, for example, was electric (see *screw the pooch*).[48]

table stakes *n.* **1.** The minimum amount needed to do business. **2.** The least amount of investment or resources needed to be competitive in an industry.

> **BS Definition: 1.** For a professional food taster, it is a mouth. **2.** A gambling term that is now used by people who, ironically, are averse to risk (see *B-school* and *bean counter*).

> **Origin:** To be clear, we are *not* talking about table *steaks* here, like the food. No, our *table stakes* is the term that comes from the world of gambling and poker, which in recent years has become the hip way to say "minimum."[1] Though in poker its definition is more of a limit[2]—you may only bet the number of chips you have on the table at the beginning of the deal in poker, and you may not bet more than that (although you may go "all in" to compete for the pot regardless of chip count)—table stakes can apply to gambling in general as a way to say a minimum necessary to enter a particular game. An example would be a high-stakes blackjack game in which a required amount is set for each bet.

> What's interesting is that there is little documented evidence of who created this term and exactly why. According to the *OED*, the first known citation comes from 1874 in author Dick Williams's *The American Hoyle: or, Gentleman's Hand-Book of Games*, by Trumps: "It may save much time, for each player to expose his capital and play 'table stakes'; this is now Club-House usage." Almost 100 years later, the term began to appear in a business context. The 1970 book *The BRMP Guide to the BRM Body of Knowledge*, published by the Business Relationship

Management Institute, states, "Table stakes represent the essential needs of the Business Partner, without which, meeting the higher order value expectations may not be meaningful or palpable."[3]

take this offline *v.* To postpone addressing an issue until later (see *parking lot* and *put a pin in it*).

BS Definition: When you use this phrase, you're really thinking that you'd just love to snap your fingers and have the whole thing disappear.

Origin: Offline itself has an interesting origin going back to its use in the context of railroads in the 19th century (see *offline*). Some have suggested, though, that the popularity of this phrase evolved more rapidly in recent times from other influences—control systems in the 1960s or assembly lines in the 1970s—with the need to take inventory or systems offline. One of the early published citations that we could find for taken offline comes from the book *Instrumentation in the Petroleum and Chemical Industries, vol. 8,* by Irving G. Young, published in 1972: "Alarm messages in this category include: 1. Alarms for equipment which is being taken offline."[4]

takeaway *n.* **1.** The conclusions or action points from a meeting or discussion. **2.** The headlines from a business meeting.

BS Definition: At the end of the day, it's the bottom-line, the postmortem, where the rubber meets the road, the upshot . . . you get the point.

Origin: The problem of combining two common words, *take* and *away*, to create the noun *takeaway* is that the resulting word can be used in a variety of ways over time.[5] In the 1500s, *takeaway* appeared in writing as a verb. An example comes from 1576's *XXVII. Lectvures: Or Readings, Vpon Part of the Epistle Written to the Hebrues* by Edward Dering: "Againe, take-away the preaching of the Gofpel, and you takeaway faith . . ."[6] Fast-for-

T

ward to the early 1900s, and it was a mathematical term to describe a number being taken away from a larger group. In the 1930s, it became a train car that was carrying logs away. By the 1940s, a "takeaway" in Ireland and Britain referred to food not eaten on premises (like "takeout" in the United States). In the 1970s, a "takeaway" could refer to an exam, a golf swing, or a player taking a ball or puck away from an opposing team.

Finally, during this time, takeaway started to establish itself in business as another way to say a lesson or principle learned. One example of such usage is cited in the Grammarphobia blog that comes from *Nature* magazine in 1976: "The takeaway message of the Dunbars' monograph is that superficially similar social systems may be the product of different behavioural arrangements."[7]

tallest midget *n.* The best choice you can make from a selection of bad choices.

BS Definition: 1. A phrase that, when used, will guarantee you insult and alienate any little person you work with. **2.** Similar to *open the kimono*, a phrase that should go the way of the dodo bird.[8]

Origin: The mid-1800s weren't exactly a time of great tolerance and understanding. Slavery existed, women weren't allowed to vote, and Joseph Merrick (an English man with severe deformities) was exhibited publicly as the "Elephant Man."[9] With this backdrop, the word *midget*—to describe people with achondroplasia (the genetic condition that causes dwarfism)—entered the English lexicon.[10]

The root of the word is midge, which is a tiny biting insect resembling a gnat. That's not exactly the most flattering origin, right? The irony is that Harriet Beecher Stowe, who wrote *Uncle Tom's Cabin* (a book that portrayed the evils of slavery and may have been an impetus for the Civil War to end it[11]), is the person credited with making the word popular.

That's right. While fighting slavery with her pen, Stowe used *midget* repeatedly to describe children and extremely short people, like in this example from 1854's *Sunny Memories of Foreign Lands*: "Here six or eight midgets were jumping the rope while papa and mamma swung it for them."

The term *tallest midget* started to appear in books around the early 1900s. One early reference comes from the *Buzzer*, a monthly publication produced by members of the Fair Employees Benefit Association, in 1919: "Stevie Rail—Tallest midget in the world."

That said, the person who may have best established the BS version of tallest midget in the public consciousness was none other than Mike Royko, the famed columnist for the *Chicago Daily News*, the *Chicago Sun-Times*, and the *Chicago Tribune*. Royko—who projected a gruff, tell-it-like-it-is, everyman persona—was considered at one time to be America's greatest columnist, having published more than 7,500 pieces in his 30-year career from the 1960s to the 1990s. He used the phrase *tallest midget in the circus* often in his columns and in interviews—referring to himself, Chicago City Council aldermen, and even other writers, like the *Washington Post's* Thomas Boswell, as such.[17]

Here's hoping this is the last edition of *The BS Dictionary* with this phrase in it.

the third degree *n.* **1.** Intense interrogation. **2.** A series of fast and accusatory questions.

BS Definition: What you get when you're suspected of taking someone's phone charger.

Origin: You can credit the Freemasons for this one. Most dictionary sources say *the third degree* is related to the somewhat mysterious fraternal organization of builders, whose members undergo rigorous questioning and examinations before becoming "third degree" master masons.[13] When a candidate receives the third degree (a status established sometime in the 1770s) in a Masonic lodge, he is subjected to an interrogation as well as physical challenges that are more difficult than the first two degrees.

Even though the words *third degree* appear in writing (with a different meaning) as far back as 1576, it wasn't until 1880, and a mention from *Harvard Lampoon* magazine in February of that year, that the third degree was documented with today's BS meaning of an intense interrogation: "He met the large and celebrated brother of one of his houries. He stopped to greet him, and was surprised at receiving a clip over the head from the brother's cane. This was followed by a personal chastisement in the third degree."[14]

thought leader *n.* **1.** A person or firm that is recognized as an authority in the field and whose expertise is sought and often rewarded. **2.** A go-to individual or organization for guidance and direction on an issue. **3.** A person with intellectual influence over a group or an organization (see *KOL* and *influencer*).

BS Definition: 1. Is sometimes confused with the person who has the loudest voice in the room (aka blowhard). **2.** If you have to label yourself a thought leader, you may not really be a thought leader. **3.** Sometimes the person who has watched the most TED Talks in your office.

Origin: The earliest written evidence of *thought leader* comes from an 1876 publication called *The Theistic Annual*, which discusses one of America's most famous essayists and philosophers: "Ralph Waldo Emerson is getting into years, but manifests to-day, as he did half a century ago, the wizard power of a thought-leader."[15] However, the use of the term in a more BS-related context doesn't appear until almost 100 years later.[16] In 1964, McKinsey & Company launched the *McKinsey Quarterly*, which is widely considered the first example of thought-leadership marketing, paving the way for other consultancy companies to start similar journals. In 1994, Joel Kurtzman, editor-in-chief of the magazine *Strategy & Business*, wrote:

> A thought leader is recognized by peers, customers and industry experts as someone who deeply understands the business they are in, the needs of their customers and the broader marketplace in which they operate. They have distinctively original ideas, unique points of view and new insights.

That, ladies and gentlemen, is some thought leadership on the definition of thought leader in the business world.[17]

throw under the bus *v.* **1.** To put the blame on someone else for a mistake. **2.** To sacrifice a friend or an ally for selfish reasons.

BS Definition: What too many managers do to their employees when confronted with a misstep.

Origin: Like many of the *BS Dictionary* terms, there is some discrepancy as to who originated this rather descriptive phrase. William Safire, former presidential speechwriter and language columnist for the *New York Times*, suggested that the first usage came from baseball.[18] He quoted slang expert Paul Dickson and referenced a 1980 article in the *Washington Post*, which called for ballplayers to board the team bus with "Bus leaving. Be on it or under it," as the source material.

Others say the first use of the phrase came from the *Times* of London in June 1982, when Julian Critchley wrote: "President Galtieri had pushed her under the bus which the gossips had said was the only means of her removal." Later, journalist David Remnick used the term in an article about recording artist Cyndi Lauper in the *Washington Post* in 1984: "In the rock 'n' roll business," Remnick wrote, "you are either on the bus or under it. Playing 'Feelings' with Eddie and the Condos in a buffet bar in Butte is under the bus."[19]

throwing shade *idiom* **1.** To express contempt or disapproval toward someone. **2.** To disrespect, insult, or criticize a person or thing in an artful manner.

> **BS Definition:** To channel your inner Beyoncé and creatively slam your co-worker's font choice on a PowerPoint slide.[20]

> **Origin:** Contrary to popular opinion, the term *throwing shade* isn't quite as recent as one might believe (and, no, it didn't originate with *RuPaul's Drag Race*). Its recent popularity can be credited to the Latino and black gay communities of New York City—more specifically, the drag culture of Harlem—in the late 1980s. In the documentary film *Paris Is Burning*, one of the central characters (a queen named Dorian Corey) explains what shade means: "Shade is I don't tell you you're ugly, but I don't have to tell you because you know you're ugly and that's shade."[21]

> However, actual references to "throwing shade" go back to well before the '80s. In Jane Austen's novel *Mansfield Park*, Edmund Bertram is displeased with a dinner guest's disparagement of the uncle who took her in: "With such warm feelings and lively spirits it must be difficult to do justice to her affection for Mrs. Crawford, without throwing a shade on the Admiral."[22] Yeah, you go, Edmund Bertram. You go.

tiger team *n.* **1.** A team of specialists who work on targeted goals. **2.** In the IT world, a group of experts who test a system by use of hacking strategies to penetrate it.

> **BS Definition:** A bunch of excitable zealots who waste time trying to fix imaginary problems rather than actually work.

Origin: A 1964 Society of Automotive Engineers paper, "Program Management in Design and Development," by J.R. Dempsey, W.A. Davis, A.S. Crossfield, and Walter C. Williams, is considered to contain one of the first documented citations of *tiger team*, defining it as "a team of undomesticated and uninhibited technical specialists, selected for their experience, energy, and imagination, and assigned to track down relentlessly every possible source of failure in a spacecraft subsystem."[23]

toe the line *idiom* 1. To adhere to the rules and standards set by your leader or organization. 2. To conform to the ideas, aims, and principles of a group or person.

BS Definition: What you must do when you're afraid of getting fired.

Origin: While we'd love to say this phrase originates with the famous Rocky Burnette song from 1980, "Tired of Toein' the Line" (it's one of our favorites from that era), unfortunately, we cannot.[24] It's a military term that derives from the practice of soldiers keeping their toes on a line as they submitted to inspections. What's perhaps surprising is that the term goes back to at least the 1700s. Timothy Pickering's 1775 book, *An Easy Plan of Discipline for a Militia*, contains the following passage: "At their first step they must bring all their toes to the line, e g, at the second step they toe the line."[25]

touch base *v.* 1. To contact someone (see *ping*). 2. Another way of saying "talk," "meet," or "visit."

BS Definition: Usually used when the speaker has little intention to set a specific date or time to actually visit.

Origin: American baseball is the source for this phrase. According to the *OED*, the first written reference in a sports page is from the *Lincoln* (Nebraska) *Daily State Journal* newspaper in 1875: "McFarland touched

T

base and put him out." The *OED* says that the first known use of the phrase in a BS context came in 1918, in the publication, *America in France* (by Frederick Palmer), about the U.S. armed forces in France: "He touched base at every desk in headquarters without ever having the chance to discuss the war situation"[26]

troll *v.* **1.** To post a deliberately erroneous or antagonistic message online with the intention of eliciting a hostile or corrective response. **2.** To monitor or attempt to sabotage a competitor's online activities.

or

troll *n.* Someone who deliberately upsets people online to get a reaction.

BS Definition: Who you will most likely have an interaction with if you stay online long enough (see *roll with the punches*).

Origin: The original inspiration for this BS term could stem from a variety of first usages for the word *troll*, including:

   » a means of fishing: "Consider how God by his Preachers trowleth for thee," *A Booke of Angling or Fishing* by Samuel Gardiner (1606).
   » singing in a full, rolling voice: "They speak well out, trolling the words clearly over the tongue," *The Autobiography of Leigh Hunt* by Leigh Hunt (1850).

However, it's the fictional troll character out of Norse mythology and Scandinavian folklore that is most commonly associated with its BS origin. The troll is a being who lives alone, deep in the wilderness and ranges in appearance from monstrous to eccentric and cute. However, no matter how charming they may look, trolls are almost always unfriendly, and encounters with them rarely end well. They've been around since the 1600s, sources say.[36]

Now, fast-forward to the early 1990s and the era of Usenet groups (precursors of the modern Internet forums of today). Back then, *flame wars* was a term more commonly used to refer to vicious and personal online attacks than *trolling*, and *net weenies* was the earliest documented title given to the people responsible.[37] Some sources say it was only after anonymous users on a popular imageboard website called 4chan defined a very specific understanding of the term *troll* that the noun (and verb) version of the word became popular as a way to capture this activity.[38] For these users, trolling was something that one actively chose to do. More important, a troll was something one chose to *be*.[39]

Over the years, a distinctive subculture of people has latched onto that idea by proudly (and we must say, oddly) identifying as trolls. They've used their creative energy to make popular Internet memes, and their exchanges with victims have become online entertainment for some. Matter of fact, the first written reference of trolling online, from the *OED*, suggests that even in 1992 it was turning into a hobby of sorts. From one Usenet group in October 1992: "Maybe after I post it, we could go trolling some more and see what happens."

turn a blind eye *idiom* **1.** To consciously ignore some wrongdoing. **2.** To pretend not to see something.

BS Definition: The opposite of quality assurance (see *QA*).

Origin: Famously, this phrase is attributed to British Admiral Horatio Nelson, who was said to have ignored orders to discontinue the fighting from the more cautious Admiral Sir Hyde Parker during the Battle of Copenhagen in 1801.[40] In ignoring the order, Nelson was thought to have looked through a telescope using his blind eye, thus ensuring he would not see any signal from his superior to withdraw. Nelson continued to press the attack and eventually battled to a truce. Parker, disgraced by the order he gave, eventually was recalled, and Nelson was

T

made the commander in chief of the Baltic.[41] In the biography *The Life of Nelson*, published in 1814, Robert Southey documents Nelson's words and actions at the time:

> "Leave off action? Damn me if I do! You know, Foley," turning to the captain, "I have only one eye,—and I have a right to be blind sometimes:" and then putting the glass to his blind eye, in that mood of mind which sports with bitterness, he exclaimed: "I really do not see the signal."

A great story for sure, and most certainly Nelson deserves credit for popularizing the phrase, but what's pretty clear is that he didn't actually create it.[42] Earlier references exist, according to the *OED*, that are closer to the "turn a blind eye" meaning, including this one from *Practical Discourses Upon Several Divine Subjects, 1st ed.*, by British clergyman and philosopher John Norris (published in 1698, a full century before Nelson's use): "To turn the deaf Ear, and the blind Eye to all those Pomps and Vanities of the World which we ren.c'd at our Baptism."[43] Poor Norris. It seems once Nelson's story got around, people turned a blind eye to this use years before.

turnkey *adj.* **1.** Ready for immediate use. **2.** A common modifier for solutions that are ready to go, out-of-the-box (aka plug and play).

BS Definition: Almost never as easy as just turning a key.

Origin: The word *turnkey* started to appear in books around the 1600s, according to the *OED*, and most observers agree it originally referred to a jailer (the one who literally turned the key on the cell).[44] One early citation comes from the 1655 book *The Reign of King Charles*, by Hamon L'Estrange: "Mr. Atturney was turn-key, pro tempore, and let them in single at one door, and they went away at another."

The use of the term as a jailer continued into the 20th century, but for unknown reasons, it started to take on its BS meaning—"ready for immediate use"—in the 1930s. Indeed, *Webster's New International Dictionary of the English Language* notes the use of the term to describe a job starting in 1934. Fifty years later, in 1984, professor of construction law, Duncan Wallace, gave *turnkey* even more shape in the BS world by defining its use with contracts: "[Turnkey is] . . . a contract where the essential design emanates from, or is supplied by, the Contractor and not the owner, so that the legal responsibility for the design, suitability and performance of the work after completion will be made to rest . . . with the contractor. . . . 'Turnkey' is treated as merely signifying the design responsibility as the contractor's."[45]

Today, the term is applied broadly in business and you'll see it used in a variety of fields, including computers, investments, websites, real estate, drilling, and more.[46]

tycoon *n.* **1.** Someone who has made a fortune in business (aka baron). **2.** A rich, powerful person of great standing and influence (aka mogul).

BS Definition: In today's business world, it's more often than not a 23-year-old who designed an app.

Origin: Deriving from the Japanese word *taikun* (pronounced similarly), with *tai* meaning "great" or "big" and *kun* indicating a prince or lord, *tycoon* entered the English lexicon in 1857.[47] In that year, Commodore Matthew Perry—this was before he starred on *Friends*[48] (see *pulling your leg*)—returned to the United States from Japan, where he had "opened up" the country to the West.[49] Before Perry, Japan had been completely closed off to outsiders, and the commodore—this was before Lionel Richie joined the band[50] (see *pulling your leg*, again)—refused to meet with lesser Japanese officials, insisting instead on "a dignitary of the highest rank in the empire." At the time, Japan was effectively being run by the Tokugawa Shogunate rather than its mostly ceremonial Emperor

Kōmei.[51] The problem was that *shogun* effectively translated into English as "general," so the Japanese made up a completely new term, *taikun*, to fulfill Perry's request. Perry brought the word back to the United States, and it created a certain buzz among President Abraham Lincoln's aides, John Hay and John Nicolay, who would refer to the president as "the tycoon" moving forward.[52] From John Hay's *1861 Diary*: "Gen. Butler has sent an imploring request to the President to be allowed to bag the whole nest of traitorous Maryland Legislators. This the Tycoon forbade." Over time, the term evolved to refer to individuals who were typically neither great, nor a lord or prince, but simply rich.[53]

T

BS BEYOND OUR BORDERS— PART III

Japanese officials making up a new BS word (*tycoon*) to soothe their foreign visitors from the United States is a rare occurrence. Usually outsiders have to learn local customs and sayings then adapt their business communications accordingly.

Take Germany for example. Germany is a country that loves food and shows it in its business speak. In a business meeting in Germany, you might hear someone say they would like to *add their mustard* (to put their two cents in) or be *clear as dumpling broth* (crystal-clear). You definitely don't want to come across as someone who *has tomatoes on one's eyes* (to be oblivious to what is going on around you) or *talks around the hot porridge* (beats around the bush).

However, Germans aren't the only ones who love to talk about food in their BS. Italians will sometimes say, *everything makes soup* as a way to say every little bit helps, and they may describe a nitpicky person as *looking for hairs in the egg*. Portuguese speakers may also use that phrase, as well as *to stuff a sausage* as a way of saying that someone is talking on and on without really saying anything. The Polish say *it's a roll with butter* when they want to say it's really easy, and the Dutch will sometimes mention buying something *for an apple and an egg*, which translates to I bought it very cheaply. The French also like their food-themed BS—*the carrots are cooked!* (the situation can't be changed!).

U

under the radar *idiom* **1.** Going unnoticed. **2.** Doing something without anyone noticing.

BS Definition: Slipping that calculator from work into your computer bag because your child needs it for homework.

Origin: Radar itself—which stands for "radio detection and ranging"— started with experiments by German scientist Heinrich Hertz in the late 19th century. Hertz showed that radio waves could be reflected by metallic objects, but it wasn't until June 17, 1935, that the first radio-based detection and ranging system was first demonstrated in Britain, thanks to the work of Robert Watson-Watt, a physicist specializing in radio waves.[1]

The individual who coined the term *under the radar* is under the radar. The *OED* says the phrase didn't appear in print for the first time until 1981, in the *Washington Post*: "Like some giant weapons system that can come in under the radar, Janet Cooke's invention eluded detection by the normal protective procedures and techniques that are designed to catch more commonplace slides and lapses."

Even so, many believe it's a term that originated during World War II, when combatants discovered that if planes flew low to the ground, they would not be detected by radar because the ground interfered with the signals.[2] The first serious attempt to evade radar detection (ushering in the era of stealth fighters) was perhaps the Horten Ho 229 flying wing fighter bomber developed in the last years of World War II in Nazi Germany.[3] The aircraft, which featured a unique wooden skin that was bonded together using plywood resins, was designed with the purpose of absorbing radar waves. In addition, it could also fly at low altitudes (50–100 feet), meaning it could avoid detection by Britain's radar system at the time.

under the weather *idiom* 1. Sick; not feeling well. 2. With a hangover.

BS Definition: A more discreet way of telling work, "Hi, I've woken up in a place I don't recognize and I'm still hungover. I won't be in the office today."

Origin: This is one of those funny BS terms that makes us feel sorry for any nonnative English speakers trying to understand. ("You say you're 'under the weather.' Does that mean you're pinned down by storm debris or something?") However, once you learn the origin story of this phrase, it starts to make a lot more sense.[4]

Experts suggest that *under the weather* originated from the language of sailors.[5] Back in the day, when storms occurred on the open sea and the water got rough, the seamen would go below deck to ride out the storm so they didn't become seasick. Authors Bill Beavis and Richard G. McCloskey suggest that the term in its entirety is actually "under the weather bow." According to their 2014 book, *Salty Dog Talk: The Nautical Origins of Everyday Expressions*, the weather bow was "the side upon which all the rotten weather is blowing."[6]

The phrase, as we know it, started to pop up in literature in the early 1800s.[7] The *OED* notes an 1827 piece (that wasn't published until 1924) by American colonist and Texas revolutionary war hero Benjamin Rush Milam, in the *Austin Papers*, as its first citation: "The fredonians is all here rather under the wether."[10] By the 20th century, the term became popular enough to be included in dictionary references.

U

unicorn *n.* **1.** Someone with a unique set of skills or experience that makes that person extremely rare and valuable. **2.** A tech startup that is valued at $1 billion or more.

BS Definition: A mythical creature that 10-year-old girls are obsessed with and Silicon Valley entrepreneurs like to pretend they are.

Origin: Of course, we wouldn't have unicorns in the business world without the mythical, horse-like horned animal that has been part of European and Asian folklore for three millennia.[9] The earliest known drawings of what we consider unicorns come from the Indus Valley civilization—those who populated the northwestern regions of South Asia from 3300 to 1300 BC. Later, ancient Greek writer Ctesias, in his 5th century BC book *Indica*, was said to have described unicorns in India as if they were real: "Wild asses, fleet of foot, having a horn a cubit and a half (28 inches) in length, and colored white, red and black."[10]

Surprisingly, it wasn't until recently—more than 2,500 years removed from its first reference in writing—that *unicorn* started to acquire its BS meanings. In 2013, venture capitalist Aileen Lee was looking for a way to describe newly formed, ventured-backed companies that had attained a $1 billion valuation.[11] Because finding these companies was somewhat of a statistical rarity, she published an article on the website TechCrunch in November 2013 that compared members of the club to the mythical creature: "Welcome to the Unicorn Club: Learning From Billion-Dollar Startups."[12] By early 2020, there were 450 companies that had joined the Unicorn Club, according to CB Insights, a tech market intelligence platform. Those companies included famous names such as DoorDash, Airbnb, SpaceX, and Peloton.[13]

U

upper hand *idiom* **1.** To have an advantage or control in a situation. **2.** To be in a dominating or leading position.

> **BS Definition:** To be so poorly paid that you're not a threat to be fired come layoffs.

> **Origin:** There are different theories as to where this phrase comes from. Some believe it originates from whose hand is on top when a couple holds hands, the implication being that the upper hand is that of the dominant person. Others suggest the term comes from the ancient childhood game used to determine who goes first in something: Beginning from the bottom, each player takes a turn grasping a stick or bat with one hand until the last hand on top (aka the upper hand) wins.

> Whatever the case, we know the use of the term itself goes back centuries, at least to the 1400s.[14] The *OED* cites a 1481 document, *Tulle on Old Age*, by John Tiptoft, which contains the following: "Marcus Attilius . . . had the vppirhande and victorye of the men of cartage." There's another "upper hand" example in history from about 100 years later, in 1575 (*An Introduction to the holy Understanding of the Glasse of Righteousnes* by Henry Nicholis), that has how we spell the phrase today: "to a great Miserie, Affliction, Sorrowe, and Heaupnes' over the Children of Men. For the wickednes hath the Upper Hand."

> It's interesting to note, reading this, that, even though times have changed from 400+ years ago, people still worry about some of the same things—namely, that wickedness "hath the Upper Hand."

upshot *n.* **1.** The benefit or outcome of something. **2.** The gist of an argument or thesis (see *takeaway*).

> **BS Definition:** Upshot? It's more like *upchuck* when some people hear this word.

U

Origin: Most agree that this word, dating back to the 16th century, derived from archery, in which an upshot was the word given to the final shot in a match. By 1603, it was in Shakespeare's *Hamlet* as a way to communicate the final result: "And in this upshot, purposes mistooke, Falne on the Inventors heads." But why did they call the final shot of an archery match an "upshot" to begin with? There are quite a few theories out there.[15] Some believe it was because the matches back then were big deals, affecting the social standing of the men who took part, so if a fellow won a given round on the final shot, he would move "up" in standing in the game and in society. Others suggest that "up" was simply referring to the end of the match, similar to the construction of "time's up." The upshot of all this conjecture? It has successfully given you something to ponder the next time you hear the word *upshot*.

USP *n.* U-S-P **1.** Acronym for "unique selling point (or proposition)." **2.** A term used commonly in marketing to define what makes your product different and beneficial to customers.

BS Definition: Beneficial to have when the phrase *because we said so* doesn't work.

Origin: The concept of a "unique selling proposition" was the brainchild of Rosser Reeves, an American pioneer of television advertising, who believed consumers had unique reasons why they bought a particular product.[16] Reeves first proposed the "USP" in the early 1940s at Ted Bates & Company, where he was chairman, as a way to explain successful advertising campaigns. His theory was that successful ads defined a unique product benefit to the customer and then used that benefit to help the product stand out from the competition. Once you found your USP, Reeves said, everything else was just wordsmithing.

U

The slogans that Reeves's teams created using this technique survive even today, such as M&M's "melts in your mouth, not in your hand."[17] In 1958, Reeves defined the USP concept for the first time in print in a book titled *Madison Avenue, USA*, by Martin Mayer: "There are three rules for a USP. First, you need a definite proposition. . . . Then, second, it must be a unique proposition. . . . Third, the proposition must sell."[18]

U

V

value add *n.* **1.** The added value. **2.** A benefit that results in greater acceptance of something.

BS Definition: Putting a word at the end of another word for-add no-add real-add reason-add.

Origin: In terms of first mention—where the two words *value* and *add* appear together—one early reference comes from Sir Isaac Newton's *Tables for Renewing and Purchasing of Leases* (published posthumously in 1735). The renowned mathematician used a line item in a table labeled as "The 2 Years Value add, viz." when discussing the addition of rents year-over-year.

Most experts think *value add*, as we know it in its BS context today, evolved from the term *value-added*.[1] However, none of these sources has hard evidence for a direct connection. The oldest of the possible relations is from economics, where the *OED* says *value-added* was first written about in 1873 as a way to describe the amount by which the value of an article is increased at each stage of its production, exclusive of the cost of materials and bought-in parts and services.

The telecommunications and computing industry has a term called *value-added network*—which describes a system that provides services (like email) in addition to a standard telephone system—that was first labeled in writing in 1974, according to the *OED*. Valued-added also applies to shareholder value—specifically any action that increases profits (or adds value) for the people who own a company[2]—refining raw goods, and the reselling process as well. The value add of all these possibilities? Looking for the origin of value add can keep you busy for a while.

vertical *n.* A group of companies and customers that are all interconnected around a specific niche.

or

vertical *adj.* When a company buys and controls other businesses along its supply chain.

> **BS Definition:** When you use this word in business, some may want to lay you out horizontal.

> **Origin:** In business today, there are two primary ways vertical is used. The first use is *vertical market*—sometimes shortened to just the vertical, reflecting the first definition (the noun version).[3] The second is in *vertical integration*—sometimes said as just "going vertical," reflecting the second definition (the adjective version).[4]

> *Vertical* originated as a mathematical term in the 1500s. In 1704, it started to appear as a way to describe anything that was straight up and down.[5]

> *Vertical integration* was first used as a business practice in the late 1800s by none other than the great industrialist Andrew Carnegie. Carnegie used this approach to acquire, basically, the entire supply and distribution chain for the Carnegie Steel Company (ore and coal mines on the supply end, railroad and shipping companies on the distribution end).[6] Some sources claim Carnegie coined this phrase, but the earliest reference to vertical integration cited by the *OED* is not from Carnegie, but rather the London newspaper *Westminster Gazette*, in 1920: "The vertical Trusts constructed by Stumm, Thyssen and the other raw-material magnates."

> Who coined the vertical market term is not definitive either, although the earliest written mention we found is from 1940 in *Brewer's Digest, Vol. 15* from Siebel Publishing Company: "One of the simplest plans for supervising both horizontal and vertical markets is as follows. . . .

V

After the horizontal market area is established, the next step is a vertical market analysis." The *OED* cites an even earlier reference to vertical—in 1927's *Social Mobility* by Pitirim Aleksandrovich Sorokin—that may apply to this use of the word as well: "There are two principal types of social mobility, horizontal and vertical."

VIP *n.* V-I-P **1.** Abbreviation for "very important person" (see *honcho, KOL,* or *tycoon*). **2.** A person who is given special privileges or access because of status or importance (see *Master of the Universe, influencer,* or *rock star*).

> **BS Definition: 1.** The person at your workplace with the best view out the window. **2.** If your life involves velvet ropes, first-class travel, and fancy celebrity pals, then you, my friend, are a VIP. If it involves long lines, mind-numbing commutes, and eating your lunch out of Tupperware, then you're probably like the rest of us—just "important," but not "very."

> **Origin:** While the term *VIP* is more modern, the concept of a "very important person" goes back to 1839. A British journal, *The Analyst: A Quarterly Journal of Science, Literature, Natural History, and Fine Arts*, introduced the idea this way:

>> and we all sat around the low hearth, discussing the best thing to be done; the good people regretting that they had no accommodation to offer, and advising us to go on still to the village, which was not more than a quarter of an hour distant, and where we should be more comfortable than anywhere else in the neighborhood, since there was a house built of stone and belong-to a rich and very important person.[7]

Experts believe it was the military that gave us the shortening of this phrase into VIP—using it as shorthand to describe high-ranking officials or dignitaries. The first person to mention it in writing was a man who served in British Intelligence in the eastern Mediterranean during World War I and was later accused of giving away state secrets in a book he wrote in 1932 called *Greek Memories*.[8] Compton Mackenzie followed up that book in 1933 with an absurdist spy-novel parody, *Water on the Brain*, in which the following passage appears:

> "At the moment he has a VIP with him" . . . Miss Glidden seemed to divine his perplexity, for she turned round and whispered through a pursed up mouth, "Very Important Personage."

virus *n.* **1.** A self-replicating computer program that's harmful to routine computer use. **2.** An unauthorized program that embeds itself into a computer system and interferes with normal operations.

BS Definition: 1. What caused your computer to do those things that made *The Exorcist* look tame. **2.** What Steve brought into the office when he refused to call in sick.

Origin: "I'm the creeper, catch me if you can!" Called "the Creeper," this experimental self-replicating program was the first computer virus ever written. It was produced in 1971 by a man named Bob Thomas, who wanted to test a theory first proposed by mathematician John von Neumann in 1949.[9] However, it would be a few years before this practice was labeled a "virus." To understand that journey, you have to go back to around the year 1400.

That's when *virus* was used for the first time in the English language. It came from the world of medicine as a way to describe the discharge from a wound.[10] This from *Science of Cirurgie* by Lanfranc of Milan:

V

"If þe virus be wiþoute heete . . . waische it [an ulcer] wiþ watir." By the 1700s, virus evolved into more of a figurative term for anything that spread infection. John Heneage Jesse wrote the following in 1778's *George Selwyn and His Contemporaries: with Memoirs and Notes*: "Venice is a stink-pot, charged with the very virus of hell!" (Uh, wow. Jesse *really* hated Venice, huh? Anyway...) Fast-forward to modern times, more specifically 1983, at the University of Southern California (USC), and you have the next chapter in this story.

Len Adleman was a teacher at USC who liked to call self-reproducing computer programs "viruses" because of their ability to "infect" computer systems. One of his students, Fred Cohen, wrote a paper that leaned on that language, called "Computer Viruses—Theory and Experiments." Cohen would go on to a prolific career developing cybersecurity techniques, and the popularity of the *virus* term would grow with him. Likewise with Adleman, who went on to become one of the creators of the R.S.A. encryption algorithm, a popular means used by modern computers to encrypt and decrypt messages.[11]

BS FROM BASEBALL

You're correct if you've noticed a fair amount of baseball terms influencing our *BS Dictionary*. The game is the source of many words and phrases in the United States. Besides the ones we've defined in this book, here are a few more that come from the sport known as "America's pastime."

swinging for the fences	trying to accomplish something extraordinary
hit and run	to cause a traffic accident and then leave without taking responsibility
rain check	a promise to fulfill an offer at a later time
cover all the bases	to review all the possible things that can or will happen
off base	wrong or misguided
pinch hitter	standing in for someone else
out of one's league	trying to achieve something that you're incapable of doing

W

WIIFM *idiom* WIIF-M **1.** Abbreviation for "What's in it for me?" **2.** A focus on defining the benefits of something for your audience.

> **BS Definition:** Kind of the opposite of *it takes a village*.

> **Origin:** The origin of this expression goes back to at least the early 20th century, as part of an effort for sobriety. In January 1909, John M. Sutherland wrote an oft-cited poem about self-indulgent drunkards in *The Temperance Cause*—a publication of the Massachusetts Total Abstinence Society (sounds like a fun group)—with the following passage: "The saloon-keepers may all be very nice men, but what is there in it for me? I blow in my money, and wake in the Pen, but what is there in it for me? . . . All over this country, we're swimming in booze, but what is there in it for me?"[1]

> Good question, John. Here's another one for you: Who turned "What's in it for me?" into the BS acronym of WIIFM? If you find out, let us know, please, because we're unaware.

What is the ask? *questioning phrase* **1.** A request to define the request. **2.** An effort to define the price of something.

> **BS Definition:** Nouning a word that some people say should only be used as a verb.

> **Origin:** Some have suggested that the BS version of this phrase debuted as an investment term related to stock trading, where the bid is the price at which a broker will buy your stock, and the ask is the price at which

you will sell.[2] However, according to the *OED*, ask, as a noun, dates back centuries, with its earliest citations happening about 1,000 years ago. It is believed that ask became a noun because no one had invented the word *request* at that time—at least not until the 14th century, when it was borrowed from the French.

How exactly does all that transform into the BS phrase *What is the ask?* you ask? Well, according to the *OED*, the BS meaning of the ask first demonstrated itself in *The Bulletin*, a Sydney, Australia, periodical, in April 1975: "I mean, Gulcher, I'm a top earner . . . A big ask, though. They wanted a grand."[3] Then, in 1996, the book *Asking Properly: The Art of Creative Fundraising*, by George Smith, presented a potential milestone event that led to the development of the full phrase.[4] Smith says it happened at the International Fundraising Workshop in Holland, when fellow Brit, Bernard Ross, made a presentation called "Making the Ask." Smith writes, "Soon the new noun became modish. 'What's the ask?' queried the writer in search of a brief. 'Here's the ask' said the agency-wallah making the presentation. 'I think we should vary the ask,' said everyone."

wheelhouse *n.* **1.** In your area of expertise or interest (aka sweet spot). **2.** A skill or task that plays to your strengths (aka shooting fish in a barrel).

BS Definition: The thing you'd do even if the business world never paid you . . . and, unfortunately, rarely does.

Origin: The earliest use of the word *wheelhouse* comes from the world of farming. An 1808 book (*General View of the Agriculture of the County of Devon* by Charles Vancouver) about agriculture in the English countryside suggests it was a term applied to the building where, simply enough, wheels for carts were stored: "The wheel-house under the barn, 25 feet square." The word also has strong 19th-century nautical roots, whereby it was used to describe the structure in which the steering wheel of a vessel is housed.[5] This from 1835's *The South-West* by Joseph Holt Ingraham: "The pilot stands in his lonely wheel-house." However, most sources say it is the use of wheelhouse in baseball that is the likely culprit for its BS meaning.[6]

For whatever reason—perhaps because it is the heart of a hitter's strike zone, just like a wheelhouse is the heart of a ship[7]—the term *wheelhouse* started to be used in the 1950s as a way to describe a hitter's most advantageous area for a pitch at the plate. From the *San Francisco Chronicle* in 1959: "He had a couple that came right into the wheelhouse—the kind he used to knock out of sight—and he fouled 'em off." Then, a few decades later, the *OED* says *wheelhouse* finally started to appear in its figurative use in the BS world. One example comes from *Musician* magazine in 1987: "He told me he couldn't play reggae. Of course he *could*, but it wasn't his wheelhouse, and he wanted to keep his playing honest."[8]

white elephant *n.* **1.** An expensive, but impractical, gift that cannot be easily disposed of. **2.** A business or an investment that is unable to turn a profit because it is so expensive to operate and maintain. **3.** A party game where amusing, impractical gifts are exchanged.

BS Definition: The reason your boss has a coffee mug in the shape of a toilet bowl.

Origin: The King of Siam (now Thailand) may be the reason this BS term exists. As (an unconfirmed) legend has it, when visitors to his court displeased him, the king would gift that a person an albino elephant. These white elephants were considered sacred and couldn't be used for work, so taking care of one could easily wipe out your wealth with upkeep costs.[9] This story appeared in England in the 1600s, and the *OED* says *white elephant* first appeared metaphorically in writing in 1721 in the *London Journal*: "In short, Honour and Victory are generally no more than white Elephants; and for white Elephants the most destructive Wars have been often made."

According to another unconfirmed legend, the co-founder of Cornell University also plays a role in how *white elephant* entered the lexicon.[10] In the late 1820s, Ezra Cornell, who also founded Western Union, was allegedly fond of throwing lavish parties including "white elephant" gift exchanges where guests were given bad, pointless gifts as a form of amusement.

Today, these exchanges are popular in U.S. workplaces at the holidays and are sometimes called Yankee Swaps or Dirty Santa.[11] Our advice if you end up in one such "white elephant" gift exchange? Run. However, if you must participate, make sure you buy a cool Yoda bottle opener that everyone will remember and not a Chia pet!

white space *n.* **1.** The place where business needs exist, but there are no services or products present to address them. **2.** The blank areas of a page used as an element of layout and design.

BS Definition: The blank areas of your work page that are excellent spaces to doodle in as someone talks to you.

Origin: This is another term that can have multiple meanings in business depending on the context. Originally, white space (also called negative space) was an aesthetic element in print design where the empty space provided relief and focus to the things it surrounded. One early reference to this kind of white space comes from the book, *A Compleat System of Opticks: A Mechanical Treatise (Book III)*, edited by Robert Smith, from 1738. The *OED* reports that 150 years later (in 1888), the *The Clothier & Furnisher* magazine made this reference to that meaning: "I make liberal use of white space about advertisements and above and below display lines."

Today, white space is talked about quite a bit in designing website pages as well as identifying business opportunities. The latter meaning was promoted in 2009 when author Mark Johnson wrote about it in his book,

Seizing the White Space: Business Model Innovation for Growth and Renewal. Indeed, a year later, then-AOL CEO Tim Armstrong borrowed the term—"We see local as the big white space"—as a way to describe his company's decision to expand local news coverage, and others began using the term to describe business opportunities available online.[12]

white-collar *adj.* **1.** Involving nonmanual labor, usually performed in an office setting. **2.** Characteristic of an administrative, managerial, or clerical worker.

BS Definition: 1. Not to be confused with *alabaster-collar*, which is one or two collars steps *above* white collar. They deal in nothing but Gucci, Maybachs, and Jimmy Choos. **2.** Contrary to popular opinion, the word "crime" doesn't always follow white-collar. That said, there's a reason the phrase is pretty popular.

Origin: Upton Sinclair, the famed American writer, is often credited with popularizing the term white-collar in 1919 with the publication of *Brass Check: A Study of American Journalism.*[13] In that book he describes workers who went to office jobs: "The petty underlings of the business world, the poor office-clerks who, because they are allowed to wear a white collar . . . regard themselves as members of the capitalist class."[14] Sinclair certainly had influence in American society by that time. His 1906 novel, *The Jungle*, which exposed labor and sanitary conditions in the U.S. meatpacking industry, contributed at least partially to the passage of the 1906 Pure Food and Drug Act and the Meat Inspection Act.[15]

However, the term *white-collar* had existed for a few years before Sinclair's use.[16] The *OED* says it dates back to at least 1910, with this mention from the *Logansport* (Indiana) *Daily Reporter* on August 20: "He follows the lure of the white collar to the city and gets a job in which he can wear a white collar all the week." Another early metaphorical reference comes from Malcolm McDowell, a chairperson at the Association of Commerce in Chicago, who was quoted as saying the following in *Chicago Commerce* on May 8, 1914: "The white collar men are your clerks; they are your bookkeepers, your cashiers, your office men. We call them the 'white collar men' in order to distinguish them from the men who work with uniform and overalls and carry the dinner pails."

In recent times, the term *white-collar crime* has become common.[17] First coined by criminologist Edwin Sutherland in 1939, it was defined as "a crime committed by a person of respectability and high social status in the course of his occupation."[18] In everyday terms, it refers to nonviolent offenses, such as bribery, money laundering, fraud, electronic theft, embezzlement, income-tax evasion, and insider trading.

wiggle room *n.* **1.** Space to negotiate or operate. **2.** Freedom of action.

BS Definition: What you wish you had after missing an important project deadline.

Origin: The shoes on your feet may be the reason *wiggle room* exists in our language. The earliest written citations of the phrase appeared in shoe advertising in the 1940s. *Wiggle room* and *wriggle room* were used as a way to sell the benefits of toe space in shoes.[19] Indeed, the *OED* says the first known mention comes from a 1941 advertisement that ran in the *Reno Evening Gazette* newspaper in Nevada on September 3: "Pumps look petite . . . give you lots of wiggle room."

According to William Safire, the late speechwriter and *New York Times* columnist on language, *wiggle room* came of age as a BS term in the 1970s through the world of politics. He cites the first use as a story from *Businessweek*, September 11, 1978: "'Congress has drafted regulatory legislation in a way that gives agencies . . . as little 'wiggle room' as possible." *Newsweek*, he noted, followed a week later with: "When it came to plugging Demo-

cratic candidates, Rosalynn Carter was sensitive enough to give each a little
wiggle room—to dodge clear of her husband's political liabilities."[20]

However, we found an even earlier reference—in *Life* magazine, July 17,
1969, in an interview with then-Secretary of State, Dean Rusk, in which
he says, "I'm skeptical about gadgetry in procedure. You have to have a
great deal of wiggle room to take into account, say, a coup in Ghana that
unseats Nkrumah or a Russian decision to go into Czechoslovakia."[21] In
addition, the *OED* says the oldest citation in our BS context is from a
more obscure publication, the *Gettysburg Times* in Pennsylvania, in April
1965: "Clark said 'We've gone about to the outer limit' in military action
against the Communist guerillas. He said he wants 'wiggle room' left for
negotiations to avoid a major war."

Given this new evidence, we're sure even the late William Safire would have
wanted some wiggle room to change his origin history on this BS term.

wild goose chase *idiom* **1.** A foolish, useless, or hopeless quest (see *herding cats/squirrels*). **2.** A hopeless enterprise for something unattainable (see
red herring).

> **BS Definition:** When you're sent to a restau-
> rant to pick up food for the office and the navigation
> system takes you to a gas station instead.

> **Origin:** One of the many phrases introduced (or popularized)
> in the lexicon by William Shakespeare, *wild goose chase* first appears
> in *Romeo and Juliet* (1597), during a conversation between Romeo and
> Mercutio, in which the latter says: "Nay, if thy wits run the wild-goose
> chase, I have done, for thou hast more of the wild-goose in one of thy
> wits than, I am sure, I have in my whole five. Was I with you there
> for the goose?" Like most of Shakespeare, it sounds pretty, but it's also
> nice to have a modern translation of his words to better understand it.

258 | The BS Dictionary

According to Sparknotes's No Fear Shakespeare series, in today's words, Mercutio might be saying, "Now, if our jokes go on a wild-goose chase, I'm finished. You have more wild goose in one of your jokes than I have in five of mine. Was I even close to you in the chase for the goose?"[22]

Unlike a lot of the terms credited to him, historians say Shakespeare didn't invent *wild goose chase*; rather, he borrowed it from an existing expression. It's said to have evolved from a type of race in which horses followed a lead horse at a set distance, mimicking the formation of wild geese.[23] We could go on a wild goose chase tracking down the very first reference to that kind of race, but we think it best to leave it with another well-known phrase from *Romeo and Juliet*: "Parting is such sweet sorrow that I shall say goodnight till it be morrow."

win-win *n.* **1.** A situation where both sides benefit. **2.** Good for everyone involved.

BS Definition: The opposite of the Kobayashi Maru. (Don't worry, it's a *Star Trek* nerd joke. . . .)

Origin: The Internet is a wonderful resource for information. The problem with it is, you can't always trust the information you get—even when it comes from multiple sites (see *straight from the horse's mouth*). *Win-win* is an example of that situation.[24] Several online sources say negotiation expert Herb Cohen coined the term in 1963 while teaching about negotiations in a two-week course for claims adjusters and attorneys sponsored by his employer, Allstate Insurance Company.[25] However, the *OED* says the first written reference to "win-win" was a year before that in *Deterrence, Arms Control & Disarmament*, by J.D. Singer: "In zero-sum games, every win for one side is a loss for the other; there can be no such thing as a 'win-win' outcome. . . . Objectively, a win-win outcome was available, but the prisoners played as if it were not."[26] So, while Cohen may have helped popularize the term with his work, he certainly did not originate it. That means our research on *win-win* is more like a lose-lose for those sites that list Cohen as the source for it. Sorry.

witch hunt *n.* **1.** The act of unfairly looking for and punishing people who are accused of minor crimes or having opposing views to your own. **2.** A campaign directed against a person or group holding unorthodox or unpopular views.

BS Definition: What you conduct in the office when someone talks smack about you to your boss (aka opening up a can of whoop-ass).

Origin: If you lived in Europe or colonial North America from about 1450 to 1750, your sport options were pretty limited. You could maybe go horseback riding, do some archery, or, if you were really lucky, hunt some  witches! "Witch hunts"—in which (innocent) people labeled as witches were sought out, with many burned in ritual ceremonies—lasted centuries in Europe and North America, resulting in anywhere from 35,000 to 100,000 executions. Amazingly, witch hunts still occur in some countries in sub-Saharan Africa and Papua New Guinea, and legislation against witchcraft can still be found in Saudi Arabia and Cameroon.[27]

The first written reference to "the sport of witch-hunting" was in 1637 in a book by Benjamin Jonson called, aptly enough, *The Workes of Benjamin Jonson*: "You speake Alken, as if you knew the sport of Witch-hunting, Or starting of a Hag."[28] One of the earliest figurative references comes from *King Solomon's Mines*, the popular 1885 novel by Sir H. Rider Haggard. In the book, protagonist Allan Quartermain exclaims: "Alas! the land cries out with his [King Twala's] cruelties. Tonight ye will see. It is the great witch-hunt, and many will be smelt out as wizards and slain. No man's life is safe."[29]

A name that has become synonymous with a metaphorical "witch hunt" in the United States is Joseph McCarthy. The former U.S. senator from Wisconsin spearheaded a movement in the 1950s attempting to root out Communism in the United States. McCarthy accused hundreds of prominent figures of having sympathies for the political ideology. The chief counsel for the army, Joe Welch, effectively finished off this campaign (and McCarthy's career) when he famously told the senator live on television: "Have you no decency, sir, at long last? Have you no sense of decency left?"[30]

with a grain of salt *idiom* **1.** To take a statement with a certain amount of reserve. **2.** View something with a skeptical attitude.

BS Definition: How you listen to pretty much any sales pitch.

Origin: Pliny the Elder is the person must commonly credited with the invention of this phrase. Pliny was a famed naval and army commander of the early Roman empire.[31] In his book *Naturalis Historia (Natural History)*, published around AD 77 to 79, one translation of a passage reads as follows:

> After the defeat of that mighty monarch, Mithridates, Gnaeus
> Pompeius found in his private cabinet a recipe for an antidote in
> his own handwriting; it was to the following effect: Take two dried
> walnuts, two figs, and twenty leaves of rue; pound them all together,
> with the addition of a grain of salt; if a person takes this mixture
> fasting, he will be proof against all poisons for that day.[32]

The suggestion of this passage is that the ill-effects of a poison could be moderated "with the addition of a grain of salt."[33]

However, others—such as Amy Ione in her 2016 book, *Art and the Brain*[34]—suggest that this phrase was actually mistranslated, leading to Pliny being credited as the inventor of this phrase incorrectly. Regardless, the phrase doesn't show up until centuries later in its wider, metaphorical form as a means of taking a statement with a healthy dose of skepti-

W

cism. In 1647, English theologian John Trapp wrote in *A Commentary or Exposition Upon All the Epistles and the Revelation of John the Divine*: "To know nothing is the bravest life, as the Greek prov. hath it. But this must be taken with a grain of salt."[35] We're not sure exactly what Trapp meant back then, but that's perhaps why—and aptly so—we should take the origin of this phrase with a grain of salt as well.

with all due respect *idiom* **1.** A polite phrase used to mitigate the effect of criticism. **2.** Used to precede an expression of disagreement.

> **BS Definition:** Usually used when you're about to show *zero* respect to someone.

> **Origin:** Some have suggested that this phrase comes from the legal world, where an arguer for a case showed "respect" to the opponent using these words.[36] The phrase itself goes back centuries, to at least the early 1600s. The *OED* cites the first reference as 1614 in a work called *The Hogge Hath Lost His Pearle*, by Robert Tailor: "With all respect Sir, pray commaund my house." Some have suggested the first written reference to this phrase actually came one year earlier (in 1613), in a book called *Purgatories Triumph Over Hell, Maugre the Barking of Cerberus in Sir Edward Hobyes Counter-Snarle, a Letter to the Sayd Knight from I. R.* (yes, that's the whole title), by John Patrick Flood.[37] With all due respect to those people, we can't find a credible online source that backs up that claim, however, so we're going to just say the *OED*'s 1614 reference is the accurate one. Again, with all due respect (you're wrong).

wolf in sheep's clothing *idiom* **1.** A person who conceals bad intentions under an appearance of friendliness (see *with all due respect*). **2.** An enemy pretending to be a friend.

> **BS Definition:** The CEO of the company that just bought yours.

Origin: Score one for the Bible! This saying comes from Matthew 7:15. Being the Lebron James fans that we are (see *straight and narrow*), let us once again refer to the King James version of the Bible for this one: "Beware of false prophets, which come to you in sheep's clothing, but inwardly they are ravening wolves." The *OED* cites two examples from the 15th century that mark its earliest references outside of the Bible. The first is from the year 1400 from *Roman Rose*: "Who-so toke a wethers skin, And wrapped a gredy wolf therin." The second is from 1460's *Wisdom* from *The Macro Plays*: "Ther ys a wolffe in a lombys skyn."[38]

worth one's salt *idiom* **1.** Efficient or capable. **2.** Deserving respect in a certain field or area.

BS Definition: Usually expressed negatively, as in, "He's not worth his salt," and is a good substitute for terms like *moron*, *ignoramus*, and *out to lunch*.

Origin: Salt is one of the most necessary ingredients for life. It not only preserves food, but also regulates the balance of fluid in our bodies. Simply put, without salt, we would all die. Because of its high value, historians say, it was the first major commodity exchanged among civilizations, often pound-for-pound with gold. Indeed, the English word *salary* is derived from the Latin word of *salarium*, which means "of salt."[39]

So, it makes sense *worth one's salt* would become a popular way to capture a person's value in the workplace. The *OED* says it was 1830 (*King's Own* by Frederick Marryat[40]) when the phrase was used for the first time in writing. However, the U.K. website Phrase Finder doesn't think that reference is worth its salt. It quotes one from 1805's *The African Memoranda*, a report on an expedition to Guinea Bissau, by Philip Beaver: "Bennet has never done anything but crawl about the block-house; Hayles has been my most useful man, but of late not worth his salt."[41] Furthermore, a few years

W

later (1808), a reference to a female being "worth her salt" appears in the book *Miss Balmaine's Past*, by Bithia Mary Croker: "As a nurse, she might be worth her salt, and help alleviate other people's sufferings."[42]

writing is on the wall *idiom* **1.** Signs or omens that things are about to get bad. **2.** Hints that a lousy outcome is happening.

BS Definition: What your co-workers may say to you *after* you're fired, as if they knew it was going to happen (but didn't bother to tell you). #EveryoneKnewButYou.

Origin: Did we mention the Bible is a popular source for BS terms? (See the sidebar on page 123.) Well, it is, and this phrase is more proof of that.

Writing is on the wall comes from Daniel 5:25 in the Old Testament. It tells the story of Belshazzar, the king of Israel, who had sinned against God by worshipping false idols, stealing from a temple in Jerusalem, and then throwing a feast with the stolen items present (sounds like classic *influencer* behavior to us, but anyway . . .). During the festivities, the fingers of a mysterious man's hand appear and write on the wall the following words: *mene, mene, tekel, upharsin.*[43] Belshazzar, who can't read the writing (again, typical *influencer*), sends for Daniel, who is renowned for his wisdom. Daniel interprets the phrase for the king and tells him, basically, that his days are numbered (which they were).[44]

According to the Phrase Finder website, the idea "the writing is on the wall" began to be used figuratively—that is, warnings of bad things coming with no actual writing or walls involved—in the early 18th century. It cites one example as Jonathan Swift's *Miscellaneous Works*, from 1720:

> A baited Banker thus desponds
> From his own Hand foresees his Fall;
> They have his Soul who have his Bonds;
> 'Tis like the Writing on the Wall."[45]

X

X factor *n.* **1.** A special, indefinable feeling that sets someone apart from all the others. **2.** An appealing quality that can't be adequately described.

BS Definition: What they said you were missing when you asked why you were overlooked for a promotion.

Origin: No, we're not talking about the Simon Cowell reality TV show, the Marvel comic book series, the bleeding disorder, or even the album by Iron Maiden.[1] We're talking about the origin of the BS term that goes back to the 1930s and even further. To get there, we must first review a little math (aka buzzkill).

A factor is any number that divides into another number exactly (with no remainders).[2] In mathematical equations, the letter x is commonly assigned to an unknown factor (for example, x − 2 = 1). That means then that the term *x factor* is an unknown factor that needs to be solved in an equation. It's certainly plausible the BS term *X factor*, in its current use today, originated from such equations. After all, determining the X factor does have a certain *je ne sais quoi* to it.

There's no record of who exactly coined the term for use outside of math, but we do know that the phrase started to take on its greater metaphorical use—in everything from philosophy to forestry—beginning in the 1930s.[3] The *OED* cites its earliest non-mathematical mention as coming from The *New York Times* on January 21, 1930: "We have to deal here with an unknown element in the disease. It is the same X factor which so regularly arises to sober man's pride."

X

xerox *v.* **1.** To copy or reproduce. **2.** To photocopy something.

BS Definition: Something you sit on to make photocopies of your butt.

Origin: The word *xerox* begins its origin story in 1936 in the law libraries of New York Law School. That's where a law student by the name of Chester Carlson started investigating ways to make copying notes from his law books easier than writing them out longhand. After conducting several smelly (and occasionally explosive) experiments in his apartment kitchen, Carlson invented a process for printing images called electrophotography. A few years later, in 1946, the Haloid Photographic Company of Rochester, New York, saw the commercial promise of Carlson's invention and signed an agreement with him to develop it. Looking for a term to differentiate its new system, Haloid coined the term *xerography* from two Greek roots meaning "dry writing" and then abbreviated it to just the word *xerox*. Haloid subsequently changed its name to Haloid Xerox in 1958 and then Xerox Corporation in 1961.

In 1963, Xerox introduced the first desktop plain-paper copier and the company started to take off, becoming synonymous with photocopying in the business world.[4] The *OED* says the first evidence of *xerox* as a verb was in 1966 in the book *Helen*, by E.V. Cunningham: "Anything you want copies of, why we'll Xerox it out."[5]

BS AND BRAND NAMES

Xerox and *dumpster fire* are just two examples of company brand names that have become synonymous with business speak. The BS world is littered with several other examples. Think about it, how many times have you said something like this lately.

FedEx and UPS	"I'll FedEx/UPS it to you first thing tomorrow morning."
Google	"I googled it and found the solution."
Skype	"I'll Skype you so we can talk."
Tweet (from Twitter)	"The boss loves tweeting out his thoughts late at night."
Uber	"Let's just Uber it from the airport."
Velcro	"I velcroed it together to make it stay."

Y

yada yada *idiom* **1.** Further details that are trivial and uninteresting, usually said dismissively (akin to phrases such as *blah, blah, blah*). **2.** Predictable, inconsequential.

BS Definition: Usually said when recounting IT's reason for your work computer not getting fixed until next week.

Origin: What *blah blah blah* was to the early 20th century, *yada yada* was to the late 20th century. The phrase really took hold in the modern American lexicon after the TV show *Seinfeld* aired a popular episode in 1997 that focused on the phrase, but it was prevalent before then.[1]

The Phrase Finder website says it emerged during or just after World War II, and was preceded by alternative forms of the phrase—*yatata, yatata; yaddega, yaddega*; and so forth. It cites an advertisement in the August 1948 edition of the *Long Beach* (California) *Independent* newspaper as the earliest evidence of it in writing: "Yatata . . . yatata . . . the talk is all about Chatterbox, Knox's own little Tomboy Cap with the young, young come-on look!"[2]

In the 1960s, famous comedian Lenny Bruce became synonymous with the phrase after he used it on his bestselling comedy album, *Essential Lenny Bruce*: "They're no good, the lot of them—'Yaddeyahdah'—They're animals!" We could go on about other places this phrase has been mentioned or written up since, but, yada yada, you get the point.

yak shaving *idiom* **1.** Performing a task that leads you to perform another related task and so on until you are distracted from your original goal (#GoingDownARabbitHole). **2.** An annoying succession of tasks you need to accomplish in order to get to your actual goal.

BS Definition: To say something so obscure that even you have to google it from time to time to remind yourself what it means.

Origin: Honestly, we hesitated even including this term, but the fact that some use it is probably evidence that we've all lost our collective minds (and that we needed another BS term to fill out the *Y* section of this book).

Yak shaving was coined by Carlin Vieri, an MIT PhD, who was inspired by a 1991 episode of *The Ren & Stimpy Show*.[3] The "Yak Shaving Day" story line involves a Christmas-like holiday where participants hang diapers instead of stockings, stuff rubber boots with coleslaw, and watch for a shaven yak to float by in his enchanted canoe.[4] Vieri explained how "yak shaving" applied to business in an interview with an American Express blogger and developer, Donovan West, in 2018:

> "Yak shaving" should be things that are related to your primary objective, not just distractions. . . . [for example,] where tools are out of date, or there are other minor hurdles that take you on a path away from your primary task, but that can be traced back to that task.[5]

Z

(a) **zero** *n.* **1.** A loser. **2.** Someone or something that is of no value.

BS Definition: If you're ever called this by someone at work, counter with "I'm rubber. You're glue. Everything you say bounces off me and sticks to you." It works *every time*.

Origin: If anyone ever calls you "a zero," know that it may be the biggest compliment you ever get, for the invention of the zero in mathematics is widely considered one of the greatest innovations in human history. Without the zero, there would be no Renaissance, no moon landing, no personal computer. The concept of zero—to represent the absence of a number—has been around since ancient times. However, it took two millennia for  "zero," as we know and use it, to really come into being. In seventh-century India, an astronomer named Brahmagupta started to promote the idea of zero (*shunya*) as not only a placeholder to signify nothing in a position, but also a number by itself that you could use in calculations.[1] This idea spurred a whole new field of mathematics that led to new knowledge and discoveries. Once this understanding of zero gained traction in South Asia, it crossed into the Middle East, where it was championed by Islamic scholars, and created part of the Arabic number system.

However, zero faced a real struggle crossing into Europe because, at the same time, the Christian crusades were going against Islam. Any Arab ideas, even in mathematics, were met with widespread skepticism and mistrust. For example, in 1299, zero was banned in Florence, Italy—along with all Arabic numerals—because it was said to encourage fraud. In addition, zero was seen as the gateway to negative numbers, which legitimized the concept of debt and money lending.[2] Thankfully, cooler (and smarter) heads prevailed in the 15th century, and zero, along with all the other Arabic numbers, was finally accepted, going from "zero to hero" in history.[3]

The *OED* says the first written use of *zero*, in its BS context of describing a loser, happened in this bit of 1650 smack-talk from *The Power of the Christian Magistrate in Sacred Things*, by Lewis Du Moulin: "This makes the Magistrate but a cipher or zero in sacred things" (see *throwing shade*).

zeitgeist *n.* **1.** The defining spirit of the time, reflected in the social and cultural trends of that period. The general feeling of a place and time as seen through the prevailing ideas, beliefs, and attitudes of the people.

BS Definition: To say a word that could just as likely be the name of a craft beer at your local brewery.

Origin: Ah, to capture the zeitgeist is to truly win the battle for the hearts and minds of the masses! The term itself derives from German—*zeit* meaning "time," and *geist* meaning "spirit" (spirit of the times). Most credit the popularization of the term to German philosopher Georg Wilhelm Friedrich Hegel (so important he had four names!), who in 1807's *Phenomenology of the Spirit* uses various forms of *geist* to define his thoughts:

» weltgeist (world spirit)
» volksgeist (national spirit)
» the phrase geist der zeiten or zeitgeist (spirit of the times).[4]

The Hegelian view of spirit integrates psychology, politics, history, art, religion, and philosophy, among other areas. The *OED* says one of zeitgeist's first written references (outside of Hegel's own book or reviews of it) was in 1834 in the book, *Sartor Resartus*, by Thomas Carlyle: "Often have I fancied how, in thy hard life-battle, thou wert shot at and slung at, wounded, handfettered, hamstrung, browbeaten and bedevilled, by the Time-Spirit (Zeitgeist) in thyself and others."

With that said, the term was only used sporadically in English through most of the 19th and 20th centuries. However, when hipsters in Silicon Valley began adopting it to describe how their new products and services captured the public imagination in the new millennium, it took off.[5] Indeed, the term clearly is enjoying its own zeitgeist moment right now, with Google hosting an annual thought leadership conference called the "Google Zeitgeist"—an intimate gathering of top global thinkers and leaders started in 2007—which may spell the end of the zeitgeist for the word zeitgeist, actually.[6]

ACHTUNG, BABY!

Zeitgeist is just one of several German words in the BS world that are still going strong. Look at these others.

angst	dissatisfaction or disenchantment
doppelgänger	a person who is the spitting image of another person
kaput	broken or busted
kitschy	oversentimental, cheap, poorly produced, or appealing to mass tastes
schadenfreude	being happy that something bad happened to someone else
über	the ride service; a preposition or prefix in German that means "higher" or "greater"
wanderlust	a restlessness that causes a desire to travel and see the world

NOTES

Introduction

1. The phrase "history is written by the victors" has been credited to Winston Churchill, Niccolò Machiavelli, Voltaire, and others, but there doesn't seem to be any documented proof that any actually uttered the phrase. Search results primarily give the credit to Winston Churchill.
2. USDA, "Nebraska Women Lunch n Learn," *Extension Service Review* 44, no. 7-8 (1973): 3. https://archive.org/stream/CAT10252415499/CAT10252415499_djvu.txt
3. However, we do want to note that the *OED* is not always the "be all end all"—in many cases we were able to find older references than even that vaunted resource (thanks to the power of Google). Who'd have thought that two guys sitting at home at their computers could do that?
4. Don't even think about laying claim to the term "thrash disco." It was coined by Iron Hammer, an obscure band out of Lakewood, Ohio, in the late 1980s. How do we know this? Tim Ito has the band's liner notes to prove it.

#

1. "NBA League Averages - Per Game," Basketball Reference, accessed April 7, 2019. www.basketball-reference.com/leagues/NBA_stats_per_game.html.
2. "Where does 24/7 come from?" BBC News UK magazine, July 25, 2007. http://news.bbc.co.uk/2/hi/uk_news/magazine/6915516.stm.
3. Shanyu Ji, "What Is the Origin of the 360 Degree Measurement?" University of Houston Department of Mathematics, July 6, 2015, www.math.uh.edu/~shanyuji/History/Appendix/Appendix-1.pdf; Bob Sillery, editor, "Who Determined That a Circle Should Be Divided Into 360 Degrees?" *Popular Science*, February 5, 2002. www.popsci.com/scitech/article/2002-02/who-determined-circle-should-be-divided-360-degrees.
4. Beautiful Science, "Do You Know Why 360 Is Special?" video, September 19, 2017. www.youtube.com/watch?v=WzkW3P7HPvs.

A

1. "Above board," The Word Detective, October 21, 2009. www.word-detective.com/2009/10/above-board; "The Meaning and Origin of the Expression: Above board," The Phrase Finder. www.phrases.org.uk.
2. "Across the board" Phrase Finder. www.phrases.org.uk.
3. "Action," Online Etymology Dictionary. www.etymonline.com.
4. "Action Man," Phrase Finder, www.phrases.org.uk.

5. "William Lambarde," Wikipedia, https://en.wikipedia.org/wiki/William_Lambarde; "William Lambarde · Archion: or, a commentary upon the high courts of justice in England," OED, www.oed.com.

6. The OED says "Charles Frederick" but it actually looks to be Christine Frederick according to this excerpt of the 1913 *Ladies Home Journal* issue we found published by the National Humanities Center (Research Triangle Park, NC, 2005): Christine Frederick, "The New Housekeeping: Efficiency Studies in Home Management 1913 | Excerpts," *Ladies Home Journal* Sept–Dec, 1912. http://nationalhumanitiescenter.org/pds/gilded/progress/text4/frederick.pdf; "Actionable," Online Etymology Dictionary. www.etymonline.com.

7. Armistead Maupin, *Tales of the City* (New York: Harper & Row, 1978).

8. "Administrator" Online Etymology Dictionary, www.etymonline.com; "Administrator," OED, www.oed.com; "History of IAAP," IAAP, www.iaap-hq.org/?page=HistoryIAAP; Abby Quillen, "From Secretary to Administrative Assistant: How the Admin Role Has Evolved Over Time," Quill.com (blog), June 30, 2017. www.quill.com/blog/office-tips/from-secretary-to-administrative-assistant-how-the-admin-role-has-evolved-over-time.html.

9. "Against the grain," The Phrase Finder, www.phrases.org.uk. "What Does Against the Grain Mean?" Writing Explained. https://writingexplained.org/idiom-dictionary/against-the-grain.

10. "Coriolanus," Wikipedia. https://en.wikipedia.org/wiki/Coriolanus.

11. William Shakespeare, *Coriolanus, a Tragedy*, act II, scene VIII. (London: J. Tonson, 1734)

12. "All Hands," *Merriam-Webster*. www.merriam-webster.com; "What Does All Hands on Deck Mean?" Writing Explained. https://writingexplained.org/idiom-dictionary/all-hands-on-deck.

13. The OED cites the following as the earliest reference of all hands being used in the colloquial reference: Samuel Hartlib, *The Reformed Common-Wealth of Bees, Presented in Severall Letters and Observations to [and ed. by] Sammuel Hartlib. With The Reformed Virginian Silk-Worm* (London: Printed for Giles Calvert at the Black-Spread-Eagle at the West-end of Pauls, 1655).

14. Greg Sandoval, "Insiders Say the Press Leaks During Google's All-Hands Meeting Backfired and Handed Sergey Brin the Moral High Ground." *Business Insider India*, August 17, 2018. www.businessinsider.in/insiders-say-the-press-leaks-during-googles-all-hands-meeting-backfired-and-handed-sergey-brin-the-moral-high-ground/articleshow/65443254.cms.

15. As cited in "Have an Axe to Grind," The Phrase Finder. www.phrases.org.uk.

16. "Anointing," Wikipedia. https://en.wikipedia.org/wiki/Anointing; "Anoint," Online Etymology Dictionary. www.etymonline.com/word/anoint.

17. Richard Creed, "YOU ASKED: Origin of Using 'Ask' as Noun Sort of Muddy," W*inston-Salem Journal*, December 13, 2009. www.journalnow.com/archives/you-asked-origin-of-using-ask-as-noun-sort-of/article_5fab1a08-2d75-5bfc-9e10-e75bd5445b2b.html; Colin Schultz, "People Have Been Saying "Ax" Instead of "Ask" for 1200 Years," Smart News, *Smithsonian* magazine, February 6, 2014. www.smithsonianmag.com/smart-news/people-have-been-saying-ax-instead-ask-1200-years-180949663; Henry Hitchings, "Those Irritating Verbs-as-Nouns," Opinionator, *New York Times*, March 30, 2013. https://opinionator.blogs.nytimes.com/2013/03/30/those-irritating-verbs-as-nouns.

18. Raymond Chen, "Words I'd Like to Ban in 2004," The Old New Thing (blog), Microsoft, January 7, 2004. https://devblogs.microsoft.com/oldnewthing/20040107-00/?p=41173.

19. Ebenezer Erskine, *The Whole Works of the Rev. Ebenezer Erskine: Consisting of Sermons and Discourses on Important and Interesting Subjects* (Philadelphia: W.S. & A. Young, 1836).

20. Patricia T. O'Conner and Stewart Kellerman, "At the End of the Day," Grammarphobia, November 13, 2012. www.grammarphobia.com/blog/2012/11/at-the-end-of-the-day.html.

22. "Authoritative," Online Etymology Dictionary. www.etymonline.com; "Authoritative," Dictionary.com; "Authoritative," Merriam-Webster. www.merriam-webster.com.

23. You can watch the *Bull Durham* scene here: www.youtube.com/watch?v=85RZMIAL7vM; Dwight's seen can be found here: https://youtu.be/ez6Xdf_p7Yg.

B

1. "Business School," Wikipedia. https://en.wikipedia.org/wiki/Business_school.

2. As cited in the *OED*: "Biz-to-Biz Info Exchange Launched," *Marketing News*, September 12, 1994.

3. "BtoB (band)," Wikipedia. https://en.wikipedia.org/wiki/BtoB_(band).

4. "25 Interesting Facts About Cold War," Kickass Facts Encyclopedia, July 3, 2014. www.kickassfacts.com/25-interesting-facts-about-cold-war; "Hedy Lamarr," Wikipedia. https://en.wikipedia.org/wiki/Hedy_Lamarr; "Korean Air Lines Flight 007," Wikipedia. https://en.wikipedia.org/wiki/Korean_Air_Lines_Flight_007; David Collins, "Grizzly End: Bears Were Fired Out of US Supersonic Jet in Ejector Seat Tests," *Mirror*, December 21, 2012. www.mirror.co.uk/news/world-news/bears-were-fired-out-of-us-supersonic-1501169.

5. "Back Burner," The Phrase Finder, October 31, 2000, www.phrases.org.uk/bulletin_board/6/messages/582.html; "Back Burner, (Put Something On the)." www.idioms.online/back-burner.

6. Gordon Bock, "The History of Old Stoves," *Old House Journal*, August 3, 2012, updated May 9, 2019. www.oldhouseonline.com/kitchens-and-baths-articles/history-of-the-kitchen-stove.

7. "Back-of-the-Envelope," *Merriam-Webster*. www.merriam-webster.com; Sarah K. Cowan, "Phrase Origins: Why Is it Called a 'Back of the Envelope' Calculation?" Quora, February 3, 2011. www.quora.com/Phrase-Origins-Why-is-it-called-a-back-of-the-envelope-calculation.

8. "Laser History & Development," Interview with Charles H. Townes, Laser Fest. http://laserfest.org/lasers/video-history.cfm.

9. "Bait-and-Switch," Wikipedia. https://en.wikipedia.org/wiki/Bait-and-switch.

10. "Ballpark Figure," The Idioms. www.theidioms.com/ballpark-figure.

11. "History of the Ruhr." Wikipedia. https://en.wikipedia.org/wiki/History_of_the_Ruhr.

12. "Keep the Ball Rolling," The Phrase Finder. www.phrases.org.uk/meanings/keep-the-ball-rolling.html.

13. "A Brief History of Juggling," Juggling Information Service. www.juggling.org/books/artists/history.html.

14. "The New Meaning of 'Bandwidth,'" *Merriam-Webster*, November 21, 2017. www.merriam-webster.com/words-at-play/what-is-the-new-meaning-of-bandwidth.

15. "What Is the Origin of 'More Bang for the/Your Buck'?" May 4, 2016, https://english.stackexchange.com/questions/323520/what-is-the-origin-of-more-bang-for-the-your-buck; Prose, "More Bang for Your Buck," Minds.com, February 11, 2016. www.minds.com/blog/view/544493942322769920.

16. Eric Partridge, *A Dictionary of Slang and Unconventional English* (New York: Routeledge, 1937) as cited in the *OED*.

17. Brian O'Dalaigh, "Why Is County Clare Often Called 'The Banner County'?" Clair County Library FAQ, February 1, 2001. www.clarelibrary.ie/eolas/coclare/history/faqs/bannerc.htm;

"Banner Year," Q&A About Words, Wordsmith.org. October 17, 2005. https://wordsmith
.org/board/ubbthreads.php?ubb=showflat&Number=148975.

18. Thomas Chalmers, *Congregational Sermons* (London: Hamilton, Adams, and Co, 1848), xi.

19. Charles D. Clark, "The Red Headed Girl," Running column in the *Lewiston Saturday Journal*,
June 1, 1907. https://news.google.com/newspapers?nid=oQQVFBP0nzwC&dat=19070601
&printsec=frontpage&hl=en; "Bean Counter," The Phrase Finder. www.phrases.org.uk.

20. "Beat a Dead Horse," Ginger, Phrase of the Day, March 10, 2013, www.gingersoftware.com
/content/phrases/beat-a-dead-horse.

21. "Beauty Contest," Dictionary.com; Times Reporter, "The Origin of Beauty Pageants," *The
New Times*, February 2, 2012. www.newtimes.co.rw/section/read/101038.

22. As cited in the *OED*: The librarian quote is from a 1914 issue of the *Bulletin American
Library Association* 8 274/2. The *Forbes* quote is from the article "Off Coors" in the June 1976
issue.

23. Alfred Pollard, *Bombers Over the Reich* (London: Hutchinson & Co, 1941).

24. William Ellis, *Agriculture Improv'd: or, The Practice of Husbandry Display'd* (Printed for T.
Osborne, 1746).

25. Robert Mearns Yerkes, "Psychological Examining in the United States Army," vol. xv of the
Memoirs of the National Academy of Sciences (Washington, DC: US Government Printing
Office, 1921), p. 67.

26. "What's the Origin of 'Beta' to Describe a 'User-Testing' Phase of Computer Development?"
English Language and Usage, August 30, 2011, https://english.stackexchange.com/questions
/40013/whats-the-origin-of-beta-to-describe-a-user-testing-phase-of-computer-devel.

27. Peppersack, "An Introduction to Data Science: Making Big Data Usable," DSF Whitepaper,
July 2, 2017. https://datascience.foundation/sciencewhitepaper/an-introduction-to-data-
science:-making-big-data-usable; Mark van Rijmenam, "A Short History of Big Data,"
Datafloq, January 6, 2013. https://datafloq.com/read/big-data-history/239; Steve Lohr, "The
Origins of 'Big Data': An Etymological Detective Story," Bits (blog), February 1, 2013,
https://bits.blogs.nytimes.com/2013/02/01/the-origins-of-big-data-an-etymological-detective
-story; "Big Data," Wikipedia. https://en.wikipedia.org/wiki/Big_data.

28. Charles Tilly, "The Old New Social History and the New Old Social History," CRSO
Working Paper No. 218, October 1980. Accessed via www.scribd.com/document/227409180
/The-Old-New-History-Charles-Tilly.

29. "Steve Jobs - It's Not Binary," video, January 3, 2016, www.youtube.com/watch?v=GE6VHtUlO4M.

30. "Claude Shannon," Wikipedia. https://en.wikipedia.org/wiki/Claude_Shannon; "A
Symbolic Analysis of Relay and Switching Circuits," Wikipedia. https://en.wikipedia.org
/wiki/A_Symbolic_Analysis_of_Relay_and_Switching_Circuits.

31. *David Epstein,* Range: Why Generalists Triumph in a Specialized World (New York:
Riverhead Books, 2019), p. 45.

32. "Bio Break," *Merriam-Webster*, Words We're Watching. www.merriam-webster.com/words
-at-play/bio-break-meaning-and-origin.

33. Satoshi Nakamoto, "Bitcoin: A Peer-to-Peer Electronic Cash System," Whitepaper, November
1, 2008. https://bitcoin.org/bitcoin.pdf.

34. Anderson Cooper, "Bitcoin's Wild Ride," CBS News, *60 Minutes*, May 19, 2019. www.cbsnews
.com/news/bitcoins-wild-ride-60-minutes-2019-05-19; Lee Grant, "What is Blockchain? -

Definition, Origin, and History," TechBullion, September 6, 2016. www.techbullion.com /blockchain-definition-origin-history.

35. Chris Morris, "Winklevoss Twins Used Facebook Payout to Become Bitcoin Billionaires," *Fortune*, December 4, 2017. https://fortune.com/2017/12/04/winklevoss-twins-bitcoin -billionaires; Jake Frankenfield, "Bitcoin Definition," Investopedia, October 26, 2019. www.investopedia.com/terms/b/bitcoin.asp.

36. OK, we just love the song "Cuts Like a Knife" by Bryan Adams. www.youtube.com /watch?v=6VZhSkREYBc.

37. "Is There a Difference Between 'Leading Edge' and 'Bleeding Edge'?" English Language and Usage, August 29, 2011. https://english.stackexchange.com/q/39918; Thomas C. Hayes, "Hope at Storage Technology," *New York Times*, March 21, 1983. www.nytimes.com/1983/03 /21/business/hope-at-storage-technology.html.

38. Laura Metz, "What Does 'Bleeding Edge' Mean?" wiseGEEK, February 29, 2020. www.wisegeek.com/what-does-bleeding-edge-mean.htm; "Bleeding Edge," Dictionary.com.

39. Grant, "What is Blockchain?"

40. "W. Scott Stornetta Bio," World Crypto Index. www.worldcryptoindex.com/creators/w-scott -stornetta; "Blockchain," Wikipedia. https://en.wikipedia.org/wiki/Blockchain.

41. Troy Segal, "Blue Sky Laws Definition," Investopedia." February 16, 2020. www.investopedia .com/terms/b/blueskylaws.asp; ESC, "Blue Sky," posted on December 6, 2003, in reply to "Grey Skies Thinking?" posted by pdianek on December 6, 2003, The Phrase Finder. www.phrases.org.uk/bulletin_board/26/messages/921.html.

42. Margaret Rouse, "Boil the Ocean," WhatIs.com, December 2013. https://whatis.techtarget.com/definition/boil-the-ocean.

43. Robert Link was quoted in the March 1930 issue of *Scouting* magazine.

44. Christopher Klein, "Where Did the Word 'Boondoggle' Come From?" History Stories, September 17, 2015, updated August 29, 2018. www.history.com/news/where-did-the-word -boondoggle-come-from; "Boondoggle," Dictionary.com.

45. "Pull Yourself Up by Your Bootstraps," The Phrase Finder. www.phrases.org.uk; Sarah Alvarez, "Where Does the Phrase 'Pull Yourself Up by Your Bootstraps' Actually Come From," State of Opportunity, April 7, 2015. https://stateofopportunity.michiganradio.org/post/where-does -phrase-pull-yourself-your-bootstraps-actually-come.

46. "What Is the Origin of the Phrase, 'The Bottom Line'?" English Language and Usage, September 28, 2017. https://english.stackexchange.com/questions/411911/what-is-the -origin-of-the-phrase-the-bottom-line.

47. "To hold a man a man irresponsible during a brainstorm is practically to maintain that a man is not responsible for losing his self-control." From "Remedies Proposed," *The Outlook*, February 26, 1910, in *The Outlook: A Weekly Newspaper* January–April, 1910, p. 420.

48. David Segal, "In Pursuit of the Perfect Brainstorm," *New York Times*, December 19, 2010. www.nytimes.com/2010/12/19/magazine/19Industry-t.html.

49. Jennifer Bridges, "Top 10 Brainstorming Ideas for Your Team," ProjectManager, February 26, 2018. www.projectmanager.com/training/top-brainstorming-ideas-team; "Brainstorm," *Merriam-Webster*. www.merriam-webster.com; "Brainstorm," Online Etymology Dictionary. www.etymonline.com.

50. "Bullish," Dictionary.com; "Bullish," Online Etymology Dictionary. www.etymonline.com; Daven Hiskey, "Origin of the Stock Market Terms 'Bull' and 'Bear,'" Today I Found Out,

April 16, 2013. www.todayifoundout.com/index.php/2013/04/origin-of-the-stock-market
-terms-bull-and-bear.

51. "The Burning Platform," Problem Solving Techniques, April 19, 2009. www.problem-solving
-techniques.com/Burning-Platform.html; Daryl Conner, "The Real Story of the Burning
Platform," Conner Partners (blog), August 15, 2012. www.connerpartners.com/frameworks
-and-processes/the-real-story-of-the-burning-platform.

C

1. "Cannibal" and "Cannibalize" Online Etymology Dictionary. www.etymonline.com.
2. *Select Works of Edmund Burke*, vol. 2, *Reflections on the Revolution in France* (Indianapolis:
   Liberty Fund, 1999).
3. "Cannibalize," *Merriam-Webster.* www.merriam-webster.com.
4. Jeff Haden, "That Elon Musk Advice to Just Walk Out of Unproductive Meetings Sounds Great
   But Is Actually Career Suicide," Inc., May 1, 2018. www.inc.com/jeff-haden/that-elon-musk
   -advice-to-just-walk-out-of-unproductive-meetings-sounds-great-but-is-actually-career-suicide.html.
5. We found the actual newspaper clipping from *The Huronite* and *The Daily Plainsman* on
   the *OED* website.
6. "Word of the Day: Catalyst," Macmillan Dictionary Blog, April 3, 2017. www.macmillan
   dictionaryblog.com/catalyst.
7. Floyd C. Mann and Franklin W. Neff, *Managing Major Change in Organizations: An
   Underdeveloped Area of Administration and Social Research* (Ann Arbor, MI: Foundation
   for Research on Human Behavior, 1961).
8. "Client," *Merriam-Webster.* www.merriam-webster.com; "client," Online Etymology
   Dictionary. www.etymonline.com.
9. Peter Drucker, *The Practice of Management* (Burlington, MA: Butterworth-Heinemann).
10. "Cookie Cutter," The Phrase Finder. www.phrases.org.uk; "Cookie-Cutter," Dictionary.com.
11. *Religious Pamphlets*, vol. 43, *A Conversation on Decrees and Free Agency, Between James and
    John; In Which the Doctrine of the Presbyterian Church Is Explained and Scripturally Defended*
    (New York 1834), p. 160.
12. "Core Competency," Wikipedia. https://en.wikipedia.org/wiki/Core_competency;
    Margaret Rouse, "Core Competency (Core Competencies)" Tech Target, SearchCIO,
    March 2017. https://searchcio.techtarget.com/definition/core-competency.
13. Maeve Maddox, "Cost-Effective vs. Cost-Efficient," Daily Writing Tips, October 2015.
    www.dailywritingtips.com/cost-effective-vs-cost-efficient; "Cost-Effective," *Merriam-Webster.*
    www.merriam-webster.com.
14. "Creativity," Wikipedia. https://en.wikipedia.org/wiki/Creativity.
15. "Can 'Creative' Be a Noun?" *Merriam-Webster,* Usage Notes, October 17, 2018. www.merriam
    -webster.com/words-at-play/can-creative-be-a-noun-usage-history; "Creative," *Merriam-Webster.*
    www.merriam-webster.com.
16. "Critical Mass (Disambiguation)," Wikipedia. https://en.wikipedia.org/wiki/Critical_mass
    _(disambiguation).
17. "Critical Mass," Wikipedia. https://en.wikipedia.org/wiki/Critical_mass.

18. Alex Wellerstein, "Critical Mass," Restricted Data: The Nuclear Secrecy Blog, April 10, 2015. http://blog.nuclearsecrecy.com/2015/04/10/critical-mass.

19. "Critical Mass (Sociodynamics)," Wikipedia. https://en.wikipedia.org/wiki/Critical_mass _(sociodynamics).

20. "Cross-Functional Team," Wikipedia. https://en.wikipedia.org/wiki/Cross-functional_team; "Cross-Functional Teams," Inc.com, Encyclopedia of Business Terms, March 28, 2019. www .inc.com/encyclopedia/cross-functional-teams.html. Accessed 29 May. 2019; "Cross Functional Teams Law and Legal Definition," US Legal, October 20, 2005. https://definitions.uslegal.com /c/cross-functional-teams.

21. "Pollination," Wikipedia. https://en.wikipedia.org/wiki/Pollination; "Cross-Pollination," *Merriam-Webster.* www.merriam-webster.com; "Cross-Pollination," Dictionary.com.

22. *U.S. House of Representatives Committee on Interstate and Foreign Commerce and U.S. Senate Committee on Interstate and Foreign Commerce. Automobile Dealers Territorial Security Hearings ... Eighty-sixth Congress, Second Session, June 20-22, 1960* (Washington, D.C.: U.S. Government Printing Office, 1960). www.google.com/books/edition/Automobile_Dealers_Territorial _Security/I9cuAAAAMAAJ?hl=en&gbpv=0.

23. Justas Markus, "Cross-Selling," eCommerce Wiki, December 23, 2016, www.oberlo.com /ecommerce-wiki/cross-selling; Margaret Rouse, "Cross-Sell," WhatIs.com. https://search customerexperience.techtarget.com/definition/cross-sell.

24. "Cutting Edge / Leading Edge," The Word Detective, December 18, 2011. www.word-detective .com/2011/12/cutting-edge-leading-edge.

25. Charles Coulton Gillispie, *The Edge of Objectivity: An Essay in the History of Scientific Ideas* (Princeton, NJ: Princeton University Press, 1960) p. 54.

D

1. "A Timeline of Database History," Quick Base, October 3, 2010. www.quickbase.com /articles/timeline-of-database-history.

2. "What is a Database Dump?" Techopedia, October 25, 2012. www.techopedia.com /definition/23340/database-dump.

3. "A Deep Dive on 'Deep Dive,'" *Merriam-Webster*, Words We're Watching, August 20, 2018. www.merriam-webster.com/words-at-play/what-is-a-deep-dive-history-words-were-watching.

4. "Deliverable," Online Etymology Dictionary, www.etymonline.com; "Deliverable," Dictionary.com.

5. This might be Tim's favorite scene ever: "De Plane De Plane | Tatoo on Fantasy Island." https://youtu.be/USfKJYZcUmI.

6. "William Caxton," Wikipedia. https://en.wikipedia.org/wiki/William_Caxton; "Deploy," Online Etymology Dictionary. www.etymonline.com.

7. Marc Prensky, "Digital Natives, Digital Immigrants," *On the Horizon* 9, no. 5 (October 2001). www.marcprensky.com/writing/Prensky%20-%20Digital%20Natives,%20 Digital%20Immigrants%20-%20Part1.pdf.

8. John Perry Barlow, "A Declaration of the Independence of Cyberspace," Electronic Frontier Foundation, February 8, 1996. www.eff.org/cyberspace-independence; Oliver Joy, "What does it mean to be a digital native?" CNN.com, December 8, 2012. www.cnn.com/2012 /12/04/business/digital-native-prensky/index.html; "Digital Native," Wikipedia. https://en.wikipedia.org/wiki/Digital_native.

9. "Disruptive Innovation," Wikipedia. https://en.wikipedia.org/wiki/Disruptive_innovation; Alexandra Twin, "Disruptive Innovation," Investopedia, June 5, 2019. www.investopedia .com/terms/d/disruptive-innovation.asp.

10. As cited in the *OED*.

11. "Dog and Pony Show," Wikipedia. https://en.wikipedia.org/wiki/Dog_and_pony_show.

12. Grant Barrett, "Dog and Pony Show Origins," A Way With Words, September 29, 2012. www.waywordradio.org/dog-and-pony-show-origins.

13. "Dogfooding: Take Pride in Your Code," DevIQ, February 20, 2013. https://deviq.com /dogfooding; "Alpo Dog Food Commercial (Lorne Greene, 1976)," video, September 23, 2017. www.youtube.com/watch?v=cHUMaKWgfS0.

14. "Eating Your Own Dog Food," Wikipedia. https://en.wikipedia.org/wiki/Eating_your_own _dog_food; Tim Slavin, "Dogfooding," *beanz* magazine, August 15, 2019. www.kidscodecs .com/dogfooding; Dale Haines, "A Brief History of Dog Fooding," KwikTag, June 25, 2018. www.kwiktag.com/a-brief-history-of-dog-fooding; Iman Gadzhi, "Why I Eat Dog Food." LinkedIn Pulse, March 1, 2019. www.linkedin.com/pulse/why-i-eat-dog-food-iman-gadzhi.

15. "Dovetail," Wiktionary. https://en.wiktionary.org/wiki/dovetail.

16. "Dovetail," Online Etymology Dictionary. www.etymonline.com; "Dovetail," *Merriam-Webster*. www.merriam-webster.com.

17. "Downsize (Automobile)," Wikipedia. https://en.wikipedia.org/wiki/Downsize_(automobile).

18. "Downsize," Online Etymology Dictionary. www.etymonline.com.

19. Nicholas Rossolillo, "Is Eastman Kodak Company a Buy?" The Motley Fool, October 11, 2018. www.fool.com/investing/2018/10/11/is-eastman-kodak-company-a-buy.aspx.

20. As cited in the *OED*.

21. "Jonestown," Wikipedia. https://en.wikipedia.org/wiki/Jonestown.

22. "Drinking the Kool-Aid," Wikipedia. https://en.wikipedia.org/wiki/Drinking_the_Kool-Aid.

23. "Ducks in a Row, Part 2," The Word Detective, July 31, 2007. www.word-detective.com /2007/07/ducks-in-a-row-part-2; "Ducks in a Row," Historically Speaking (blog), August 22, 2011. https://idiomation.wordpress.com/tag/nine-pine-bowling.

24. "Due Diligence," Word of the Day (blog), EVS Translations, April 10, 2014. https://evs-translations.com/blog/due-diligence.

25. Joanna Bourke-Martignoni, "The History and Development of the Due Diligence Standard in International Law and Its Role in the Protection of Women Against Violence," in *Due Diligence and Its Application to Protect Women From Violence*, edited by Carin Benninger-Budel (Boston: Martinus Nijhoff, 2008).

26. Bill Muller of the *Arizona Republic* reviewing *The Texas Chainsaw Massacre* on Rotten Tomatoes, October 16, 2003. www.rottentomatoes.com/m/texas_chainsaw_massacre/reviews?type=top _critics&sort=&page=2; Claire Fallon, "Where Did 'Dumpster Fire' Come From? Where Is It Rolling?" HuffPost, June 24, 2016. www.huffpost.com/entry/dumpster-fire-slang-history_n_57 6474d4e4b015db1bc97923.

BS Abbreviations

1. Justin, "The 37 Most Common English Acronyms and Abbreviations," RealLife English, June 2, 2014. https://reallifeglobal.com/acronyms.

E

1. "English Journal," Wikipedia. https://en.wikipedia.org/wiki/English_Journal.
2. "Daniel Goleman," Wikipedia. https://en.wikipedia.org/wiki/Daniel_Goleman; "Emotional Quotient: Meaning, Definition, Components and Benefits." Your Article Library, April 2, 2014. www.yourarticlelibrary.com/human-resources/emotional-quotient-meaning-definition-components-and-benefits/32401.
3. "Peter Salovey," Wikipedia. https://en.wikipedia.org/wiki/Peter_Salovey; "John D. Mayer," Wikipedia. https://en.wikipedia.org/wiki/John_D._Mayer; "John Mayer," Wikipedia. https://en.wikipedia.org/wiki/John_Mayer.
4. "Critical review of Daniel Goleman," EQI.org, February 1, 2002. http://eqi.org/gole.htm.
5. "Easter Egg (Media)," Wikipedia. https://en.wikipedia.org/wiki/Easter_egg_(media).
6. SC Messina Capital, "Who Invented the Term EBITDA? Was It KKR? Milken?" ValueWalk, September 22, 2015. www.valuewalk.com/2015/09/ebitda-milken.
7. Chris B. Murphy, "What Is the Difference Between EBIT and EBITDA?" Investopedia, June 24, 2019. www.investopedia.com/ask/answers/020215/what-difference-between-ebit-and-ebitda.asp.
8. Murphy, "What Is the Difference Between EBIT and EBITDA?"
9. John English, "How Did the Phrase 'the Elephant in the Room' Come to Originate?" Quora, September 10, 2016. www.quora.com/How-did-the-phrase-the-elephant-in-the-room-come-to-originate; "Elephant in the Room," Wikipedia. https://en.wikipedia.org/wiki/Elephant_in_the_room; "Elephant in the Room," Know Your Phrase, August 14, 2019. https://knowyourphrase.com/elephant-in-the-room.
10. Presenting: Rob, "Elevator Pitches: A Brief History." Tips and Tricks for Presentations and Pitches (blog), January 14, 2016. http://presentingrob.blogspot.com/2016/01/elevator-pitches-brief-history.html.
11. "Elevator Pitch," Wikipedia. https://en.wikipedia.org/wiki/Elevator_pitch; Graham Wilson, "The History of the Elevator Speech," The Confidant (blog), November 25, 2012. www.the-confidant.info/2012/the-history-of-the-elevator-speech.
12. "Emerging," Dictionary.com; "Emerging," *Merriam-Webster*. www.merriam-webster.com; "Samuel Bolton (1606-1654)," A Puritan's Mind, April 16, 2015. www.apuritansmind.com/puritan-favorites/samuel-bolton-1606-1654.
13. Ben Russell, "Dozens Burned in Tony Robbins' Hot-Coals Walk in Dallas," NBC DFW, June 24, 2016. www.nbcdfw.com/news/local/several-injured-after-walking-across-hot-coals-dallas-police/2020166.
14. "Work of the Day: Empower," Macmillan Dictionary Blog, January 10, 2018. www.macmillandictionaryblog.com/empower; "Empower," Vocabulary.com; Nicola Denham Lincoln, Cheryl Travers, Peter Ackers, and Adrian Wilkinson, "The Meaning of Empowerment: The Interdisciplinary Etymology of a New Management Concept," *International Journal of Management Reviews*, 2002. https://doi.org/10.1111/1468-2370.00087; "Empowerment," Wikipedia. https://en.wikipedia.org/wiki/Empowerment.
15. "End-to-End Principle," Wikipedia. https://en.wikipedia.org/wiki/End-to-end_principle; Simson Garfinkel, "The End of End-to-End?" *MIT Technology Review*, July 1, 2003. www.technologyreview.com/s/401966/the-end-of-end-to-end.
16. CU Ergo, "Ergonomics Origin and Overview," Cornell University Ergonomics Web, Class Notes from DEA 3250/6510. http://ergo.human.cornell.edu/dea3250flipbook/dea3250notes

/ergorigin.html; "History of Ergonomics," Japan Human Factors and Ergonomics Society, July 25, 2011. www.ergonomics.jp/e_index/e_outline/e_ergono-history.html.

Commonly Confused BS Terms

1. Christina DesMarais, "43 Embarrassing Grammar Mistakes Even Smart People Make," Inc .com, July 11, 2017. www.inc.com/christina-desmarais/43-embarrassing-phrases-even-smart -people-use.html.

F

1. DARPA, "ARPANET: About Us." www.darpa.mil/about-us/timeline/arpanet.
2. "FAQ," Wikipedia. https://en.wikipedia.org/wiki/FAQ; "Faq," Dictionary.com.
3. Shara Tibken, "FaceTime Creator Details Its History, Including Code Name," CNET, April 22, 2014. www.cnet.com/news/apple-engineer-details-facetimes-history-including- original -codename.
4. "Face Time," *Merriam-Webster*. www.merriam-webster.com.
5. William Safire, "On Language; Face Time," *New York Times*, September 9, 1990. www.nytimes.com/1990/09/09/magazine/on-language-face-time.html.
6. As cited in the *OED*.
7. Shari Waters, "What Does Facing Mean in Retail?" The Balance Small Business, May 8, 2019. www.thebalancesmb.com/what-is-meant-by-facing-in-retail-stores-2890188; "Facing (Retail)," Wikipedia. https://en.wikipedia.org/wiki/Facing_(retail).
8. "Fake News," Wikipedia. https://en.wikipedia.org/wiki/Fake_news.
9. The previous two quotes were cited in "The Real Story of 'Fake News,'" *Merriam-Webster*, Words We're Watching (blog), March 23, 2017. www.merriam-webster.com/words-at-play /the-real-story-of-fake-news.
10. Donald Trump (@realDonaldTrump), "Reports by @CNN that I will be working on The Apprentice during my Presidency, even part time, are ridiculous & untrue - FAKE NEWS!" Twitter, December 10, 2016, 3:11 p.m.
11. Christopher Rosen, "All the Times Donald Trump Has Called the Media 'Fake News' on Twitter," *Entertainment Weekly*, July 24, 2017. https://ew.com/tv/2017/06/27/donald -trump-fake-news-twitter.
12. "Feeding Frenzy," Ginger Phrase of the Day, January 1, 2013. www.gingersoftware.com /content/phrases/feeding-frenzy; "Feeding frenzy," The Phrase Finder. www.phrases.org.uk; "Media Feeding Frenzy," Wikipedia. https://en.wikipedia.org/wiki/Media_feeding_frenzy.
13. Nick Saint, "10 First-to-Market Products That Lost," *Business Insider*, December 1, 2009. www.businessinsider.com/10-first-to-market-companies-that-lost-out-to-latecomers-2009-11.
14. Marvin B. Liberman and David B. Montgomery, "First-Mover Advantages," *Strategic Management Journal Summer* 1988. https://doi.org/10.1002/smj.4250090706.
15. Steve Blank, "Steve Blank: Here's Why The First-Mover Advantage Is Extremely Overrated," Business Insider, The Cheat Sheet, October 19, 2010. www.businessinsider.com/steve-blank -first-mover-advantage-overrated-2010-10; "First-Mover Advantage," Wikipedia. https://en .wikipedia.org/wiki/First-mover_advantage; George Anders, "He Who Moves First Finishes

Last," Fast Company, Consultant Debunking Unit, August 31, 2000. www.fastcompany.com/40793/he-who-moves-first-finishes-last.

16. Although this could be the flavor every month, which would in fact render "flavor of the month" rather meaningless.

17. "Flavor of the Month," The Phrase Finder. www.phrases.org.uk; Pascal Treguer, "Meanings and Origin of 'Flavour of the Month/of the Week.'" Word Histories, September 22, 2018, https://wordhistories.net/2018/09/22/flavour-month-week.

18. Oliver Smith, "Ben & Jerry's Bets on Blockchain to Cancel Out the Carbon in Every Scoop," *Forbes*, May 29, 2018. www.forbes.com/sites/oliversmith/2018/05/29/ben-jerrys-bets-on-blockchain-to-cancel-out-the-carbon-in-every-scoop.

19. Dan Herman, "Introducing Short-Term Brands: A New Branding Tool for a New Consumer Reality," *Journal of Brand Management* May 1, 2000. https://doi.org/10.1057/bm.2000.23.

20. Peter Kozodoy, "The Inventor of FOMO Is Warning Leaders About a New, More Dangerous Threat," Inc.com, October 9, 2017. www.inc.com/peter-kozodoy/inventor-of-fomo-is-warning-leaders-about-a-new-more-dangerous-threat.html; "Fear of Missing Out," Wikipedia. https://en.wikipedia.org/wiki/Fear_of_missing_out; Roger Dooley, "Episode 107: The Unexpectedly Smart Way to Become an Entrepreneur," Brainfluence Podcast Transcript, April 21, 2016. www.rogerdooley.com/wp-content/uploads/2016/04/EP107-BrainfluencePodcastTranscript.pdf.

21. "Which Is Correct: 'Could Care Less' or 'Couldn't Care Less'?" English Language and Usage, August 13, 2010. https://english.stackexchange.com/questions/706/which-is-correct-could-care-less-or-couldnt-care-less.

22. "For all Intents and Purposes," The Phrase Finder. www.phrases.org.uk; "Intensive Purposes," The Word Detective. www.word-detective.com/2009/01/intensive-purposes.

23. "10 Best Quotes From Terminator Movies," Time Out Bahrain, June 28, 2015. www.timeoutbahrain.com/films/features/64412-10-best-quotes-from-terminator-movies.

24. Nicholas Davis, "What Is the Fourth Industrial Revolution?" World Economic Forum, January 19, 2016. www.weforum.org/agenda/2016/01/what-is-the-fourth-industrial-revolution.

25. Logical Design Solutions, "The Industry Leap From Vertical Markets to Ecosystems," LDS whitepaper, September 27, 2018. www.lds.com/pov/industry-leap-vertical-markets-ecosystems; Bernard Marr, "The 4th Industrial Revolution Is Here - Are You Ready?" Forbes, August 13, 2018. www.forbes.com/sites/bernardmarr/2018/08/13/the-4th-industrial-revolution-is-here-are-you-ready.

26. "Purchase Funnel," Wikipedia. https://en.wikipedia.org/wiki/Purchase_funnel.

G

1. "Game Plan," Merriam-Webster. www.merriam-webster.com.

2. "Game Plan," Collins English Dictionary. www.collinsdictionary.com.

3. "Game," Online Etymology Dictionary. www.etymonline.com.

4. "What Game Did 'Game Changer' Originally Refer To?" English Language and Usage, June 24, 2016. https://english.stackexchange.com/questions/333671/what-game-did-game-changer-originally-refer-to; Hendrik Hertzberg, "Nobody Said That Then!" *The New Yorker*, February 10, 2014. www.newyorker.com/news/hendrik-hertzberg/nobody-said-that-then.

5. As cited in the *OED*.

6. Kurt Lewin, "Forces Behind Food Habits and Methods of Change," chap. 8 in *The Problem of Changing Food Habits: Report of the Committee on Food Habits* 1941–1943 (Washington, D.C.: National Research Council, 1943). www.nap.edu/read/9566/chapter/8.

7. "Communication Theories Sorted by Category," University of Twente. www.utwente.nl/en/bms /communication-theories; "Gatekeeping (Communication)," Wikipedia. https://en.wikipedia .org/wiki/Gatekeeping_(communication); "Kurt Lewin," Wikipedia. https://en.wikipedia.org /wiki/Kurt_Lewin.

8. "Generation X: Tales for an Accelerated Culture," Wikipedia. https://en.wikipedia.org/wiki /Generation_X:_Tales_for_an_Accelerated_Culture.

9. Rich Cohen, "Why Generation X Might Be Our Last, Best Hope," *Vanity Fair,* August 11, 2017. www.vanityfair.com/style/2017/08/why-generation-x-might-be-our-last-best-hope; "Generation X," Wikipedia. https://en.wikipedia.org/wiki/Generation_X.

10. Sir. William Johnson, *Papers of Sir William Johnson* (Albany, NY: The Division of Archives and History). https://archive.org/stream/papersofsirwilli07johnuoft/papersofsirwilli07 johnuoft_djvu.txt.

11. Christine Ammer, *The Dictionary of Clichés: A Word Lover's Guide to 4,000 Overused Phrases and Almost-Pleasing Platitudes* (New York: Skyhorse Publishing, 2013).

12. "Get the Ball Rolling and Start the Ball Rolling," Grammarist. https://grammarist.com/idiom /get-the-ball-rolling-and-start-the-ball-rolling; "Croquet," Wikipedia. https://en.wikipedia .org/wiki/Croquet; "Get (Keep) the Ball Rolling," The Phrase Finder, November 10, 2000. www.phrases.org.uk/bulletin_board/6/messages/706.html; "William Henry Harrison," Wikipedia. https://en.wikipedia.org/wiki/William_Henry_Harrison.

13. Anne Fletcher, "Setting the AA Record Straight: Clearing Up Misconceptions," Pro Talk, National Rehabs Directory, November 4, 2019. www.rehabs.com/pro-talk-articles/setting-the -aa-record-straight-clearing-up-misconceptions-part-1; Joan White, "Get With the Program," *New York Times,* August 18, 1991. www.nytimes.com/1991/08/18/magazine/l-get-with-the -program-987091.html.

14. William Safire, "On Language; Poetic Allusion Watch, Explained," *New York Times,* July 21, 1991. www.nytimes.com/1991/07/21/magazine/on-language-poetic-allusion-watch -expanded.html.

15. Maj. Charles H. Metzger, "Is Your NOTAM Showing?" *Aerospace Safety: United States Air Force* (January 1963), p. 25.

16. "Ghost," Wikipedia. https://en.wikipedia.org/wiki/Ghost.

17. Gardner R. Dozois, *Geodisic Dreams: The Best Short Fiction of Gardner Dozois* (New York: Macmillian, 1992), p. 211.

18. Valeriya Safronova, "Exes Explain Ghosting, the Ultimate Silent Treatment," *New York Times,* June 26, 2015. www.nytimes.com/2015/06/26/fashion/exes-explain-ghosting-the -ultimate-silent-treatment.html.

19. "Gif," Dictionary.com; "GIF," Wikipedia. https://en.wikipedia.org/wiki/GIF; Amy Kay, "What Is a GIF?" Techwalla, February 9, 2017. www.techwalla.com/articles/what-is-a-gif.

20. Logitech, "The History of the GIF and How to Make Your Own," Logitech Blog, June 26, 2013. https://blog.logitech.com/2013/06/26/the-history-of-the-gif-and-how-to-make-your-own.

21. "Temporary Work," Wikipedia. https://en.wikipedia.org/wiki/Temporary_work; "What Is a Gig Economy? Definition and Examples," Market Business News, December 11, 2016. https://marketbusinessnews.com/financial-glossary/gig-economy-definition-meaning; "Gig

Economy," Dictionary.com; "Gig Economy," *Macmillan Dictionary* Buzzword, January 17, 2017. www.macmillandictionary.com/buzzword/entries/gig-economy.html.

22. Angela Tung, "10 Phrases That Come From Horse Racing," Wordnik, May 1, 2014. https://blog.wordnik.com/10-phrases-that-come-from-horse-racing.

23. "Glad-Hand," Grammarist, September 18, 2012. https://grammarist.com/words/glad-hand; "Glad Hand," Online Etymology Dictionary. www.etymonline.com.

24. "10 of the Biggest Mistakes Ever Made in History," Unbelievable Facts, September 5, 2017. www.unbelievable-facts.com/2017/09/biggest-mistakes-in-history.html.

25. Josh Chetwynd, *The Field Guide to Sports Metaphors: A Compendium of Competitive Words and Idioms* (New York: Ten Speed Press, 2016).

26. Hayden Bird, "A *Merriam-Webster* Editor Explained Tom Brady's Role in 'GOAT' Entering the Dictionary," Boston.com, September 7, 2018. www.boston.com/sports/new-england -patriots/2018/09/07/tom-brady-goat-dictionary.

27. "G.O.A.T. (Greatest of All Time)," Grammarphobia (blog), July 22, 2016. www.grammarphobia.com/blog/2016/07/goat.html.

28. As they sang in *My Fair Lady*, "The rain in Spain stays mainly in the plain."

29. "Golden Parachute," Wikipedia. https://en.wikipedia.org/wiki/Golden_parachute; "Howard Hughes," Wikipedia. https://en.wikipedia.org/wiki/Howard_Hughes.

30. "Charles Tillinghast, Jr." Slide 1 of 10 in "Biggest Golden Parachutes," *Time*, October 9, 2008. http://content.time.com/time/specials/packages/article/0,28804,1848501_1848500 _1848418,00.html; "What Is a Golden Parachute?" Corporate Finance Institute, March 8, 2018. https://corporatefinanceinstitute.com/resources/knowledge/deals/golden-parachute.

31. "Guerrilla," Online Etymology Dictionary. www.etymonline.com; "Guerrilla Marketing," Wikipedia. https://en.wikipedia.org/wiki/Guerrilla_marketing; "Guerrilla Marketing." http://gmarketing.com.

BS Reporting for Duty

1. Tom Hawking, "Our Casual Use of Military Jargon Is Normalizing the Militarization of Society," *Quartz*, November 30, 2016. https://qz.com/847577/our-casual-use-of-military -jargon-is-normalizing-the-militarization-of-society; David Moore, "10 Common Words and Phrases You Didn't Know Had Military Origins," Veterans United, February 19, 2013. www.veteransunited.com/network/face-the-music-and-other-common-words-and-phrases -with-military-origins.

H

1. "Hackathon," Wikipedia. https://en.wikipedia.org/wiki/Hackathon.

2. "Usenet," Wikipedia. https://en.wikipedia.org/wiki/Usenet.

3. Matt Weinberger, "'There Are Only Two Rules'—Facebook Explains How 'Hackathons,' One of Its Oldest Traditions, Is Also One of Its Most Important," *Business Insider*, June 11, 2017. www.businessinsider.com/facebook-hackathons-2017-6.

4. Garrett Reim, "Marijuana Hackathon Attracts National Attention and Crowns First-Ever Winner," Built in Colorado, October 2, 2014. www.builtincolorado.com/2014/10/01 /marijuana-hackathon-attracts-national-attention-crowns-first-ever-winner; Katherine Noyes, "NBA Holds Its First Hackathon—Should Your Company, Too?" Computer World, August 19, 2016. www.computerworld.com/article/3109872/nba-holds-its-first-hackathon-should

-your-company-too.html; Andrea Valdez, "Inside the Vatican's First-Ever Hackathon," WIRED, March 12, 2018. www.wired.com/story/inside-vhacks-first-ever-vatican-hackathon.

5. Lia Eustachewich and Mara Siegler, "Fyre Festival paid $250K for Kendall Jenner Instagram Post," Page Six, May 4, 2017. https://pagesix.com/2017/05/04/fyre-festival-co-founder-blew-through-millions-on-models-yachts.

6. "Halo Effect," Wikipedia. https://en.wikipedia.org/wiki/Halo_effect.

7. "Hammer," Wikipedia. https://en.wikipedia.org/wiki/Hammer; "Hammer," Online Etymology Dictionary. www.etymonline.com; "Bring the Hammer Down," The Word Detective, November 22, 2009. www.word-detective.com/2009/11/bring-the-hammer-down.

8. "Hammer Out," Merriam-Webster. www.merriam-webster.com.

9. "Handle," Tech Terms, April 8, 2015. https://techterms.com/definition/handle; Douglas Currens, "What Is the Origin of the Term 'Handle' in CB Radio Communication?" Quora, January 30, 2015. www.quora.com/What-is-the-origin-of-the-term-handle-in-CB-radio-communication; "Citizens Band Radio," Wikipedia. https://en.wikipedia.org/wiki/Citizens_band_radio.

10. Chetwynd, The Field Guide to Sports Metaphors.

11. "Doubleday Myth," Wikipedia. https://en.wikipedia.org/wiki/Doubleday_myth.

12. "Baseball Before We Knew It," Wikipedia. https://en.wikipedia.org/wiki/Baseball_Before_We_Knew_It.

13. "Who Invented Baseball?" History, March 27, 2013, updated March 28, 2019. www.history.com/news/who-invented-baseball; "Baseball (ball)," Wikipedia. https://en.wikipedia.org/wiki/Baseball_(ball); "Play Hardball," Dictionary.com.

14. This clip of Jabba the Hut's laugh from Star Wars is a great example: https://youtu.be/OPcod8IS214

15. VOA English, "Does This Story Have Legs?" VOA Learning English, Words and Their Stories (blog), April 16, 2016. https://learningenglish.voanews.com/a/does-this-story-have-legs/3287704.html.

16. Belle Beth Cooper, "The Surprising History of Twitter's Hashtag Origin and 4 Ways to Get the Most out of Them," Buffer Research, September 24, 2013. https://buffer.com/resources/a-concise-history-of-twitter-hashtags-and-how-you-should-use-them-properly.

17. "Chris Messina (Open Source Advocate)," Wikipedia. https://en.wikipedia.org/wiki/Chris_Messina_(open-source_advocate)

18. Amy Edwards, "#Fail: When Hashtags Go Wrong," Social Media Today, July 28, 2013. www.socialmediatoday.com/content/fail-when-hashtags-go-wrong; John Souza, "6 Tips to Getting Twitter Hashtags Right," Social Media Impact, December 3, 2014. www.socialmediaimpact.com/6-tips-getting-twitter-hashtags-right/#.

19. "Heavy Hitter," Dictionary.com; "Heavy Hitter," Merriam-Webster. www.merriam-webster.com.

20. Robert Hendrickson, God Bless America: The Origins of Over 1,500 Patriotic Words and Phrases (New York: Skyhorse Publishing, 2013).

21. "Mickey Cochrane," Wikipedia. https://en.wikipedia.org/wiki/Mickey_Cochrane.

22. Mark Nichol, "30 Baseball Idioms," Daily Writing Tips, April 28, 2016. www.dailywritingtips.com/30-baseball-idioms.

23. "Hedge Your Bets," The Phrase Finder. www.phrases.org.uk.

24. "What Does Hedge Your Bets Mean?" Writing Explained, September 18, 2017. https://writingexplained.org/idiom-dictionary/hedge-your-bets.

25. Jon Emmons, "Cat Herding," Life After Coffee (blog), March 31, 2006. www.lifeaftercoffee.com
    /2006/03/31/cat-herding; "Herd Cats," Wiktionary. https://en.wiktionary.org/wiki/herd_cats.
26. Brad Lemley, *Washington Post Magazine*, June 9, 1985; "Origin of the Term 'Herding
    Cats,'" Google Answers, February 18, 2003.
27. Warren Clements, "Cat's Got Our Tongue," *The Globe and Mail*, June 8, 2000. www.theglobe
    andmail.com/arts/cats-got-our-tongue/article25464248; Ben Reed, "50 Cat Idioms and Phrases,"
    Owlcation, January 19, 2019. https://owlcation.com/humanities/50-Cat-Idioms-and-Phrases.
28. "Squirrel Away," The Free Dictionary. www.thefreedictionary.com.
29. "Hired Gun," Dictionary.com; "Hired Gun," *Merriam-Webster*. www.merriam-webster.com;
    "Hired Gun," *Collins English Dictionary*. www.collinsdictionary.com.
30. "Honcho," *Merriam-Webster*. www.merriam-webster.com.
31. "Clifford Stoll," Wikipedia. https://en.wikipedia.org/wiki/Clifford_Stoll; "The Cuckoo's
    Egg," Wikipedia. https://en.wikipedia.org/wiki/The_Cuckoo%27s_Egg.
32. "Honeypot (Computing)," Wikipedia. https://en.wikipedia.org/wiki/Honeypot_(computing);
    Caleb Townsend, "What Is a Honeypot?" *United States Cybersecurity Magazine*, August 2, 2018.
    www.uscybersecurity.net/honeypot.
33. "Wednesday," Wikipedia. https://en.wikipedia.org/wiki/Wednesday.
34. "Hump Day," The Phrase Finder, July 4, 2001. https://www.phrases.org.uk/bulletin_board/9
    /messages/498.html; "Who Is Wednesday Named For?" Everything After Z, Dictionary.com.
    "Happy Hump Day," Slang Dictionary, Dictionary.com. www.dictionary.com/e/slang/happy
    -hump-day.

I

1. Paul Yeager, "Ideation and Ideating," Everything Language and Grammar (blog), February
   16, 2008. https://languageandgrammar.com/2008/02/16/ideation-and-ideating.
2. "In a Nutshell," The Phrase Finder. www.phrases.org.uk; David Bevington, "Hamlet,"
   Britannica.com. www.britannica.com/topic/Hamlet-by-Shakespeare.
3. Ruth Walker, "Going Deep Into the Weeds," *The Christian Science Monitor*, February 1, 2008.
   www.csmonitor.com/The-Culture/The-Home-Forum/2008/0201/p18s02-hfes.html; "In the
   Weeds," The Phrase Finder, November 25, 2003. www.phrases.org.uk/bulletin_board/26
   /messages/576.html; "Getting Into the Weeds," The Word Detective, May 4, 2011. www
   .word-detective.com/2011/05/getting-into-the-weeds.
4. "What's the Origin of the Phrase 'Into the weeds'?" English Language and Usage, February 6,
   2015. https://english.stackexchange.com/questions/225595/whats-the-origin-of-the-phrase-into
   -the-weeds.
5. *In the Weeds* (2000), IMDb. www.imdb.com/title/tt0210756.
6. Merrill Perlman, "The '-ize' Have It," *Columbia Journalism Review*, July 6, 2010. www.cjr.org
   /language_corner/the_ize_have_it.php; "The Differences in British and American Spelling,"
   Oxford International English Schools. www.oxfordinternationalenglish.com/differences-in
   -british-and-american-spelling.
7. Tarpley Hitt, "The Inscrutable Rise of the Online 'Influencer,'" The Daily Beast, Oxtober
   5, 2018. www.thedailybeast.com/the-inscrutable-rise-of-the-online-influencer; "Cambridge
   Platonists," Wikipedia. https://en.wikipedia.org/wiki/Cambridge_Platonists; "Henry More,"
   Wikipedia. https://en.wikipedia.org/wiki/Henry_More.

8. Zameena Mejia, "How Kylie Jenner Became the World's Youngest Self-Made Billionaire at 21," CNBC, March 5, 2019. www.cnbc.com/2019/03/05/forbes-kylie-jenner-is-the-worlds -youngest-self-made-billionaire.html.

9. "Kevin Ashton," Wikipedia. https://en.wikipedia.org/wiki/Kevin_Ashton.

10. Allison DeNisco Rayome, "How the Term 'Internet of Things' Was Invented," TechRepublic, July 27, 2018. www.techrepublic.com/article/how-the-term-internet-of-things-was-invented; "Internet of Things," Wikipedia. https://en.wikipedia.org/wiki/Internet_of_things.

11. As cited in the *OED*.

12. William Safire, "It Is What It Is," *New York Times*, March 5, 2006. www.nytimes.com/2006 /03/05/magazine/it-is-what-it-is.html.

13. *It Is What It Is* (2001), IMDb. www.imdb.com/title/tt0309722; Lyrics to "It Is What It Is" by The String Cheese Incident can be found at www.justsomelyrics.com/2262478/the-string -cheese-incident-it-is-what-it-is-lyrics.html.

14. Liane Gabora, "The Hidden Meaning of 'It Is What It Is,'" *Psychology Today*, May 23, 2014. www.psychologytoday.com/us/blog/mindbloggling/201405/the-hidden-meaning-it-is-what-it-is.

J

1. "Where Does 'Jet Lag' Come From and When Was It Coined?" English Language and Usage, September 5, 2017. https://english.stackexchange.com/questions/374473/where-does-jet-lag -come-from-and-when-was-it-coined; "Jet Lag," *Merriam-Webster*. www.merriam-webster.com.

2. "Jockey for Position," English Club. www.englishclub.com/ref/esl/Idioms/American/jockey_for _position_645.php; "Jockey for Position," The Free Dictionary. https://idioms.thefreedictionary .com/jockey+for+position.

3. "John Hancock," Wikipedia. https://en.wikipedia.org/wiki/John_Hancock.

4. F.N. Litten, "Front Page Stuff," *Boy's Life*, May 1932, p. 14.

5. Lyrics to "Happiness Is a Warm Gun" by The Beatles can be found at www.songfacts.com /lyrics/the-beatles/happiness-is-a-warm-gun.

Rooted in the Bible

1. Amanda N. "32 Biblical Idioms and Sayings," Improving Your English," March 19, 2016. https://improving-your-english.com/biblical-idioms.

K

1. "KISS Principle," Wikipedia. https://en.wikipedia.org/wiki/KISS_principle.

2. "Elihu Katz," Wikipedia. https://en.wikipedia.org/wiki/Elihu_Katz; Elihu Katz, Personal Influence: *The Part Played by People in the Flow of Mass Communications* (New York: Routledge, 2005); "Opinion Leadership," Wikipedia. https://en.wikipedia.org/wiki /Opinion_leadership.

3. William Congreve, *The Old Bachelor*, Project Gutenberg, www.gutenberg.org/files/1192/1192-h /1192-h.htm; "The Old Bachelor," Wikipedia. https://en.wikipedia.org/wiki/The_Old_Bachelor.

4. "Handle With Kid Gloves," The Phrase Finder. www.phrases.org.uk.

5. We love this scene from the 1971 version of *Willy Wonka and the Chocolate Factory* (https:// youtu.be/JASsbo7fvc4). People may be more likely to remember the Wonka golden tickets, but we think the geese laying golden eggs were cooler.

6. "The Goose That Laid the Golden Eggs," Wikipedia. https://en.wikipedia.org/wiki/The _Goose_That_Laid_the_Golden_Eggs; "Kill the Goose That Lays the Golden Egg," The Idioms. www.theidioms.com/kill-the-goose-that-lays-the-golden-egg.

7. "AltaVista," Wikipedia. https://en.wikipedia.org/wiki/AltaVista; Sean Fennessey, "Reality Bites: 'Captain Marvel' and the Lie of the '90s," The Ringer, March 7, 2019. www.theringer.com /movies/2019/3/7/18254204/captain-marvel-90s-culture-music-mcu-black-panther-avengers.

8. Mark Wilkinson, "20 of the Worst (But Funniest) Email Mistakes People Have Made at Work," Coburg Banks, November 23, 2016. www.coburgbanks.co.uk/blog/friday-funnies /20-of-the-worst-email-mistakes.

9. "Bird Play," Grammarphobia (blog), August 2, 2013. www.grammarphobia.com/blog/2013/08 /bird-play.html; "Daedalus," Wikipedia. https://en.wikipedia.org/wiki/Daedalus.

10. "Knockoff," Dictionary.com; "Knock Off," The Phrase Finder. www.phrases.org.uk.

11. "What Are the Origins for the Phrases 'Knock it off' and 'Cut it Out,'" English Language and Usage, January 6, 2013. https://english.stackexchange.com/questions/96696/what-are -the-origins-for-the-phrases-knock-it-off-and-cut-it-out.

12. "Peter Drucker," Wikipedia. https://en.wikipedia.org/wiki/Peter_Drucker; "Knowledge Economy," Wikipedia. https://en.wikipedia.org/wiki/Knowledge_economy; Rick Wartzman, "What Peter Drucker Knew About 2020," Harvard Business Review, October 16, 2014. https://hbr.org/2014/10/what-peter-drucker-knew-about-2020.

13. "Kudos," Dictionary.com; "Kudos," Online Etymology Dictionary. www.etymonline.com.

L

1. You can find the rules to the *NYPD Blue* drinking game, created by Alan Sepinwall, here: www.stwing.upenn.edu/~sepinwal/drink.html.

2. Adam Hanft, "Neolawisms," Legal Affairs, January/February 2003. www.legalaffairs.org/issues /January-February-2003/scene_hanft_janfeb2003.msp; Ben Zimmer, "Lawyering Up With the Help of 'NYPD Blue,'" *Wall Street Journal*, June 22, 2017. www.wsj.com/articles/lawyering -up-with-the-help-of-nypd-blue-1498150876.

3. Connie Schultz, "Review: Sheryl Sandberg's 'Lean In' Is Full of Good Intentions, But Rife With Contradictions," *The Washington Post*, March 1, 2013. www.washingtonpost.com /opinions/review-sheryl-sandbergs-lean-in-is-full-of-good-intentions-but-rife-with -contradictions/2013/03/01/3380e00e-7f9a-11e2-a350-49866afab584_story.html.

4. Olivia Solon, "Sheryl Sandberg: Facebook Business Chief Leans Out of Spotlight in Scandal," *The Guardian*, March 29, 2018. www.theguardian.com/technology/2018/mar/29/sheryl -sandberg-facebook-cambridge-analytica.

5. "The Lunacy of the Leave Behind," Better Presenting, November 17, 2009. www.better presenting.com/editorial/leave-behind.

6. "Snipe Hunt," Wikipedia. https://en.wikipedia.org/wiki/Snipe_hunt.

7. "Bagholder," Wikipedia. https://en.wikipedia.org/wiki/Bagholder; "Left Holding the Bag," World Wide Words, November 30, 2002. www.worldwidewords.org/qa/qa-lef1.htm; "What's the Origin of the Idiom 'to Be Left Holding the Bag'?" English Language and Usage, March 10, 2017. https://english.stackexchange.com/questions/377789/whats-the-origin-of-the-idiom -to-be-left-holding-the-bag.

8. "Long in the Tooth," The Free Dictionary, Idioms. https://idioms.thefreedictionary.com/long +in+the+tooth.

9. Lucas Reilly, "The Origins of 12 Horse-Related Idioms," *Mental Floss,* May 22, 2014. http://mentalfloss.com/article/56850/origins-12-horse-related-idioms.

10. Learn more about Longshot's powers, enemies, and history at www.marvel.com/characters/longshot.

11. The Washington Generals franchise has lost well over 17,000 games to the Globetrotters. The last game they won against the team was on January 5, 1971: "Get to Know the History Behind the Washington Generals." www.washingtongenerals.com/history.

12. "Long Shot," Online Etymology Dictionary. www.etymonline.com; "Not by a Long Shot and Not by a Long Chalk," Grammarist. https://grammarist.com/idiom/not-by-a-long-shot-and-not-by-a-long-chalk.

13. Max Mallet, Brett Nelson, and Chris Steiner, "The Most Annoying, Pretentious and Useless Business Jargon," *Forbes,* January 26, 2012, www.forbes.com/sites/groupthink/2012/01/26/the-most-annoying-pretentious-and-useless-business-jargon.

14. As cited in the *OED.*

15. As cited in the *OED.*

16. Mark Liberman, "Memetic Dynamics of Low-Hanging Fruit," Language Log, September 30, 2009. https://languagelog.ldc.upenn.edu/nll/?p=1778; "Low-Hanging Fruit," Grammarist. https://grammarist.com/idiom/low-hanging-fruit.

17. MJB2010, "Whoever Invented the Lunch and Learn," All Nurses, February 24, 2012. https://allnurses.com/whoever-invented-lunch-learn-t421555/?page=2

18. The full text for the *Extension Service Review* is available at https://archive.org/stream/CAT10252415499/CAT10252415499_djvu.txt.

Latin-Based BS Terms

1. Erica Urie, "24 Latin Phrases You Use Every Day," Inklyo, October 7, 2015. www.inklyo.com/latin-phrases-you-use-every-day.

M

1. "Modus Operandi," *Merriam-Webster.* www.merriam-webster.com.

2. "Magic Bullet," Science Museum, March 2, 2009. http://broughttolife.sciencemuseum.org.uk/broughttolife/techniques/magicbullet; "Magic Bullet (Medicine)," Wikipedia. https://en.wikipedia.org/wiki/Magic_bullet_(medicine).

3. "Magic Bullet," Wikipedia. https://en.wikipedia.org/wiki/Magic_bullet.

4. "Seinfeld - The Magic Loogie, Reconstructed." (video) April 19, 2011. www.youtube.com/watch?v=tBz3PqA2Fmc.

5. Ilyce Glink, "10 of the World's Most Expensive Homes," CBS News, November 22, 2014. www.cbsnews.com/media/10-of-the-worlds-most-expensive-homes.

6. "The Bonfire of the Vanities," Wikipedia. https://en.wikipedia.org/wiki/The_Bonfire_of_the_Vanities; Tom Wolfe, "A Selection from The Bonfire of the Vanities: A Novel," B&N Readouts. www.barnesandnoble.com/readouts/the-bonfire-of-the-vanities-a-novel; Minda Zetlin, "Even if You've Never Read Tom Wolfe, You Probably Use These Phrases He Invented," Inc., May 15, 2018. www.inc.com/minda-zetlin/tom-wolfe-death-influence-terms-coined-vocabulary.html.

7. "Masters of the Universe," Wikipedia. https://en.wikipedia.org/wiki/Masters_of_the_Universe.

8. "Meeting of the Minds," Wikipedia. https://en.wikipedia.org/wiki/Meeting_of_the_minds; "Oliver Wendell Holmes Jr.," Wikipedia. https://en.wikipedia.org/wiki/Oliver_Wendell _Holmes_Jr.; Richard Orsinger, "170 Years of Texas Contract Law," State Bar of Texas, April 11, 2013. www.orsinger.com/PDFFiles/170-Years-of-Texas-Contract-Law.pdf.

9. Caitlin Berens, "Buffett, Zuckerberg & the Meeting of Billionaires," Inc.com, July 7, 2012. www.inc.com/caitlin-berens/buffett-zuckerberg-and-the-meeting-of-billionaires.html; Rakesh Krishnan, "Bilderberg Conference 2019: What Happens in the Secretive Meet of the World's Most Powerful People?" *Business Today,* June 6, 2019. www.businesstoday.in/opinion/columns /bilderberg-conference-2019-secretive-meeting-of-worlds-most-powerful-people-western-elite -us-mike-pompeo-satya-nadella-microsoft-donald-trump/story/354219.html.

10. Maya Kachroo-Levine, "What Is a Meme? Here's What the Thing Is You Always Hear People Talking About So You Can Stop Smiling and Nodding," Bustle, May 27, 2015. www.bustle .com/articles/86077-what-is-a-meme-heres-what-the-thing-is-you-always-hear-people-talking -about-so; "Meme," Wikipedia. https://en.wikipedia.org/wiki/Meme.

11. "Kilroy Was Here," Wikipedia. https://en.wikipedia.org/wiki/Kilroy_was_here.

12. "Millennial," Online Etymology Dictionary. www.etymonline.com; "Millennials," Wikipedia. https://en.wikipedia.org/wiki/Millennials.

13. Robert L. Heath, *Encyclopedia of Public Relations,* 2nd ed., (New York: SAGE Publications).

14. Ryan Holiday, "What Is Growth Hacking? A Definition and a Call to Action," HuffPost, September 4, 2013. www.huffpost.com/entry/what-is-growth-hacking-a_b_3863522; "Edward Bernays," Wikipedia. https://en.wikipedia.org/wiki/Edward_Bernays.

15. "Boat," Dictionary.com.

16. "John Henry Newman," Wikipedia. https://en.wikipedia.org/wiki/John_Henry_Newman.

17. Pascal Treguer, "Origin of 'to Miss the Buss' (to Miss an Opportunity)," Word Histories, September 15, 2016. https://wordhistories.net/2016/09/15/to-miss-the-bus.

18. "Mission Critical," Wikipedia. https://en.wikipedia.org/wiki/Mission_critical.

19. "Trade," Wikipedia. https://en.wikipedia.org/wiki/Trade.

20. Robert Spector, *The Mom & Pop Store: True Stories from the Heart of America* (New York: Walker Books, 2010).

21. "Mom-and-Pop," Dictionary.com; "White Collar: The American Middle Classes," Wikipedia. https://en.wikipedia.org/wiki/White_Collar:_The_American_Middle_Classes.

22. Peter Jensen Brown, "The History and Origin of 'Monday Morning Quarterback,'" Early Sports and Pop Culture History Blog, July 21, 2014. https://esnpc.blogspot.com/2014/07/the-history -and-origin-of-monday.html; "Monday-Morning Quarterback," Idioms Online. www.idioms .online/monday-morning-quarterback; Chetwynd, The Field Guide to Sports Metaphors.

23. Brian McCullough, "The Real Reason Excite Turned Down Buying Google for $750,000 in 1999." Internet History Podcast, November 17, 2014. www.internethistorypodcast.com /2014/11/the-real-reason-excite-turned-down-buying-google-for-750000-in-1999.

24. "Move the Needle," Wiktionary. https://en.wiktionary.org/wiki/move_the_needle; Giovanni Rodriguez, "Office Talk: 'Moving the Needle,'" The Hubbub, November 26, 2006. https://hubbub.typepad.com/blog/2006/11/office_talk_mov.html.

N

1. "Net-Net Definition," Investopedia, April 8, 2019. www.investopedia.com/terms/n/net-net.asp.

2. "Benjamin Graham," Wikipedia. https://en.wikipedia.org/wiki/Benjamin_Graham.

3. Guru Focus, "5 Stocks Become Ben Graham Net-Nets In Market Decline," *Forbes,* December 7, 2018. www.forbes.com/sites/gurufocus/2018/12/07/5-stocks-become-ben-graham-net-nets-in-market-decline; Timothy Green, "Net-Net Investing: How to Identify Value Stocks," The Motley Fool, June 3, 2015. www.fool.com/investing/general/2015/06/03/net-net-investing-how-to-identify-value-stocks.aspx.

4. "New Normal (Business)," Wikipedia. https://en.wikipedia.org/wiki/New_Normal_(business); Mohamed A. El-Erian, "Paul Ryan's Plan and the Next 'New Normal,'" *The Washington Post,* August 13, 2012. www.washingtonpost.com/opinions/paul-ryans-plan-and-the-next-new-normal/2012/08/13/53fdfda4-e566-11e1-936a-b801f1abab19_story.html; Jon Hartley, "How 'The New Normal' Of Economic Growth Took Shape," *Forbes,* February 29, 2016. www.forbes.com/sites/jonhartley/2016/02/29/falling-productivity-underlying-slow-gdp-growth-and-how-monetary-policy-became-the-only-game-in-town; ALG Research, "Can the Trump Trade Agenda Sustain the Current Economic Boom, Grow the Labor Force, and Get America Back to Work," ALG Research Foundation, September 26, 2018. http://algresearch.org/2018/09/can-the-trump-trade-agenda-sustain-the-current-economic-boom-grow-the-labor-force-and-get-america-back-to-work; Mohamed A. El-Erian, "The End of the New Normal?" Project Syndicate, February 2, 2016. www.project-syndicate.org/commentary/the-end-of-the-new-normal-by-mohamed-a--el-erian-2016-02.

5. J.E. Luebering, "Henry Chettle," *Encyclopedia Britannica.* www.britannica.com/biography/Henry-Chettle.

6. "The Woman Hater," Wikipedia. https://en.wikipedia.org/wiki/The_Woman_Hater.

7. First uses of earshot and prostitute confirmed by *OED* and included in Wikipedia; "Nip in the Bud," The Phrase Finder. www.phrases.org.uk.

8. Barry Popik, "This Ain't My First Rodeo," The Big Apple, September 4, 2006. www.barrypopik.com/index.php/new_york_city/entry/this_aint_my_first_rodeo2.

9. Jonathan Becher, "This Ain't My First Rodeo," *Forbes,* April 22, 2015. www.forbes.com/sites/sap/2015/04/22/this-aint-my-first-rodeo; "Frank Yablans," Wikipedia. https://en.wikipedia.org/wiki/Frank_Yablans.

BS Terms From Horseracing

1. Tung, "10 Phrases That Come From Horse Racing"; Elizabeth Harrison, "7 Expressions You Might Not Know Came From Horse Racing," History, May 2, 2014. www.history.com/news/7-expressions-you-might-not-know-came-from-horse-racing; Mark McGuire, "Horse Racing Terms Common in Everyday Language," *The Daily Gazette,* August 12, 2015. https://dailygazette.com/article/2015/08/12/0812_horselingo.

2. *Bad actor* has been used in the industry and certainly popularized, but it remains unclear whether the actual origin came from horse racing.

3. Note that the term *upset* was likely popularized by horse racing—most notable was the "upset" of the great Man O' War in 1919, but it was also referenced 40 years before in horse racing as well. "Sports Legend Revealed: Did the Term 'Upset' in Sports Derive From a Horse Named Upset Defeating Man o' War?" *Los Angeles Times,* May 10, 2011. https://latimesblogs.latimes.com/sports_blog/2011/05/sports-legend-revealed-did-the-term-upset-in-sports-derive-from-a-horse-named-upset-defeating-man-o-.html.

4. The claim itself was based on some loose citations, but upon inspection that doesn't appear to be the case. On the plus side, Seabiscuit was mentioned in an impressive 238 articles

that year. David Mikkelson, "Seabiscuit," Snopes, January 21, 2006. www.snopes.com
/fact-check/seabiscuit.

5. Thom Loverro, "Seabiscuit vs. War Admiral: The Horse Race That Stopped The Nation,"
The Guardian, November 1, 2013. www.theguardian.com/sport/2013/nov/01/seabiscuit
-war-admiral-horse-race-1938-pimlico.

6. "Horse Racing," Wikipedia. https://en.wikipedia.org/wiki/Horse_racing.

7. Chetwynd, *The Field Guide to Sports Metaphors*.

O

1. "Online and Offline," Wikipedia. https://en.wikipedia.org/wiki/Online_and_offline.

2. Evan Andrews, "Who Invented the Internet?" History, December 18, 2013. www.history.com
/news/who-invented-the-internet.

3. Walt Hickey, "The Longest Filibuster in History Lasted More Than a Day—Here's How It
Went Down," Business Insider, March 6, 2013. www.businessinsider.com/longest-filibuster
-in-history-strom-thurmond-rand-paul-2013-3.

4. Chetwynd, *The Field Guide to Sports Metaphors*; "Schoolboy Days; Or, Ernest Bracebridge
by W.H.G. Kingston," Goodreads, September 1, 2015. www.goodreads.com/book/
show/29821655
-schoolboy-days-or-ernest-bracebridge.

5. "Onboarding," Wikipedia. https://en.wikipedia.org/wiki/Onboarding.

6. Robert D. Marx, Todd Jick, Peter J. Frost, *Management Live: The Video Book* (Englewood
Cliffs, NJ: Prentice Hall, 1991), p. 283.

7. Conner Burt, "The History of Employee Onboarding, Pt. 1," Lessonly, September 30,
2014. www.lessonly.com/blog/the-history-of-employee-onboarding-pt-1.

8. "20 English Idioms With Their Meanings and Origins," Oxford Royale Academy, January 23,
2014. www.oxford-royale.co.uk/articles/bizarre-english-idioms-meaning-origins.html;
"American Idioms (Meanings and Origins) [I thru P]," Pride UnLimited. www.pride-unlimited
.com/probono/idioms2.html; Emily Upton, "The Origin of the Phrase 'Once in a Blue Moon,'"
Today I Found Out, June 10, 2013. www.todayifoundout.com/index.php/2013/06/the-origin
-of-the-phrase-once-in-a-blue-moon; Donovan Alexander, "The Reason Why We Say 'Once in
a Blue Moon.'" Interesting Engineering, December 13, 2017. https://interestingengineering.com
/the-reason-why-we-say-once-in-a-blue-moon; "Once in a Blue Moon," The Phrase Finder.
www.phrases.org.uk.

9. Mark Nichol, "25 Idioms About Bread and Dessert," Daily Writing Tips, December 29, 2012.
www.dailywritingtips.com/25-idioms-about-bread-and-dessert.

10. Katie Halper, "A Brief History of People Getting Fired for Social Media Stupidity," *Rolling
Stone*, July 13, 2015. www.rollingstone.com/culture/culture-lists/a-brief-history-of-people
-getting-fired-for-social-media-stupidity-73456; "One-Two Punch," Dictionary.com.

11. "The Old One-Two," Know Your Phrase. https://knowyourphrase.com/the-old-one-two.

12. Aaron Rinberg and Scott Tobin, "Amazon's One-Two Punch: How Traditional Retailers
Can Fight Back," Tech Crunch, April 18, 2019. https://techcrunch.com/2019/04/18/amazons
-one-two-punch-how-traditional-retailers-can-fight-back.

13. Lydia Dishman, "The Problematic Origins of Common Business Jargon," Fast Company,
September 27, 2018. www.fastcompany.com/90239290/six-business-phrases-that-have
-racist-origins.

14. Steve Haruch, "Why Corporate Executives Talk About 'Opening Their Kimonos,'" NPR, November 2, 2014. www.npr.org/sections/codeswitch/2014/11/02/360479744/why-corporate -executives-talk-about-opening-their-kimonos; Radio Ray, "Open the Kimono," Urban Dictionary, September 24, 2005. www.urbandictionary.com/define.php?term=open%20the%20kimono.

15. "Vote for the Worst Business Jargon of all Time," Fast Company, August 3, 2015. www.fastcompany.com/3049222/vote-for-the-worst-business-jargon-of-all-time.

16. "History of IBM: 1880," IBM. www.ibm.com/ibm/history/history/decade_1880.html; "History of IBM: 1920," IBM. www.ibm.com/ibm/history/history/decade_1920.html.

17. "The Evolution of the Org Chart," Pingboard, March 3, 2017. https://pingboard.com/org -charts/evolution-org-charts; "Organizational Chart," Wikipedia. https://en.wikipedia.org /wiki/Organizational_chart.

18. "Organic," World Wide Words, March 14, 1998. www.worldwidewords.org/topicalwords /tw-org1.htm.

19. "Organic Growth," Wikipedia. https://en.wikipedia.org/wiki/Organic_growth; "Edith Penrose," Wikipedia. https://en.wikipedia.org/wiki/Edith_Penrose.

20. "Where Did the 'Unavailable' Meaning of 'Out of Pocket' Come From?" English Language and Usage, December 16, 2013. https://english.stackexchange.com/questions/68729/where-did-the -unavailable-meaning-of-out-of-pocket-come-from; Mark Liberman, "Out of Pocket," Language Log, June 22, 2009. https://languagelog.ldc.upenn.edu/nll/?p=1526; Merrill Perlman, "Empty Pockets," Columbia Journalism Review, June 5, 2012. www.cjr.org/language_corner/empty_ pockets.php; "Out of Pocket, Revisited," Grammarphobia, April 16, 2010. www.grammarphobia .com/blog/2010/04/out-of-pocket-revisited.html.

21. "O. Henry," Wikipedia. https://en.wikipedia.org/wiki/O._Henry.

22. "Think Outside the Box," The Phrase Finder. www.phrases.org.uk.

23. Mark Strauss, "Let's Take This Offline Where We Can Brainstorm a Little More Outside the Box," Mel magazine, April 21, 2016. https://melmagazine.com/en-us/story/lets-take-this -offline-where-we-can-brainstorm-a-little-more-outside-the-box; "Thinking Outside the Box," Wikipedia. https://en.wikipedia.org/wiki/Thinking_outside_the_box.

24. "John Adair (author)," Wikipedia. https://en.wikipedia.org/wiki/John_Adair_(author).

25. "Mike Vance," Creative Thinking Association of America. www.thinkoutofthebox.com /mikevance.html.

26. Luke Lewis, "The Surprising Origins of 35 English Phrases," BuzzFeed, May 13, 2013. www. buzzfeed.com/lukelewis/the-surprising-origins-of-35-english-phrases; "To Be Over a Barrel (Origin)," Grammar Monster. www.grammar-monster.com/sayings_proverbs/to_have_someone _over_the_barrel.htm; "Over a Barrel," The Phrase Finder. www.phrases.org.uk/meanings /over-a-barrel.html.

P

1. Garry Westmore, "The History and Future of the POV Film," ACMI, April 8, 2016. https://2015.acmi.net.au/acmi-channel/2016/the-history-and-future-of-the-pov-film; "Point-of-View shot," Wikipedia. https://en.wikipedia.org/wiki/Point-of-view_shot.

2. Scenes from Psycho and Rear Window.

3. Evan Andrews, "10 Common Sayings With Historical Origins," History, April 23, 2013, updated August 22, 2018. www.history.com/news/10-common-sayings-with-historical-origins.

4. "Paint the Town Red," The Phrase Finder, www.phrases.org.uk.

5. "First Parachute Jump Is Made Over Paris," History, March 4, 2010, update October 18, 2019. www.history.com/this-day-in-history/the-first-parachutist.

6. "Parachute," Wikipedia. https://en.wikipedia.org/wiki/Parachute.

7. John Naughton, "Thomas Kuhn: The Man Who Changed the Way the World Looked at Science." *The Guardian,* August 18, 2012. www.theguardian.com/science/2012/aug/19/thomas-kuhn -structure-scientific-revolutions; L. Patton, "Kuhn, Pedagogy, and Practice: A Local Reading of Structure," later published in *The Kuhnian Image of Science,* edited by Moti Mizrahi (London: Roman & Littlefield, 2017). https://core.ac.uk/download/pdf/160113784.pdf.

8. BT Editors, "Paradigm Shift Definition," Business Terms, March 4, 2019. https://business terms.org/paradigm-shift; Brian Windhorst, "LeBron James Changed the Game as a Basketball Prodigy," ESPN, March 28, 2018. www.espn.com/nba/story/_/id/22924664/lebron-james -changed-game-basketball-prodigy-nba.

9. Tania Lombrozo, "What Is A Paradigm Shift, Anyway?" NPR, July 18, 2016. www.npr. org/sections/13.7/2016/07/18/486487713/what-is-a-paradigm-shift-anyway; "Paradigm Shift," Wikipedia. https://en.wikipedia.org/wiki/Paradigm_shift;

10. "Analysis Paralysis," Wikipedia. https://en.wikipedia.org/wiki/Analysis_paralysis.

11. "The History of Parking Lots," Parking Israel, www.parkingisrael.co.il/the-history-of-parking -lots; "About Parking Network," Parking Network, www.parking-net.com/about-parking -network; "Parking Lot," Dictionary.com; "La Salle Hotel," Wikipedia. https://en.wikipedia .org/wiki/La_Salle_Hotel; PPA Staff, "#TBT: America's First Multi-Storey Parking Garage," The Philadelphia Parking Authority, March 23, 2016. www.philapark.org/2016/03/tbt -americas-first-multi-storey-parking-garage.

12. Harvey Schachter, "Don't Forget the Meeting Items You Put in the 'Parking Lot,'" *The Globe and Mail,* November 11, 2012, updated May 9, 2018. www.theglobeandmail.com/report -on-business/careers/management/dont-forget-the-meeting-items-you-put-in-the-parking -lot/article5168705.

13. "Pass the Buck," The Word Detective, November 18, 2008, www.word-detective.com/2008 /11/pass-the-buck; "Pass the Buck," The Phrase Finder. www.phrases.org.uk; "Buck Passing," Wikipedia. https://en.wikipedia.org/wiki/Buck_passing.

14. Rex Trulove, "Did You Wonder Where 'Passed With Flying Colors' Came From?" Virily, October 18, 2018. https://virily.com/other/did-you-wonder-where-passed-with-flying -colors-came-from.

15. Christine Ammer, *Fighting Words: From War, Rebellion, and Other Combative Capers* (NTC Pub Group, 1999).

16. "The Beaux' Stratagem," Wikipedia. https://en.wikipedia.org/wiki/The_Beaux%27_Stratagem; "Flying Colors; False Colors," The Phrase Finder, October 31, 2000. www.phrases.org.uk /bulletin_board/6/messages/572.html.

17. "Peeps," Wikipedia. https://en.wikipedia.org/wiki/Peeps; "Where'd Ya Get Those Peeps?" Grammarphobia (blog), March 20, 2008. www.grammarphobia.com/blog/2008/03/whered -ya-get-those-peeps.html.

18. Ben Zimmer, "Mailbag Friday: 'Phoning It In,'" Visual Thesaurus, October 17, 2008. www.visualthesaurus.com/cm/wordroutes/mailbag-friday-phoning-it-in.

19. "Piggyback," The Word Detective, March 2008. www.word-detective.com/2008/03/ piggyback; "Piggyback," The Phrase Finder. www.phrases.org.uk/meanings/piggyback.html.

20. Strauss, "Let's Take This Offline"; Katy Waldman, "The Thing About Ping," *Slate,* January 20, 2015. https://slate.com/human-interest/2015/01/history-of-ping-a-warlike-word-used-by-business-people-trying-to-be-cute.html.
21. "1800s," Pipeline101, The History of Pipelines. https://pipeline101.org/The-History-of-Pipelines/1800.
22. "Pipeline," Dictionary.com.
23. Alan Spoon, "What 'Pivot' Really Means," Inc.com. August 10, 2012. www.inc.com/alan-spoon/what-pivot-really-means.html; "What Is a 'Pivot' in a Business?" Quora, July 10, 2015. www.quora.com/What-is-a-pivot-in-a-business.
24. Adam L. Peneberg, "How Eric Ries Coined 'The Pivot' and What Your Business Can Learn From It." Fast Company, August 9, 2012, www.fastcompany.com/1836238/how-eric-ries-coined-pivot-and-what-your-business-can-learn-it.
25. Jason Nazar, "14 Famous Business Pivots," *Forbes,* October 8, 2013. www.forbes.com/sites/jasonnazar/2013/10/08/14-famous-business-pivots
26. "20 English Idioms," Oxford Royale Academy.
27. "Post-Mortem," Online Etymology Dictionary. www.etymonline.com; "Postmortem," Dictionary.com; "Postmortem," *Merriam-Webster.* www.merriam-webster.com.
28. Henry T. Cheever, *The Whale and His Captors, Or, the Whaleman's Adventures* (New York: Harper & Brothers, 1850).
29. Gary Klein, "Performing a Project Premortem," *Harvard Business Review,* September 2007. https://hbr.org/2007/09/performing-a-project-premortem; Guy Kawaski, "Startups: How to Do a Pre-Mortem (and Prevent a Post-Mortem)," Guy Kawasaki, May 20, 2015. https://guykawasaki.com/startups-how-to-do-a-pre-mortem-and-prevent-a-post-mortem.
30. "Don Quixote," Wikipedia. https://en.wikipedia.org/wiki/Don_Quixote.
31. "The Pot Calling the Kettle Black," Wikipedia. https://en.wikipedia.org/wiki/The_pot_calling_the_kettle_black.
32. "Phillie Phanatic," Wikipedia. https://en.wikipedia.org/wiki/Phillie_Phanatic.
33. "Preaching to the Choir," The Phrase Finder. www.phrases.org.uk.
34. "Organ Stop," Wikipedia. https://en.wikipedia.org/wiki/Organ_stop; "Pull Out all the Stops," The Phrase Finder. www.phrases.org.uk.
35. Jes D.A. "20 English Idioms With Surprising Origins," Inklyo, August 4, 2016. www.inklyo.com/english-idioms-origins.
36. "Push the Envelope," The Phrase Finder. www.phrases.org.uk.
37. Tom Wolfe, *The Right Stuff* (New York: Picador, 1979); Thu-Huong Ha, "Tom Wolfe Has Died, But His Best Quotes Are Eternal," Quartzy, May 15, 2018. https://qz.com/quartzy/1278495/tom-wolfe-has-died-but-his-best-quotes-are-eternal.
38. "Envelope (Mathematics)," Wikipedia. https://en.wikipedia.org/wiki/Envelope_(mathematics).
39. "Where Does the Phrase 'Let's Put in a Pin in That One' Come From?" Democratic Underground, May 30, 2014. www.democraticunderground.com/1018622299; Samara Veler, "What Does 'Put a Pin in' Mean?" Quora, October 18, 2016. www.quora.com/What-does-put-a-pin-in-mean.
40. "Pig-Faced Women," Wikipedia. https://en.wikipedia.org/wiki/Pig-faced_women.
41. Ben Zimmer, "Who First Put 'Lipstick on a Pig'?" Slate, September 10, 2008. https://slate.com/news-and-politics/2008/09/where-does-the-expression-lipstick-on-a-pig-come-from.html;

Marti Covington and Maya Curry, "A Brief History Of: 'Putting Lipstick on a Pig,'" *Time*, September 11, 2008. http://content.time.com/time/nation/article/0,8599,1840392,00.html.

42. John Crouch, "Mercurius Fumigosus: Slang Decoded," *Newsbooks @ Lancaster.* www.lancaster.ac.uk/fass/projects/newsbooks/dict.htm.

Q

1. "Quality Assurance," Wikipedia. https://en.wikipedia.org/wiki/Quality_assurance; Margaret Rouse, "Quality Assurance (QA)," TechTarget, July 2019. https://searchsoftwarequality.techtarget.com/definition/quality-assurance; M. Best and D. Neuhauser, "Avedis Donabedian: Father of Quality Assurance and Poet," *BMJ Quality & Safety* 13: 472-473. https://qualitysafety.bmj.com/content/13/6/472.

2. "Atomic Electron Transition," Wikipedia. https://en.wikipedia.org/wiki/Atomic_electron_transition.

3. Henry L. Roberts, "Russia and America: Dangers and Prospects," *Foreign Affairs,* July 1956. www.foreignaffairs.com/reviews/capsule-review/1956-07-01/russia-and-america-dangers -and-prospects; "Quantum Leap," The Phrase Finder. www.phrases.org.uk.

4. "Quantum Leap (TV Series 1989–1993) - IMDb." www.imdb.com/title/tt0096684/.

5. Mark E. Van Buren and Todd Safferstone, "The Quick Wins Paradox," *Harvard Business Review,* January 2009. https://hbr.org/2009/01/the-quick-wins-paradox.

6. Central Intelligence Agency, "Daily Report, Foreign Radio Broadcasts," Issues 136-140, July 19, 1965.

7. "Quid Pro Quo," The Phrase Finder. www.phrases.org.uk; "Quid Pro Quo," The Free Dictionary. https://legal-dictionary.thefreedictionary.com/Quid-pro-quo.

8. "The Silence of the Lambs," Wikipedia. https://en.wikipedia.org/wiki/The_Silence_of_the_Lambs_(film).

9. You can watch the quid pro quo scene here: www.youtube.com/watch?v=YlRLfbONYgM; The other scene can be found here: www.youtube.com/watch?v=bHoqL7DFevc.

10. "Qwerty," *Merriam-Webster.* www.merriam-webster.com; "QWERTY," Wikipedia. https://en.wikipedia.org/wiki/QWERTY.

R

1. "Why Do We Say: 'Raining Cats and Dogs'?" History Extra, October 22, 2014. www.historyextra .com/period/early-modern/why-do-we-say-raining-cats-and-dogs; LOC, "What Is the Origin of the Phrase 'It's Raining Cats and Dogs'?" Library of Congress, Everyday Mysteries. www.loc .gov/rr/scitech/mysteries/rainingcats.html; "20 English Idioms," Oxford Royale Academy; Lewis, "The Surprising Origins of 35 English Phrases"; "Odin," Wikipedia. https://en.wikipedia .org/wiki/Odin; "Raining Cats and Dogs," The Phrase Finder. www.phrases.org.uk.

2. "Rain of Animals," Wikipedia. https://en.wikipedia.org/wiki/Rain_of_animals.

3. "Ramp," *Merriam-Webster.* www.merriam-webster.com.

4. "Etymology of 'ramp up'?" English Language and Usage. https://english.stackexchange.com /q/44930.

5. "Ramp-Up," Urban Dictionary, August 16, 2009. www.urbandictionary.com/define.php?term =Ramp-up. Accessed 28 Jun. 2019.

6. Ben Jonson, William Bulmer, John Cuthell, R.H. Evans, William Gifford, et al. *The works of Ben Jonson: In Nine Volumes* (London: G. and W. Nicol, 1816).

7. Royal Military Academy, *Text Book of Fortification and Military Engineering.*

8. "Ramp-Up," *Merriam-Webster.* www.merriam-webster.com.

9. Andrews, "10 Common Sayings With Historical Origins"; "Read the Riot Act," The Phrase Finder. www.phrases.org.uk.

10. "American Idioms (Meanings and Origins) [A thru H]," Pride UnLimited. www.pride -unlimited.com/probono/idioms1.html; "Riot Act," Wikipedia. https://en.wikipedia.org /wiki/Riot_Act; Pascal Treguer, "Meaning and Origin of the Phrase 'To Read the Riot Act,'" Word Histories, February 11, 2017. https://wordhistories.net/2017/02/11/riot-act.

11. "Red Herring Definition," Investopedia, April 18, 2019. www.investopedia.com/terms/r /redherring.asp; "Red Herring," Dictionary.com.

12. Alison Flood, "Agatha Christie: Little Grey Cells and Red Herrings Galore," *The Guardian,* October 1, 2010. www.theguardian.com/books/2010/oct/01/agatha-christie-at-her-best; "Red Herring," Literary Devices. https://literarydevices.net/red-herring.

13. Esther Inglis-Arkell, "Linguistic Mysteries: The Origin of 'Red Herring' Was a Red Herring," Gizmodo, May 11, 2014. https://io9.gizmodo.com/linguistic-mysteries-the-origin-of-red-herring-was-a-1574673551; "The Lure of the Red Herring," World Wide Words, October 25, 2008. www.worldwidewords.org/articles/herring.htm.

14. "Red Herring," Wikipedia. https://en.wikipedia.org/wiki/Red_herring.

15. "Red Flag (Idiom)," Wikipedia. https://en.wikipedia.org/wiki/Red_flag_(idiom); James Briggs, "Red Flags," The Phrase Finder, May 23, 2003. www.phrases.org.uk/bulletin_board/21/messages /131.html.

16. Joshua J. Mark, "Hellenic World: Definition," Ancient History Encyclopedia, September 2, 2009. www.ancient.eu/Hellenic_World.

17. Andrews, "10 Common Sayings With Historical Origins"; "Why Do We Say 'Resting on Your Laurels,'" History Extra, BBC History Revealed, January 21, 2015. www.historyrevealed.com /eras/ancient-greece/why-we-say-resting-on-your-laurels.

18. Suzy Welch, "Bill Belichick Reveals His 5 Rules of Exceptional Leadership," CNBC, April 13, 2017. www.cnbc.com/2017/04/13/bill-belichick-leadership-rules.html.

19. Jes D.A. "20 English Idioms With Surprising Origins"; Shotgun Rules, "The History of Calling Shotgun," The Official Shotgun Rules, June 17, 2018. www.shotgunrules.com /history-of-shotgun.

20. Alfred Henry Lewis, *The Sunset Trail* (New York: A.L. Burt Company, 1906); "Riding Shotgun," Wikipedia. https://en.wikipedia.org/wiki/Riding_shotgun; "Ride Shotgun," Dictionary.com.

21. English Idioms Online, "Right off the Bat Idiom Meaning," video, April 15, 2018. www.youtube.com/watch?v=KShHj4kxCBI.

22. Chetwynd, *The Field Guide to Sports Metaphors.*

23. Karen Hill, "Where Does the Phrase "Right up One's Alley" Come From and What Does It Mean?" Zippy Facts. https://zippyfacts.com/where-does-the-phrase-right-up-ones-alley-come -from-and-what-does-it-mean.

24. "Alley," Dictionary.com; Suzanne Grubb, "Proverbs, Sayings and Adages: Where Did the Phrase 'Right up My Alley' Come From?" Quora, January 10, 2012. www.quora.com /Proverbs-Sayings-and-Adages-Where-did-the-phrase-right-up-my-alleycome-from.

25. Heywood Broun, *The Boy Grew Older* (Self-Published, 2017).

26. "Rightsize," Dictionary.com.
27. "Roger & Me," Wikipedia. https://en.wikipedia.org/wiki/Roger_%26_Me.
28. "American Idioms [A thru H]," Pride UnLimited.
29. "Ring a Bell," The Phrase Finder. www.phrases.org.uk.
30. Melissa Hellmann, "DJ Alan Freed's Ashes Removed From Rock and Roll Hall of Fame," *Time,* August 4, 2014. https://time.com/3078967/alan-freed-ashes-rock-and-roll-hall-of-fame-museum.
31. "The Real Reason Why 'Rock and Roll' Music Is Called 'Rock and Roll," I'm a Useless Info Junkie, July 17, 2017. https://theuijunkie.com/rock-n-roll-name-origin.
32. Suzanne Shelton, "Armadillos in Toe Shoes," *Texas Monthly,* October 1973. www.texasmonthly.com/articles/armadillos-in-toe-shoes.
33. "Yin and Yang," Wikipedia. https://en.wikipedia.org/wiki/Yin_and_yang.
34. "China's German Military Advisers Go Home," *Life,* August 1, 1938, p. 18. https://books.google.com/books?id=lk8EAAAAMBAJ&printsec=frontcover#v=onepage&q&f=false.
35. "John Calvin," Wikipedia. https://en.wikipedia.org/wiki/John_Calvin.
36. "Round-robin," The Phrase Finder. www.phrases.org.uk.
37. Steve Hargreaves, "Apple's Stock Hit by Web Rumor," CNN Money, October 3, 2008. https://money.cnn.com/2008/10/03/technology/apple; Glenn Thompson, "7 Bullshit Rumors That Caused Real World Catastrophes," Cracked.com, December 11, 2008. www.cracked.com/article_16869_7-bullshit-rumors-that-caused-real-world-catastrophes.html.
38. "Sir Francis Buller, 1st Baronet," Wikipedia. https://en.wikipedia.org/wiki/Sir_Francis_Buller,_1st_Baronet.
39. "James Gillray," Wikipedia. https://en.wikipedia.org/wiki/James_Gillray.
40. "Rule of Thumb," Wikipedia. https://en.wikipedia.org/wiki/Rule_of_thumb.
41. Catch the flagpole quote in *12 Angry Men* here: https://yarn.co/yarn-clip/e41bd190-851b-47b7-b997-728a2fa64262.
42. "What Does the Idiom Run It Up the Flagpole Mean?" Answers.com, July 8, 2008. www.answers.com/Q/What_does_the_idiom_run_it_up_the_flagpole_mean; "Run It Up the Flagpole," Wikipedia. https://en.wikipedia.org/wiki/Run_it_up_the_flagpole.
43. Andrews, "10 Common Sayings With Historical Origins"; Daven Hiskey, "What's the Origin of the Phrase 'Run Amok'?" *Mental Floss,* August 29, 2013. http://mentalfloss.com/article/51176/whats-origin-phrase-run-amok; "Running Amok," Wikipedia. https://en.wikipedia.org/wiki/Running_amok.

S
1. "Jefferson Starship," Wikipedia. https://en.wikipedia.org/wiki/Jefferson_Starship.
2. Bob Heyman, "Who Coined the Term SEO?" Search Engine Land, October 2, 2008. https://searchengineland.com/who-coined-the-term-seo-14916.
3. Hristina Nikolovska, "SEO Statistics 2018: Search Engine Evolution & Market Share in Numbers," Moto CMS (blog), November 23, 2018. www.motocms.com/blog/en/seo-statistics-local-industry-roi.
4. "Hinduism," Wikipedia. https://en.wikipedia.org/wiki/Hinduism.
5. R. Brookes, *The General Gazetteer* (London: B. Law, 1795).
6. "Sandbag," Dictionary.com; "Sandbag," *Merriam-Webster.* www.merriam-webster.com.
7. "Oswald Jacoby," Wikipedia. https://en.wikipedia.org/wiki/Oswald_Jacoby.

8. Brooke Julia, "What Is the Origin of Sandbagging?," SportsRec, June 17, 2009. www.sportsrec
.com/origin-sandbagging-5097732.html; Max Rappaport, "The Definitive History of 'Trust
the Process,'" Bleacher Report, August 23, 2017. https://bleacherreport.com/articles/2729018
-the-definitive-history-of-trust-the-process.

9. "Edsel," Wikipedia. https://en.wikipedia.org/wiki/Edsel; "New Coke," Wikipedia.
https://en.wikipedia.org/wiki/New_Coke; "Alliance of American Football," Wikipedia.
https://en.wikipedia.org/wiki/Alliance_of_American_Football.

10. "Scalable," *Merriam-Webster.* www.merriam-webster.com; "Scalable," Dictionary.com;
"Scalable," Online Etymology Dictionary. www.etymonline.com/word/scalable.

11. Gene M. Amdahl, "Validity of the Single Processor Approach to Achieving Large Scale
Computing Capabilities," Paper presented at the AFIPS Spring Joint Computer Conference,
1967. www-inst.eecs.berkeley.edu/~n252/paper/Amdahl.pdf; "Designing Your Application for
Growth," Leaseweb (blog), May 22, 2014. https://blog.leaseweb.com/2014/05/22/designing
-application-growth.

12. "The Wealth of Nations," Wikipedia. https://en.wikipedia.org/wiki/The_Wealth_of_Nations;
"Economies of Scale," Wikipedia. https://en.wikipedia.org/wiki/Economies_of_scale; Joe S.
Bain, "Economies of Scale," Encyclopedia.com. www.encyclopedia.com/social-sciences-and
-law/economics-business-and-labor/businesses-and-occupations/economies-scale; Troy Segal,
"External Economies of Scale," Investopedia, April 18, 2019. www.investopedia.com/terms/e
/externaleconomiesofscale.asp.

13. Wolfe, *The Right Stuff;* Watch the clip here: https://getyarn.io/yarn-clip/3b2a2f4f-96ce
-4a1a-ab9d-411db33d0040.

14. John, "Screw the Pooch," The Phrase Finder, May 17, 2010. www.phrases.org.uk/bulletin
_board/61/messages/865.html; "Origin of 'Screw the Pooch,'" English Language and Usage,
December 18, 2013. https://english.stackexchange.com/questions/142312/origin-of-screw
-the-pooch.

15. Ben Zimmer, "A Reporter Said "Screw the Pooch" on Face the Nation. Where Does That
Phrase Come From?" *Slate,* January 14, 2014. https://slate.com/human-interest/2014/01
/screw-the-pooch-etymology-of-the-idiom-dates-back-to-nasa-and-the-military.html.

16. "Show Your True Colors, to," Idioms Online. www.idioms.online/show-your-true-colors-to;
"5 Idioms With Unexpected Origins," AutoCrit, January 10, 2018. www.autocrit.com/blog
/5-idioms-unexpected-origins.

17. "Thomas Elyot," Wikipedia. https://en.wikipedia.org/wiki/Thomas_Elyot; Christine Ammer,
Seeing Red or Tickled Pink: A Rainbow of Colorful Terms (Self-Published, 2012); "Sir Thomas
Elyot," *Encyclopedia Britannica.* www.britannica.com/biography/Thomas-Elyot.

18. On page 91 of the April 3, 1942, issue of the *Lowell Sun Newspaper.* https://newspaperarchive
.com/lowell-sun-apr-03-1942-p-91; "Fraser's Magazine," Wikipedia. https://en.wikipedia.org
/wiki/Fraser%27s_Magazine; "Snail Mail," Wikipedia. https://en.wikipedia.org/wiki/Snail_mail.

19. "Spitball," Online Etymology Dictionary. www.etymonline.com; "Spitball," Baseball
Reference, November 28, 2015. www.baseball-reference.com/bullpen/Spitball.

20. "Spitballing," Historically Speaking (blog), June 10, 2013. https://idiomation.wordpress.com
/2013/06/10/spitballing; "How Did Spitballing Originate," English Language and Usage,
July 23, 2017. https://english.stackexchange.com/questions/382067/how-did-spitballing
-originate.

21. "John Dennis (Dramatist)," Wikipedia. https://en.wikipedia.org/wiki/John_Dennis_(dramatist).

22. Lewis, "The Surprising Origins of 35 English Phrases"; "Steal One's Thunder," The Phrase Finder. www.phrases.org.uk.

23. Troy Segal, "Enron Scandal: The Fall of a Wall Street Darling," Investopedia, May 29, 2019. www.investopedia.com/updates/enron-scandal-summary; "Lehman Brothers Declares Bankruptcy," History, January 19, 2018. www.history.com/this-day-in-history/lehman-brothers-collapses; Robert Lenzner, "Bernie Madoff's $50 Billion Ponzi Scheme," *Forbes,* December 12, 2008. www.forbes.com/2008/12/12/madoff-ponzi-hedge-pf-ii-in_rl_1212croesus_inl.html.

24. "Matthew 7:14," Bible Hub. https://biblehub.com/matthew/7-14.htm; "Matthew 7:14," Wikipedia. https://en.wikipedia.org/wiki/Matthew_7:14; "Straight and Narrow: Phrases," English for Students. www.english-for-students.com/Straight-and-Narrow.html.

25. "Getting in Tune," Wikipedia. https://en.wikipedia.org/wiki/Getting_in_Tune.

26. "What Does Straight From the Horse's Mouth Mean?" Writing Explained. https://writing explained.org/idiom-dictionary/straight-from-the-horses-mouth; Jes D.A. "20 English Idioms With Surprising Origins."

27. "Straight From the Horse's Mouth," The Phrase Finder. www.phrases.org.uk; "Straight From the Horse's Mouth," Bloomsbury Idiom of the Week, www.bloomsbury-international .com/en/index/25-en/ezone/idiom-of-the-week/1703-straight-from-the-horse-s-mouth.html; "Horse," The Free Dictionary. https://idioms.thefreedictionary.com/horse.

28. Mignon Fogarty, "'Straw Man' Origin," Grammar Girl, Quick and Dirty Tips, February 11, 2016. www.quickanddirtytips.com/education/grammar/straw-man-origin.

29. "Ada (Programming Language)," Wikipedia. https://en.wikipedia.org/wiki/ Ada_(programming_language).

30. "Strawman: The Technical Requirements—April 1975." DoD, Overview of the ADA Language Competition. http://iment.com/maida/computer/requirements/straw man.htm; "Straw Man Proposal," Wikipedia. https://en.wikipedia.org/wiki/Straw_man_proposal.

31. "Strike While the Iron Is Hot," The Phrase Finder. www.phrases.org.uk.

32. "What Is Leech Therapy?" Healthline, April 21, 2017. www.healthline.com/health/what-is -leech-therapy.

33. "About the Unicorn Hunters," Lake Superior State University. www.lssu.edu/banished-words -list/unicorn-hunters.

34. Jasper Pickering and Fraser Moore, "This Is Why Some People Believer the World Is Flat, According to an Astronomer," *Business Insider,* January 8, 2018. www.businessinsider.com /why-some-people-believe-the-world-is-flat-according-to-an-astronomer-2018-1.

35. "American Friends Service Committee," Wikipedia. https://en.wikipedia.org/wiki/American _Friends_Service_Committee; To see a copy of an AFSC work camp brochure for June 28– August 23, 1940, visit the American Friends Service Committee website: www.afsc.org/sites /default/files/documents/1940%20Work%20Camp%20Brochure_0.pdf.

36. "Sweat Equity," *Merriam-Webster.* www.merriam-webster.com; "Sweat Equity," Wikipedia. https://en.wikipedia.org/wiki/Sweat_equity

37. "Swim Lane," Wikipedia. https://en.wikipedia.org/wiki/Swim_lane.

38. "Geary Rummler," Rummler-Brache. www.rummlerbrache.com/geary-rummler; "Alan Brache," Rummler-Brache. www.rummlerbrache.com/alan-brache; "What Is a Swimlane Diagram," Lucidchart. www.lucidchart.com/pages/swimlane-diagram.

39. "'Stay in Your Lane': A History," *Merriam-Webster,* Word History (blog), December 12, 2018. www.merriam-webster.com/words-at-play/stay-in-your-lane-origin-phrase-history.

40. Bob, "You Say Tomato, I Say Tomahto," The Phrase Finder, April 26, 2006. www.phrases
    .org.uk/bulletin_board/47/messages/878.html.
41. "What Does SWAT Stand for in Case of Launching a New Business," Answers.com, May 1,
    2010. www.answers.com/Q/What_does_swat_stand_for_in_case_of_launching_a_new_business.
42. "Albert S. Humphrey," Wikipedia. https://en.wikipedia.org/wiki/Albert_S._Humphrey;
    Sidharth Thakur, "SWOT – History and Evolution," Bright Hub Project Management,
    December 22, 2010. www.brighthubpm.com/methods-strategies/99629-history-of-the
    -swot-analysis.
43. Tim Friesner, "History of SWOT Analysis," Marketing Teacher, September 3, 2008.
    www.marketingteacher.com/history-of-swot-analysis; "SWOT Analysis," Wikipedia.
    https://en.wikipedia.org/wiki/SWOT_analysis.
44. "SWAT," Wikipedia. https://en.wikipedia.org/wiki/SWAT.
45. Ben Zimmer, "The Meaning of 'Synergy': Working Together, for Good and Ill," *Wall Street
    Journal,* December 14, 2018. www.wsj.com/articles/the-meaning-of-synergy-working
    -together-for-good-and-ill-11544804040; "Synergy," Online Etymology Dictionary.
    www.etymonline.com; Strauss, "Let's Take This Offline."
46. "Henri Mazel," Wikipédia. https://fr.wikipedia.org/wiki/Henri_Mazel; Menri Mazel, *La
    Synergie Sociale. . . .* French ed. (Charleston, SC: Nabu Press, 2010).
47. "Raymond Cattell," Wikipedia. https://en.wikipedia.org/wiki/Raymond_Cattell; Emma
    Green, "The Origins of Office Speak," *The Atlantic,* April 24, 2014. www.theatlantic.com
    /business/archive/2014/04/business-speak/361135.
48. Stephen Grocer, "What Happened to AOL Time Warner?" *New York Times,* June 15, 2018.
    www.nytimes.com/2018/06/15/business/dealbook/aol-time-warner.html.

T

1. "Table Stakes," Wikipedia. https://en.wikipedia.org/wiki/Table_stakes.
2. Albert H. Morehead, Oswald Jacoby, William N. Thompson, "Poker," *Encyclopedia
    Britannica,* August 6, 2019. www.britannica.com/topic/poker-card-game.
3. *Business Relationship Management: BRM Professional* (Atlanta, GA: BRM Institute).
4. "Origin of 'Let's Take It Offline,'" English Language and Usage, February 18, 2011.
    https://english.stackexchange.com/questions/13193/origin-of-lets-take-it-offline.
5. "Takeaway," Dictionary.com.
6. "Edward Dering (Priest)," Wikipedia. https://en.wikipedia.org/wiki/Edward_Dering_(priest).
7. "What's the Takeaway?" Grammarphobia (blog), April 17, 2012. www.grammarphobia.com
    /blog/2012/04/takeaway.html.
8. The dodo is believed to have gone extinct during the second half of the 17th century. Emily
    Anthes, "The Smart, Agile, and Completely Underrated Dodo," *The Atlantic,* June 8, 2016.
    www.theatlantic.com/science/archive/2016/06/the-dodos-redemption/486086.
9. "Joseph Merrick," Wikipedia. https://en.wikipedia.org/wiki/Joseph_Merrick.
10. "Achondroplasia," Wikipedia. https://en.wikipedia.org/wiki/Achondroplasia.
11. Robert McNamara, "Did Uncle Tom's Cabin Help to Start the Civil War?" ThoughtCo.,
    April 30, 2019. www.thoughtco.com/uncle-toms-cabin-help-start-civil-war-1773717.
12. Robert Reed, "Recalling the Golden Age of Chicago's Best Columnist," Crain's Chicago
    Business, September 11, 1999. www.chicagobusiness.com/article/19990911/ISSUE01
    /1000424/recalling-the-golden-age-of-chicago-s-best-columnist; "Mike Royko," Chicago

Literary Hall of Fame, April 29, 1997. https://chicagoliteraryhof.org/inductees/profile/mike
-royko; Mike Royko, "Factor Made A's the World Chumps," *Chicago Tribune,* October 22,
1990. www.chicagotribune.com/news/ct-xpm-1990-10-22-9003280527-story.html.

13. Andrews, "10 Common Sayings With Historical Origins."

14. "Third-Degree," Dictionary.com; "The Third Degree," The Phrase Finder. www.phrases.org.uk.

15. "Thought Leader," Wikipedia. https://en.wikipedia.org/wiki/Thought_leader.

16. Peter Cook, "A Brief History of Thought Leadership," Thought Leaders (blog), August 15, 2012.
https://petercook.com/blog/a-brief-history-of-thought-leadership; Bob Buday, "A Brief
History of Thought Leadership Marketing," The Bloom Group, November 25, 2008.
https://bloomgroup.com/content/history-thought-leadership-marketing-consulting-and-it
-services; Margaret Rouse, "Thought Leader (Thought Leadership)," Tech Target.
https://searchcio.techtarget.com/definition/thought-leader.

17. "5 Characteristics of a Thought Leader," Langhout International (blog), October 13, 2015.
www.langhoutinternational.com/blog/2016/9/2/5-characteristics-of-a-thought-leader.

18. "William Safire," Wikipedia. https://en.wikipedia.org/wiki/William_Safire; William Safire,
"Netroots," *New York Times,* November 19, 2006. www.nytimes.com/2006/11/19
/magazine/19wwln_safire.html.

19. "Throw Under the Bus," Wikipedia. https://en.wikipedia.org/wiki/Throw_under_the_bus.
"What's the Origin of 'Throwing Someone Under the Bus'?" English Language and Usage.
https://english.stackexchange.com/questions/30698/whats-the-origin-of-throwing-someone
-under-the-bus; "Under the Bus, to Throw," The Word Detective, February 12, 2008. www
.word-detective.com/2008/02/under-the-bus-to-throw; Lea Tassie, "Thrown Under the Bus,"
Rainforest Writer (blog), December 30, 2018. https://leatassiewriter.com/2018/12/30/thrown
-under-the-bus.

20. Steven Knott, "How to Channel Your Inner-Beyoncé," Odyssey, December 1, 2015.
www.theodysseyonline.com/how-to-channel-your-inner-beyonce.

21. Linette Lopez, "This is Where the Expression 'Throw Shade' Comes From," Business Insider,
March 4, 2015. www.businessinsider.com/where-the-expression-throw-shade-comes-from-2015-3.

22. "Edmund Bertram," Wikipedia. https://en.wikipedia.org/wiki/Edmund_Bertram; "Throw
Shade," Wikipedia. https://en.wikipedia.org/wiki/Throw_shade.

23. "Tiger Team," Wikipedia. https://en.wikipedia.org/wiki/Tiger_team.

24. "Tired of Toein' the Line," Wikipedia. https://en.wikipedia.org/wiki/Tired_of_Toein%27_the_Line.

25. Timothy Pickering, *An Easy Plan of Discipline for a Militia* (Gale ECCO, 2010).

35. Strauss, "Let's Take This Offline"; CRB, "Let's Touch Base. Or Was That Basis?" Intelligent
Instinct (blog), July 26, 2011. http://intelligentinstinct.blogspot.com/2011/07/lets-touch
-baseor-was-that-bass.html.

36. Prof. Geller, "Troll," Mythology.net, January 19, 2017. https://mythology.net/norse/norse
-creatures/troll; "Troll," Dictionary.com.

37. Ashley Feinberg, "The Birth of the Internet Troll," Gizmodo, October 30, 2014.
https://gizmodo.com/the-first-internet-troll-1652485292.

38. "4chan," Wikipedia. https://en.wikipedia.org/wiki/4chan.

39. Whitney Phillips, "A Brief History of Trolls," The Daily Dot, May 20, 2013. www.dailydot
.com/via/phillips-brief-history-of-trolls.

40. Jes D.A. "20 English Idioms With Surprising Origins."

41. "Horatio Nelson, 1st Viscount Nelson," Wikipedia. https://en.wikipedia.org/wiki/Horatio_Nelson,_1st_Viscount_Nelson.
42. "Turning a Blind Eye," Wikipedia. https://en.wikipedia.org/wiki/Turning_a_blind_eye; Andrews, "10 Common Sayings With Historical Origins"; "Turn a Blind Eye," The Phrase Finder. www.phrases.org.uk; "20 English Idioms," Oxford Royale Academy.
43. "John Norris (Philosopher)," Wikipedia. https://en.wikipedia.org/wiki/John_Norris_(philosopher).
44. "Origins of 'Turnkey,'" English Language and Usage, June 7, 2014. https://english.stackexchange.com/questions/175580/origins-of-turnkey; "Turnkey," Dictionary.com.
45. Anthony Thornton and William Godwin, *Construction Law: Themes and Practice* (London: Sweet & Maxwell, 1998).
46. "Turnkey," Wikipedia. https://en.wikipedia.org/wiki/Turnkey.
47. "Taikun," Wikipedia. https://en.wikipedia.org/wiki/Taikun.
48. "Matthew Perry," Wikipedia. https://en.wikipedia.org/wiki/Matthew_Perry.
49. "Matthew C. Perry," Wikipedia. https://en.wikipedia.org/wiki/Matthew_C._Perry.
50. "Lionel Richie," Wikipedia. https://en.wikipedia.org/wiki/Lionel_Richie.
51. "Tokugawa Shogunate," Wikipedia. https://en.wikipedia.org/wiki/Tokugawa_shogunate; "Emperor Kōmei," Wikipedia. https://en.wikipedia.org/wiki/Emperor_K%C5%8Dmei.
52. "Tycoon," Online Etymology Dictionary. www.etymonline.com; "John Hay," Wikipedia. https://en.wikipedia.org/wiki/John_Hay; "John George Nicolay," Wikipedia. https://en.wikipedia.org/wiki/John_George_Nicolay.
53. "Business Magnate," Wikipedia. https://en.wikipedia.org/wiki/Business_magnate.

U

1. "History of Radar," Wikipedia. https://en.wikipedia.org/wiki/History_of_radar.
2. "Under the Radar," The Idioms. www.theidioms.com/under-the-radar.
3. "Stealth Aircraft," Wikipedia. https://en.wikipedia.org/wiki/Stealth_aircraft; "Horten Ho 229," Wikipedia. https://en.wikipedia.org/wiki/Horten_Ho_229.
4. "Under the Weather," Know Your Phrase. https://knowyourphrase.com/under-the-weather.
5. Susan Higgins, "Where Did the Term 'Under the Weather' Come From?" *Farmers' Almanac*, September 28, 2015. www.farmersalmanac.com/where-did-the-term-under-the-weather-come-from-21566.
6. Bill Beavis and Richard McCloskey, *Salty Dog Talk: The Nautical Origins of Everyday Expression* (London: Bloomsbury Publishing, 2014).
7. "Feeling Under the Weather," The Phrase Finder, February 10, 2004. www.phrases.org.uk/bulletin_board/28/messages/325.html.
8. "Benjamin Milam," Wikipedia. https://en.wikipedia.org/wiki/Benjamin_Milam.
9. "Unicorn—a Brief History of the Mythical Creature," Psy Minds, September 15, 2018. https://psy-minds.com/unicorn-mythical-creature; "Unicorn," Wikipedia. https://en.wikipedia.org/wiki/Unicorn.
10. "Ctesias," Wikipedia. https://en.wikipedia.org/wiki/Ctesias; "Indica (Ctesias)," Wikipedia. https://en.wikipedia.org/wiki/Indica_(Ctesias).
11. Scott Carey, "What Is a Tech Unicorn? Here's How the Tech Startup Landscape Is Changing and Why You Should Care," Tech World, April 18, 2016. www.techworld.com/startups/what-is-tech-unicorn-3638723.

12. Salvador Rodriguez, "The Real Reason Everyone Calls Billion-Dollar Startups 'Unicorns.'" International Business Times, September 3, 2015. www.ibtimes.com/real-reason-everyone -calls-billion-dollar-startups-unicorns-2079596; Aileen Lee, "Welcome to the Unicorn Club: Learning From Billion-Dollar Startups," TechCrunch, November 2, 2013. https://techcrunch.com/2013/11/02/welcome-to-the-unicorn-club.

13. "Unicorn (Finance)," Wikipedia. https://en.wikipedia.org/wiki/Unicorn_(finance); "The Global Unicorn Club," CB Insights. www.cbinsights.com/research-unicorn-companies.

14. "Get the Upper Hand," The Phrase Finder. www.phrases.org.uk.

15. "Upshot," Online Etymology Dictionary. www.etymonline.com/word/upshot; "Upshot," The Word Detective, January 2012. www.word-detective.com/2012/01/upshot; "Hamlet: Act 5, Scene 2," Spark Notes, No Fear Translation. www.sparknotes.com/nofear/shakespeare /hamlet/page_334; "What's the Upshot?" English Language and Usage, December 31, 2012. https://english.stackexchange.com/q/96200.

16. "35 Terms to Enhance Your Business English Vocabulary," Oxford Royale Academy, September 13, 2014. www.oxford-royale.co.uk/articles/business-english-vocabulary.html.

17. "Unique Selling Proposition," Wikipedia. https://en.wikipedia.org/wiki/Unique_selling_proposition.

18. Martin Mayer, *Madison Avenue, USA* (New York: Pocket Books, 1959).

V

1. Erik Deckers, "Stop Saying 'Value Add,'" Pro Blog Service, June 29, 2011. https://problogservice .com/2011/06/29/stop-saying-value-add; "Value-Added," *Merriam-Webster.* www.merriam -webster.com.

2. Emma Green, "The Origins of Office Speak," *The Atlantic,* April 24, 2014. www.theatlantic .com/business/archive/2014/04/business-speak/361135.

3. Julie Young, "Vertical Market," Investopedia, April 24, 2019. www.investopedia.com/terms/v /verticalmarket.asp; "Vertical Market," Wikipedia. https://en.wikipedia.org/wiki/Vertical_market.

4. Will Kenton, "Vertical Integration," Investopedia, May 31, 2018. www.investopedia.com /terms/v/verticalintegration.asp; "Vertical Integration," Wikipedia. https://en.wikipedia .org/wiki/Vertical_integration.

5. "Vertical," Dictionary.com.

6. "Andrew Carnegie," Encyclopedia Britannica, November 27, 2019. www.britannica.com /biography/Andrew-Carnegie; "36 c. The New Tycoons: Andrew Carnegie," U.S. History. www.ushistory.org/us/36c.asp; "Carnegie Steel Company," Wikipedia. https://en.wikipedia .org/wiki/Carnegie_Steel_Company.

7. W. Holi, *The Analyst a Quarterly Journal: Of Science, Literature, Natural History and the Fine Arts,* Classic Reprint (Charleston, SC: Bibliolife, 2017).

8. "Compton Mackenzie," Wikipedia. https://en.wikipedia.org/wiki/Compton_Mackenzie; Richard Norton-Taylor, "Mackenzie Memoirs Banned for Spilling Spy Secrets to Be Republished," *The Guardian,* November 18, 2011. www.theguardian.com/books/2011 /nov/18/mackenzie-memoirs-banned-republished; Barry Popik, "VIP (Very Important Person)," The Big Apple, April 28, 2012. www.barrypopik.com/index.php/new_york_city /entry/vip_very_important_person.

9. "Timeline of Computer Viruses and Worms," Wikipedia. https://en.wikipedia.org/wiki /Timeline_of_computer_viruses_and_worms.

10. "Virus," Wikipedia. https://en.wikipedia.org/wiki/Virus.

11. "RSA Algorithm," Simple English Wikipedia. https://simple.wikipedia.org/wiki/RSA
    _algorithm; Sabrina Pagnotta, "Professor Len Adleman Explains How He Coined the Term
    'Computer Virus,'" We Live Security, November 1, 2017. www.welivesecurity.com/2017
    /11/01/professor-len-adleman-explains-computer-virus-term.

BS From Baseball

1. Mark Nichol, "30 Baseball Idioms."
2. "Hit and Run," The Free Dictionary. www.thefreedictionary.com.
3. "Cover All the Bases," The Free Dictionary, Idioms. https://idioms.thefreedictionary.com/cover
    +all+the+bases.

W

1. John Macleod Sutherland, "What Is There in It?" Poem About Temperance, www.newspapers
    .com/clip/14281037/poem_by_john_macleod_sutherland_about.
2. Richard Creed, "You Asked: Origin of Using 'Ask' as Noun Sort of Muddy," Winston-
    Salem Journal, December 13, 2009. www.journalnow.com/archives/you-asked-origin-of-
    using-ask
    -as-noun-sort-of/article_5fab1a08-2d75-5bfc-9e10-e75bd5445b2b.html.
3. "The Bulletin (Australian Periodical)," Wikipedia. https://en.wikipedia.org/wiki/The
    Bulletin(Australian_periodical).
4. George Smith, *Asking Properly: The Art of Creative Fundraising* (London: The White Lion
    Press, 1996).
5. "Wheelhouse," Dictionary.com.
6. Anne Curzan, "In One's Wheelhouse: From Boats, to Baseball," *The Chronicle of Higher
    Education,* Lingua Franca (blog), September 9, 2013. www.chronicle.com/blogs/linguafranca
    /2013/09/09/in-ones-wheelhouse-from-boats-to-baseball-to.
7. Strauss, "Let's Take This Offline."
8. "Are You in Our Wheelhouse?" Grammarphobia (blog), January 8, 2014. www.grammarphobia
    .com/blog/2014/01/wheelhouse.html; Melissa Mohr, "Business Jargon Isn't in Her
    Wheelhouse," *Christian Science Monitor,* May 23, 2019. www.csmonitor.com/The-Culture
    /In-a-Word/2019/0523/Business-jargon-isn-t-in-her-wheelhouse.
9. Andrews, "10 Common Sayings With Historical Origins"; "A White Elephant," The Phrase
    Finder. www.phrases.org.uk; "White Elephant," Dictionary.com.
10. Maggie Lange, "White Elephant Has No Winners," *GQ,* December 8, 2016. www.gq.com
    /story/white-elephant-has-no-winners.
11. "White Elephant Gift Exchange," Wikipedia. https://en.wikipedia.org/wiki/White_elephant
    _gift_exchange; Caroline Bologna, "Why Do We Call That Holiday Game Yankee Swap,
    White Elephant, and Dirty Santa," HuffPost, December 18, 2017. www.huffpost.com/entry
    /holiday-game-yankee-swap-white-elephant-dirty-santa_n_5a2ecdb9e4b06e3bccf30ce6.
12. Chuck Leddy, "Seize the White Space: Q&A With Mark W. Johnson," National Center for the
    Middle Market, August 16, 2018. www.middlemarketcenter.org/expert-perspectives/seize
    -the-white-space-qanda-with-mark-w-johnson; Mark W. Johnson, "Where Is Your White
    Space?" *Harvard Business Review,* February 12, 2010. https://hbr.org/2010/02/where-is-your
    -white-space; Julia Boorstin, "CEO Tim Armstrong on AOL's Big Local News Bet," CNBC,

August 17, 2010. www.cnbc.com/id/38743752; "Whitespace," Business Today, August 7, 2011. www.businesstoday.in/magazine/focus/meaning-of-the-word-whitespace/story/17200.html.

13. "Designation of Workers by Collar Color," Wikipedia. https://en.wikipedia.org/wiki /Designation_of_workers_by_collar_color; "White-Collar Worker," Wikipedia. https://en.wikipedia.org/wiki/White-collar_worker.

14. Upton Sinclair, *The Brass Check: A Study of American Journalism* (Champaign: University of Illinois Press, 2003).

15. Kristen L. Rouse, "Meat Inspection Act of 1906," *Encyclopedia Britannica,* July 1, 2019. www.britannica.com/topic/Meat-Inspection-Act.

16. Rob Berger, "The Difference Between White Collar and Blue Collar," Dough Roller, November 5, 2017. www.doughroller.net/personal-finance/the-difference-between-white-collar-and-blue -collar; "White Collar," Market Business News. https://marketbusinessnews.com/financial -glossary/white-collar-definition-meaning.

17. "White-Collar Crime," Wikipedia. https://en.wikipedia.org/wiki/White-collar_crime.

18. "Edwin Sutherland," Wikipedia. https://en.wikipedia.org/wiki/Edwin_Sutherland.

19. "What Is the Difference Between 'Wriggle Room' and 'Wiggle Room,'" English Language and Usage, July 15, 2013. https://english.stackexchange.com/questions/119293/what-is-the -difference-between-wriggle-room-and-wiggle-room; "Wiggle Room," Merriam-Webster. www.merriam-webster.com.

20. "Wiggle Room," The Phrase Finder, March 8, 2004. www.phrases.org.uk/bulletin_board /29/messages/251.html; William Safire, "Secret Plan," *New York Times,* On Language, September 9, 1984. www.nytimes.com/1984/09/09/magazine/on-language-secret-plan.html.

21. You can see the quote on page 62B of the January 17, 1969, issue of *Life*: https://books .google.com/books?id=rFIEAAAAMBAJ&lpg=PA62-IA2&dq=%22wiggle%20room%22 &pg=PP1#v=onepage&q&f=false.

22. "Romeo and Juliet: Act 2 Scene 4," SparkNotes, No Fear Shakespeare. www.sparknotes.com /nofear/shakespeare/romeojuliet/page_110.

23. "Wild Goose Chase," The Phrase Finder. www.phrases.org.uk; "Wild Goose Chase: Origin and Meaning," Bloomsbury Idiom of the Week, March 17, 2014. www.bloomsbury-international .com/en/student-ezone/idiom-of-the-week/list-of-itioms/102-wild-goose-chase.html.

24. "Win-Win," *Merriam-Webster.* www.merriam-webster.com.

25. "Herb Cohen (Negotiator)," Wikipedia. https://en.wikipedia.org/wiki/Herb_Cohen_ (negotiator); "Herb Cohen: Master Negotiator," CBN, April 6, 2002. www.cbn.com/700club /guests/bios/Herb_Cohen_020404.aspx; "Biography," Herb Cohen on Negotiating and Selling. www.herbcohenonline.com/biography.htm; Chris Geraci, "The Art of 'Win-Win,'" SAP Litmos (blog), February 11, 2015. www.litmos.com/blog/healthcare/the-art-of-win-win.

26. Raymond H Dawson, "Deterrence, Arms Control, and Disarmament: Toward a Synthesis in National Security Policy. By J. David Singer. (Columbus: Ohio State University Press, and the Mershon Center for Education in National Security, 1962. Pp. Xi, 279. $5.50). The Strategy of Disarmament. By Henry W. Forbes. (Washington: Public Affairs Press, 1962. Pp. Viii. 158. $3.75.)." *American Political Science Review* 57, no. 3 (1963): 732–33. doi:10.1017 /S0003055400288242.

27. "Witch-Hunt," Wikipedia. https://en.wikipedia.org/wiki/Witch-hunt; "Witch Hunt," Online Etymology Dictionary. www.etymonline.com.

28. Ben Jonson, *The Workes of Benjamin Jonson* (London: Printed for Richard Meighen, 1640). https://archive.org/details/workesofbenjamin00jons.

29. Henry Rider Haggard, "The Witch Hunt," ch. 10 in *King Solomon's Mines* (Leipzig: Bernhard Tauchnitz, 1886).

30. "McCarthyism," Wikipedia. https://en.wikipedia.org/wiki/McCarthyism.

31. "Pliny the Elder," Wikipedia. https://en.wikipedia.org/wiki/Pliny_the_Elder.

32. "Natural History (Pliny)," Wikipedia. https://en.wikipedia.org/wiki/Natural_History_(Pliny).

33. "Take With a Grain of Salt," The Phrase Finder, www.phrases.org.uk; "Grain of Salt," Wikipedia. https://en.wikipedia.org/wiki/Grain_of_salt.

34. Amy Ione, *Art and the Brain: Plasticity, Embodiment, and the Unclosed Circle* (Leiden, Netherlands: Brill Rodopi, 2016).

35. "John Trapp," Wikipedia. https://en.wikipedia.org/wiki/John_Trapp.

36. Lewis, "With All Due Respect," The Phrase Finder, May 2, 2003. www.phrases.org.uk/bulletin_board/20/messages/870.html.

37. John Patrick Flood, *Purgatories Triumph Over Hell, Maugre the Barking of Cerberus in Sir Edward Hobyes Counter-Snarle, a Letter to the Sayd Knight from I. R.* (Nabu Press, 2010).

38. "Digital Library of Medieval Manuscripts," Johns Hopkins University. http://dlmm.library.jhu.edu/en/digital-library-of-medieval-manuscripts.

39. Elizabeth Nix, "Where Did the Expression 'Worth One's Salt' Come From?" History, October 15, 2014. www.history.com/news/where-did-the-expression-worth-ones-salt-come-from.

40. Frederick Marryat, *The King's Own,* first published 1830 (Ithaca, NY: McBooks Press, 1999).

41. "Bolama," Wikipedia. https://en.wikipedia.org/wiki/Bolama; "Philip Beaver," Wikipedia. https://en.wikipedia.org/wiki/Philip_Beaver; "Worth One's Salt," The Phrase Finder. www.phrases.org.uk/meanings/worth-ones-salt.html.

42. Bithia Mary Croker, *Miss Balmaine's Past* (Palala Press, 2018).

43. "Mene, Mene, Tekel, Upharsin," *Collins Dictionary.* www.collinsdictionary.com/us/dictionary/english/mene-mene-tekel-upharsin; Isidore Singer and M. Seligsohn, "Mene, Mene, Tekel, Upharsin," *Jewish Encyclopedia.* www.jewishencyclopedia.com/articles/10678-mene-mene-tekel-upharsin.

44. "Belshazzar's Feast," Wikipedia. https://en.wikipedia.org/wiki/Belshazzar%27s_feast; "The Handwriting on the Wall or the Writing on the Wall," Grammarist. https://grammarist.com/idiom/the-handwriting-on-the-wall-or-the-writing-on-the-wall.

45. "The Writing Is on the Wall," The Phrase Finder. www.phrases.org.uk.

X

1. "The X Factor," Wikipedia. https://en.wikipedia.org/wiki/The_X_Factor; "X-Factor (Comics)," Wikipedia. https://en.wikipedia.org/wiki/X-Factor_(comics); "Factor X Deficiency," Genetics Home Reference, NIH. https://ghr.nlm.nih.gov/condition/factor-x-deficiency; "The X Factor (Album)," Wikipedia. https://en.wikipedia.org/wiki/The_X_Factor_(album).

2. "Factor," iCoachMath.com, Math Dictionary. www.icoachmath.com/math_dictionary/factor.html; "Factor," *Encyclopedia Britannica,* April 4, 2014. www.britannica.com/science/factor-mathematics.

3. "X Factor," *Merriam-Webster.* www.merriam-webster.com.

6. "Xerox," Wikipedia. https://en.wikipedia.org/wiki/Xerox; "Xerox As a Verb: Definition and Meaning," Market Business News. https://marketbusinessnews.com/financial-glossary/xerox-verb-definition-meaning.
7. E.V. Cunningham, *Helen* (Pan Books; New Ed edition, 1968).

BS and Brand Names
1. "Xerox As a Verb," Market Business News; Mike Hoban, "Google This: What It Means When a Brand Becomes a Verb," Fast Company, January 18, 2013. www.fastcompany.com/3004901/google-what-it-means-when-brand-becomes-verb.

Y
1. "The Yada Yada," Wikipedia. https://en.wikipedia.org/wiki/The_Yada_Yada.
2. "Yada Yada," The Phrase Finder. www.phrases.org.uk.
3. Jeremy H. Brown, "GSB: 5:30pm, 7ai playroom," Email to all-ai@ai.mit.edu, February 11, 2000. https://projects.csail.mit.edu/gsb/old-archive/gsb-archive/gsb2000-02-11.html; Mike Pope, "Heavy Lifting and Shaving Yaks: Corporate Lingo," Visual Thesaurus, October 22, 2014. www.visualthesaurus.com/cm/wc/heavy-lifting-and-shaving-yaks-corporate-lingo; "The Ren & Stimpy Show," Wikipedia. https://en.wikipedia.org/wiki/The_Ren_%26_Stimpy_Show.
4. "Yak Shaving," Wiktionary. https://en.wiktionary.org/wiki/yak_shaving.
5. Donavon West, "Yak Shaving: A Short Lesson on Staying Focused," American Express Technology, August 9, 2018. https://americanexpress.io/yak-shaving.

Z
1. Jessie Szalay, "Who Invented Zero?" Live Science, September 18, 2017. www.livescience.com/27853-who-invented-zero.html.
2. Hannah Fry, "We Couldn't Live Without 'Zero'—But We Once Had to," BBC, December 6, 2016. www.bbc.com/future/story/20161206-we-couldnt-live-without-zero-but-we-once-had-to.
3. John Matson, "The Origin of Zero," *Scientific American*, August 21, 2009. www.scientificamerican.com/article/history-of-zero; "0," Wikipedia. https://en.wikipedia.org/wiki/0.
4. "Georg Wilhelm Friedrich Hegel," Wikipedia. https://en.wikipedia.org/wiki/Georg_Wilhelm_Friedrich_Hegel.
5. "Zeitgeist," Wikipedia. https://en.wikipedia.org/wiki/Zeitgeist.
6. "Great Expectations," Google Zeitgeist, https://wearesparks.com/work_experiential/google-zeitgeist-2016.

BS From German
1. Ryan Sitzman, "33 Uber-Cool Words Used in English That Are Totally German," FluentU, April 28, 2016. www.fluentu.com/blog/german/german-words-used-in-english.

ABOUT THE AUTHORS

Bob Wiltfong is a former correspondent on *The Daily Show With Jon Stewart,* an Emmy award-winning journalist, as well as a public relations expert, content specialist, and coach. His love for BS was fostered through more than 20 years of working as a consultant in presentation skills for several Fortune 500 companies, including T-Mobile, General Electric and Charles Schwab. He often confirms trending BS terms with his CMO wife and is reminded that he has a lot more to learn from his three kids.

Tim Ito is vice president of marketing at the Washington Speakers Bureau and a former vice president of content at the Association for Talent Development. He also currently teaches digital marketing to master's students at Georgetown's School of Continuing Studies. Tim ran the content marketing group for the Association for Supervision and Curriculum Development. He was a senior editor and producer at AltaVista and WashingtonPost.com and a reporter and writer for *U.S. News & World Report* magazine. He is a co-author of the ATD Press title *Focus on Them: Become the Manager Your People Need You to Be.* His wife and two kids can vouch for the fact that he is full of BS.